Thus Have I Seen

The Marvelous True Buddha Dharma

And Its Power to Transform

Zhaxi Zhuoma Rinpoche

Great River Books
Salt Lake City, Utah

Figures 9, 10, 11, 12, 13, 14, 15, 16, 17, 18, 19, 20, 21, 36, 43, 48, 66, 71, 73, 92 from the book *H.H. Dorje Chang Buddha III, A Treasury of True Buddha-Dharma* are used with permission.

Figures 1, 70, 83, 84, 93, 94 from the World Buddhism Association Headquarters are used with permission.

Figure 25 from *Revealing the Truth* by Shi Zheng Hui is used with permission.

Figure 96 published in *Learning from Buddha* by H.H. Dorje Chang Buddha III is used with permission.

For Information contact:
    Great River Books
    161 M Street
    Salt Lake City, UT 84103
    info@greatriverbooks.com

Library of Congress Control Number: 2020950736

ISBN: 978-0-91-555651-9

May this book be dedicated
to all who seek liberation and enlightenment.

Contents

Illustrations

FIGURE 1: H.H. Dorje Chang Buddha III photographed during the ceremonies at the U.S. Capitol when the Buddha received the World Peace Prize.

Preface

I want this book to be first, a description of what I have seen and heard while following my Buddha Master, H.H. Dorje Chang Buddha III (FIGURE 1). I will tell the stories, the miracles, the practices, the steps forward and back, warts and all. It includes my aspirations, the aspirations the Buddha Master has for me, and my resistance. And, most importantly, it includes an introduction to the Buddha Dharma[1] brought to this world by my Buddha Master. I must offer an important caveat; it does not attempt to discuss the entire body of Dharma imparted by H.H. Dorje Chang Buddha III. It is only about the part that this humble student is aware of, as I do not read or understand Chinese. I believe it does offer an overview of what is known to English-speakers and I hope it can help you know how to learn from the Buddha and realize that you, too, can and will become a Buddha.

But second, I want to share what I think all of this means—what I have learned or understand from all this. I am sure there are many errors in this book, so many that I cannot even ask my Buddha Master to critique or approve it. However, I believe and hope that it will be useful to others who will (I hope) soon have access to more of the Buddha's teachings and can make their own evaluation. There are many Dharma Teachings available in Chinese by my Buddha Master, but not many English translations of the books and recorded discourses have yet been published. The karmic conditions have not yet matured, but the time is near.

Late in 2019, while leading a Dharma class in San Diego on a draft translation of the book *Learning from Buddha*, [2] it became clear to me how exquisitely all the varied teachings given by my Buddha Master that I know of, fit together and supported one another. It was like solving a giant puzzle. I do not yet have all the pieces and don't fully understand some of the pieces I do have, but I had the overall vision of how the teachings we do have complemented each other. It was then that I became determined to share that vision with whomever I could. I want to be clear that I am not qualified to explain or teach the correct

---

1 *Dharma can have different meanings in different contexts. Generally, it refers to the teachings of a Buddha, or the absolute truth of reality and how to comprehend that truth. Buddha Dharma is all that, but, as I understand it, used by H.H. Dorje Chang Buddha III to specifically refer to dharma that can enable someone to become enlightened and ultimately a Buddha. We have many Dharmas that are helpful and useful, but not so many that have the power originally propagated by Shakyamuni Buddha.*

2 *This book, like others by H.H. Dorje Chang Buddha III, is described later in this book. Quotes from and titles of books written by H.H. Dorje Chang Buddha III are printed in blue ink here.*

Buddha-Dharma that can enable you to become enlightened. However, what I can do and want to do in this book is introduce you to that Dharma and share what I have seen and understand about the Dharma so that you can gain access to the wonders and joy of what the Buddhas teach. I can also transmit some of the dharmas you need to start on this path.

I started with a sort of curriculum in my head with classes at the temporary site of the Xuanfa Holy Heavenly Lake Dharma Center in Hesperia, California. There were some good old students finding ways to participate and some eager new students who seemed to have good karmic roots for learning the Dharma. Then COVID-19 hit and the classes had to stop. Only they didn't. They grew. We started holding large weekly international virtual classes via Zoom on Sunday afternoons and held smaller, more intimate Saturday morning open mike-like sessions to further discuss what we were learning and anything else that came up. The Dharma came alive. I wrote this book in the hope that by sharing my unique experiences, I can help make the Dharma come alive for others and that they will be motivated to learn and follow that Dharma to find joy and a good life and ultimately become enlightened beings. From my experience with these online classes and creating a virtual international temple online with students from all over the world joining us to chant and sing our praises to the Buddhas and Bodhisattvas and to sit together in both silent meditation and to reflect on what we have learned from the Buddha, I realized that there was much more I could and should do. This book is part of that effort.

I had for the past few years become quite frustrated—even despondent—over my own Dharma practice, my lack of progress, and my inability to bring people to the Dharma. It started when we lost the ability to provide recordings of preliminary translations of the Buddha Master's Dharma discourses to those wanting to start Dharma listening centers. True, they could still come to my temple in Sanger, California and I could read them these draft translations, but Sanger is a long way from just about anywhere and most of the students did not have the time or the resources or priorities to take the time to come to Sanger to do that. A few did and they progressed, but most did not. Besides they needed Dharma discourses and translations of the basic texts to be able to study and practice on their own and develop their own Dharma centers and bring people to the Dharma. I know I made mistakes and alienated students as well, for which I am truly sorry.

Even when I was able to have preliminary translations of the amazing *Supreme and Unsurpassable Mahamudra of Liberation* and the profound *Imparting the Absolute Truth through the Heart Sutra* at the temple, it only attracted a very few to my temple to hear or read them. The ones who came and were able to hear and read even preliminary translations were thrilled and some became quite accomplished. I can see how their practice has prospered as a result. But they were few in number. I knew others who I thought would also benefit, but they simply could or would not come to Sanger. The Seven-Dharma Seminars, discussed later, generated some interest as did the Xuanfa Five Vidyas University, but nothing sustainable. Again, we needed authorized translations of the discourses and Dharma texts. But what could we do until that happened? What can those of us who do not and probably will never be able to understand or read Chinese do? What can I share of my experiences that might be helpful? Many of these stories and events I have reported before on the temple website and more recently in my blog, "Thus Have I Seen (Heard)." That was really the beginning of this book, but some I have not shared before. Still, they were merely random news articles. I wanted to publish these events in a, hopefully, more coherent format that would be more helpful to others.

The Phoenix and the Chicken

Recently (2019), the Buddha Master gave me a scathing "Phoenix and Chicken" discourse when I went to him for advice. I tend to think "pigeon" would have been a better metaphor for me than chicken, but I finally got the idea. My translator was laughing so hard when he explained what the Buddha Master had just said that I could barely hear what he was saying. I had the distinct feeling that it was much better in Chinese, or at least more colorful. I often suspected that there was some editing on the part of the translators, but in all fairness, I think they probably also edited my questions to the Buddha Master to make them more respectful and appropriate. To be honest, I do not believe that the Buddha Master needed any translation to understand my intent. Many times, He understands my situation before I even think it, let alone understand it. Other disciples have had that experience as well. Sometimes I have received instruction and guidance that was outside of the restraints of language.

In essence, His Holiness sees me as a phoenix with all its grandeur, fancy plumage and abilities. Whereas, I still see myself as a pigeon or chicken. I guess both of the ordinary birds are appropriate, if not very flattering. I certainly share undesirable qualities attributed to both—stupidity, greed, and lack of courage or timidity. I know, chickens don't really lack courage, but we do use that expression. In fact, chickens can be vicious cannibals and deadly fighters. The Buddha Master sees me as the holy person I could be, and I, unfortunately, resist rising to that level even though He has tried so hard to teach me and give me the necessary initiations and empowerments.

The same thing happened when I was recognized as a rinpoche.[3] I still re-

---

3 Rinpoche is a Tibetan term for someone who is considered to be a reincarnated lama or Dharma teacher.

member the argument before His dais when I fiercely fought having my photo installed at Hua Zang Si, our temple in San Francisco, as an elder or something like that. Suddenly, with no warning, one of the Buddha's Dharma instruments on His dais, I think it was His bell, started flying ever so deliberately across the room on its own volition. The Buddha Master had not touched it. It must have been a Dharma Protector[4] making a statement. I shut up then and the portrait was installed.

I had not wanted to be a rinpoche. I did not think I knew enough or was virtuous enough to be one. I considered myself an "aspirational rinpoche." And that was probably true. It was the phoenix-chicken syndrome again. I have struggled with this ever since I started following the Buddha Master. I finally accepted the rinpoche role, realizing that I could probably help more people in that role than being at a lesser status. Could it be that anyone with the karmic affinity to seriously follow the Buddha Master, has enough virtue and merit from past lives to be a reincarnated lama no matter what they "knew" or how virtuous they were in this life? Maybe. I also reflected on an important teaching from the Buddha Master on the role of faith in esoteric Buddhism whereby you had to have faith not only in the Buddha and the Dharma, but also in yourself that you, too, could become a Buddha. "Divine Pride or Arrogance" is a part of some tantric practice. This is not just what you do on your cushion.

And I think there was a dark side to my rejecting the high-status positions. It wasn't all modesty or humility. There was a very real fear that I would like it. I did not need anything more to be attached to. I often joked about this, but on my part, it was pure gallows humor. I had laughed when the Buddha told me I would have assistants with parasols, but I found the idea very unlikely and ridiculous. However, when it happened, it wasn't all bad.

But it was not until I was discussing *The Supreme and Unsurpassable Mahamudra of Liberation* during a retreat at the temple that I think I really understood what the Buddha Master had been trying to teach me and it shook me to the bone. All my being cute about being an aspirational rinpoche was wrong. The Buddha Master's analogy to the Phoenix and Chicken was spot on. As long as you were just aspiring to something, you were not really committed to being that thing—you still had doubts and there was no room for doubt in this process. This is exactly what you do with your yidam[5] practice of becoming the yidam. How could you succeed, if you did not totally believe you could do so?

---

4 *Dharma Protectors are beings from another realm who guard the sacred teachings and those who follow them. I will describe them later.*

5 *A yidam is the practitioner's personal or main deity for Tantric practice; i.e., the deity with which the practitioner has the strongest connection.*

You had to take seriously and believe the Four Great Mahayana Vows even though you know no ordinary person could possibly accomplish them. These were not vows for the chicken-hearted. These are phoenix-level vows.

Defilements are countless; I vow to put an end to them.

Dharma methods are limitless; I vow to learn them.

Living beings are innumerable; I vow to save them.

Buddhahood is unsurpassable; I vow to realize it.

There is one more confessional statement I want to make. Many years ago I wanted to establish a website to tell the world about my Buddha Master and Guru and explain how a Buddha had incarnated into this world to make the teachings of Shakyamuni Buddha more relevant to our troubled times and to correct mistranslations and errors that had crept into the original teachings over the millennia. This Buddha, an incarnation of Dorje Chang Buddha, the teacher of Shakyamuni Buddha in another time and place, was living in America and I wanted other Americans to know about it. I requested guidance on how I should do this and received an image of a sun and moon riding on clouds that contained seven rainbow-colored gems. The meaning of this image was explained to me and although I found it very interesting and used it on my website for years, I never fully understood its significance or what I should do with it.

FIGURE 2: Xuanfa Institute Logo

When I redesigned my website, I dropped the logo and had not given it much thought until I started to write this book. Just as I had the flash of recognition of how all the bits and pieces of Dharma I had received over the years fit together, I was also able to see how beautiful and important the symbolism of this logo was and how useful it was to telling my story (FIGURE 2).

With this background, I begin the journey and will, hopefully, be able to end with the synthesis of what happened and what other non-Chinese speakers need to be able to find and practice the true Buddha Dharma that can enable them to become enlightened.

Introduction

It is the year 2020, the time of Covid-19, and I am currently sheltered-in-place at the Holy Vajrasana Temple and Retreat Center in the midst of fruit and nut trees, vineyards, and subdivisions creeping out from Fresno and at the beginning of the foothills, within sight of the magnificent snow-capped Sierras.

I am the abbot (abbess might be more accurate) of the Holy Vajrasana Temple, but we have closed the temple doors to outsiders, and I have no major retreats or on-site classes planned, nor do I know if and when there will be any for some time. This seems like the ideal time to finish a book I started over a decade ago and to reflect on my 80 years on this planet and share what I have of value.

That would be sharing my experiences and what I have seen, heard, and learned from being a close disciple of a living Buddha for many years and doing what I can to make that Chinese Buddha's teachings more accessible and interesting to English-speaking people. This book consists of my travels, including my journey to all fifty states to introduce H.H. Dorje Chang Buddha III and His most fundamental teachings, mainly "What Is Cultivation?" and *The Supreme and Unsurpassable Mahamudra of Liberation,* to the American people; the recognition and development of the Holy Vajrasana Temple and Retreat Center and its Holy Vajra Poles and what that offers; and my personal experiences in receiving and witnessing higher Dharmas. I want to conclude with what I have learned from these streams that can enable English-speaking seekers of truth to learn, understand, and follow the true Dharma.

I have followed this Buddha since before I even knew He was a Buddha. When I first met Master Wan Ko Yee, He was known as a Dharma King, but frankly, I did not have a clue as to what that meant either. Ever since I sat alone in the solemn and beautiful temples in Kyoto in 1983, I wanted to learn the true Buddha Dharma of Shakyamuni Buddha; the Dharma that can enlighten and enable one to attain liberation from samsara, and I felt this Dharma King could do that. I am grateful to all the other teachers who helped me on this path, but I have come to know that H.H. Dorje Chang Buddha III is truly a holy being and has the Buddha Dharma that can enable us to become Bodhisattvas and eventually Buddhas. I don't see that anywhere else, but I do see a lot of erroneous and even evil practices that do not provide the power of the Dharma that Shakyamuni Buddha brought to this world. I am alarmed at the secularization of Buddhism that has occurred in the West. It would seem that much of what is presented as Buddhism today is mainly a form of mindfulness or zen practice that is a method to develop concentration, reduce stress, and achieve serenity.

These are all worthy by-products and useful but fall far short of the wonders and marvelous existence taught by Shakyamuni Buddha. People do not believe in the power of the Buddha Dharma, because they have never experienced or seen it.

I believe that H.H. Dorje Chang Buddha III came to this world to correct the evil and erroneous views and practices that have crept into Buddhism over the centuries and to restore and propagate the true Dharma of the Holy Ones. We are now seeing more of that Dharma become available in English so that westerners can also receive those teachings. And although the trends within Western Buddhism seem to be toward a lack of belief in the mysterious and holy, or the power of Buddhism that we read about in times past, there are positive trends or glimpses of inquiry into those very magical things by some members of the scientific community. Psychoenergetic Science[6] or explorations into new realms of the science of consciousness may not be yet an accepted area of research on the scale of a second Copernican-scale revolution, but it is encouraging. I do not attempt to draw parallels here from what I have seen, but it does seem that Shakespeare may have gotten it right when he gave voice to Hamlet's insights: "There are more things in heaven and earth, Horatio, than are dreamt of in your philosophy."[7]

Why use the expression "Thus Have I Seen (or Heard)"? It is said that Ananda, Shakyamuni Buddha's cousin and attendant for His last twenty-five years on this planet, was present at most of the discourses given by the Buddha over 2,500 years ago and had an understanding with the Buddha that he would be given the discourses he missed. It is also believed that Ananda had perfect recall and after the Buddha's death was called to recite all of these discourses from memory. At that time, he began reciting these discourses with the words "Thus Have I Heard…"

Now, I am not saying that my level of realization is anything near that of the Buddha's cousin or that I have a fraction of that ability to remember, but I do realize that I am one of very few non-Chinese disciples of H.H. Dorje Chang Buddha III who has witnessed many of the holy manifestations or amazing events connected to His Holiness. And I have been able to receive private discourses and translations of other more public discourses given by this great holy being that are not available to the general English-speaking public as well as many higher initiations and empowerments. Since seeing is believing and I have seen and heard so many wondrous things, some of which are hard to believe even when seen, I decided to document some of the events and teachings that have been so important to my spiritual evolution so that others can know that

---

6 *Psychoenergetic Science relates to the relationship between human consciousness and subtle energy.*

7 *Hamlet, Act I, Scene 5.*

the true Buddha Dharma still exists in this world and that you, too, can benefit from these teachings.

But first, I must offer a caveat. Most of the quotes from H.H. Dorje Chang Buddha III given in this book (printed in blue ink) are from unapproved translations or my memory of events and may contain errors. Likewise, the contents of this book have not been reviewed or approved by the Buddha and should be considered as reference material and not Buddha Dharma. I must emphasize this. You should, dear reader, seek the correct Buddha Dharma directly from H.H. Dorje Chang Buddha III yourself and form your own conclusions. I offer this book as a guide to do that.

It is the purpose of this book to tell the English-speaking world about the magnificence of this great holy being and the teachings or Dharma that He brings to help us be free from all suffering and experience much happiness and good fortune. The book also documents some amazing events and the supernormal experiences, powerful empowerments, and incredible initiations that I and other disciples have had as well as the holy teachings that led me to follow this holy Buddha and gave me such complete faith in the existence and power of the true Buddha Dharma. Additionally, the book documents my own personal spiritual journey and the revelation that the temple and retreat center concept that I have been developing could enable ordinary beings to become holy beings, whether in central or southern California or online or wherever.

There are many who do not believe in supernatural phenomena, and others, especially certain Buddhists, who downplay their importance. Perhaps they have never seen or only rarely experience such events. This is because they did not get Shakyamuni Buddha's teachings in the correct way and developed simple and erroneous concepts by mistake. Even animals can perform miracles and prove the existence of other dimensions beyond what we experience in ordinary reality. Beings from other dimensions, even demons, may possess supernormal powers.[8] What appears as miracles to ordinary beings is merely the power of

---

8 *The five great supernormal powers or superknowledges (abhijna) are 1) rddhi-saksatkriya: the ability to be anywhere or do anything at will including flying through the air and performing other miracles; 2) divyasrotra: the ability to hear sounds anywhere including those that normally cannot be heard, such as the sounds of ants walking or sounds emanating from a far-away place, even in another realm of existence. This is also known as clairaudience or "the divine ear;" 3) paracittajnana: the ability to know the thoughts or read the minds of other beings; 4) purvanivasanu-smrtijnana: the ability to recollect previous existences or past-lives of oneself and others; and 5) divyacakus: instantaneous view of anything anywhere including the ability to see things that occur outside one's presence, such as things happening at a far-away place, even in another realm of existence. This is also known as clairvoyance or "the divine eye." The sixth supernormal power (asavakkhaya) is knowing that your defilements are extinguished and that you have attained liberation from the cycle of reincarnation. It is unique to Buddhism and enhances the powers of the other five. Non-Buddhist or anyone who develops his or*

super or enlightened beings. If you read about what happened when Shakyamuni Buddha was on this earth and study the lives of the great disciples and holy people who followed the Buddha through the ages, you will read about many examples of these enlightened ones exhibiting such powers. However, it is true that acquiring supernormal powers is not the goal of practicing Buddhism, but if one is progressing on the path toward becoming a holy being, they are a natural by-product. It is also true that one must consider such phenomena as illusory and not become attached to them in any way. My Buddha Master has repeatedly told us that they are only useful to employ as a measuring stick to mark one's progress and to determine one's own level of realization and that of others. They are a necessary component in becoming an enlightened being. They are one of the main ways of showing that you are a holy being, but not the only way. To determine if one is a holy being one must demonstrate achievements in the Five Vidyas;[9] pass certain tests in both the worldly and holy realms; and have an overall high level of cultivation and bodhichitta. Demonstrating miracles is only one component, albeit an important one, of proving you are a true holy being.

Before I begin to tell my story and what I have seen and experienced, I want to provide a very general framework of my understanding of how Buddhists see the universe—a simple Buddhist Cosmology. It will provide context and a framework for the rest of the book since this book is intended for a Western audience who may not be familiar with certain Buddhist terms. It will also help explain what it means to be a holy being and why you would want to become one.

First, there is the divide between ordinary existence or samsara that we experience as ordinary beings and the holy—what is possible for those who have realized their true nature or have become enlightened or holy beings, sometimes referred to as nirvana. What the Buddha taught is the nature of each and various paths to follow to become a holy person. I have also included Appendix B to provide some comparisons of different paths as offered in other religions and within

her powers of concentration can achieve the first five powers, but without the wisdom that comes from complete enlightenment they are not as great as those available to a Buddha.

9 The five vidyas include everything that is good and bright and helps living beings and are grouped into five categories: 1) the healing vidya of medicine, health, and fixing that which is broken (cikitsvidya or cikitsadvidya); 2) the craftsmanship vidya of arts and crafts, mathematics, science and technology (silpakarmasthanavidya or silpasthanavidya); 3) the sound vidya of speech, grammar and composition, linguistics, phonology, literary studies, and music (sabdavidya); 4) the causal vidya of logic and reasoning (hetuvidya); and 5) the inner realization vidya of metaphysics, psychology, or inner special philosophy (adhyatmavidya) which in this context means knowledge of the ultimate truths of the universe as taught by the Buddhas and the ability to apply this knowledge to help living beings, including the use of supernormal powers. The original holy meaning of the five vidyas or sciences or knowledges is much different from what is normally talked about today. More on this later.

the major branches of Buddhism that exist within the world today.

Samsara: Six Realms of Reincarnation or Existence

To understand the Buddhist world, you must have a basic belief in reincarnation or at least allow for that possibility. Sentient beings continually transmigrate to the various realms of existence known as samsara. The human realm is not the only realm that is open to us. Depending on your karma, you can also take birth in the three lower or evil realms as animals, hell-beings (narakas), or hungry ghosts (pretas). Even as humans we sometimes experience the stupidity of animals, the hatefulness and anger of hell, and the frustration and greed of hungry ghosts, but most human beings don't spend their entire lives in such states. You can also take rebirth in the good or higher realms as devas or heavenly beings, but this is not a permanent state and when your good karma expires (and you don't normally generate more good karma in those realms), you have to return to the lower realms to pay off your karmic debts.

I should probably add a definition of "karma," but I think it is pretty much part of our Western language now. It is literally a Sanskrit word for "action" or "doing." It is the law of cause and effects. You commit a cause and you reap a corresponding effect. After we die, we reincarnate according to our accumulated karma. If we live a good life, we will reincarnate in an equal or higher realm and if we don't, we devolve into the lower realms. When your karmic retribution or payback is complete, you can reincarnate again and so forth. Going to heaven is not our goal although we believe that we can receive a nice life on earth or in the heavens for good behavior, but eventually you will use up all your good merits and need to be reborn in the lower realms to pay back negative or black karma.

Sometimes the asuras or demi-gods are combined with the devas as five realms or they may be counted as a separate realm. As humans we do sometimes also get a taste of the bliss and pleasures of these higher realms. They are also known as the six paths, six courses, or six modes of existence. If you follow Buddhist precepts and live a good life, you can go to the upper realms after death, but as I already said, that is not the goal of a Buddhist. If you reach enlightenment you transcend or become liberated from samsara and its cycle of reincarnation entirely and reach nirvana. Samsara literally means "going around" as a wheel in motion. The goal of a Buddhist is to escape this cycle entirely. (FIGURE 3)

Samsara is further divided into three spheres: the formless sphere, the form sphere, and the desire sphere. The highest of the three spheres of samsara is occupied only by the highest-level celestial beings (devas or gods) of the heavenly realm. It is so named because beings therein do not have gross bodies or form, but are pure consciousness. The middle of the three spheres of samsara is the form sphere. It is so named because the beings therein (primarily devas or gods) do have material bodies or form, but no longer have desire. Their pleasures come from four stable meditative states with no need for exterior projections. The desire sphere, where we live, is the lowest of the three spheres of samsara. It is so named because beings therein are characterized by gaining pleasure from sensual experience such as seeing objects, hearing sounds, tasting and smelling, and so forth. It includes beings from the six lowest heavens, the asura realm, the human realm, the animal realm, the hungry ghost realm, and the hell realms.

The lower realms are known to us, but the heavenly realms perhaps not as much. The Buddhist view of many levels of Hell are similar to that described in Dante's *Inferno*. We also have eight types of celestial or heavenly beings: 1)

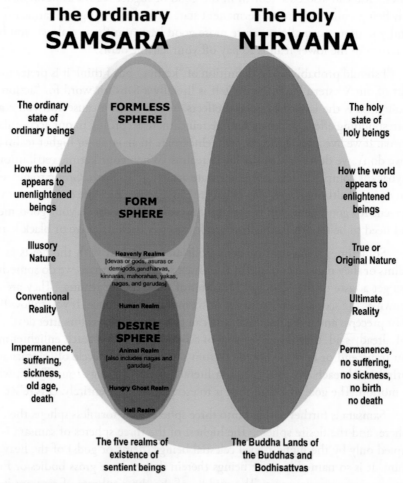

FIGURE 3: Realms of Samsara and Nirvana

gods or devas; 2) nagas or snake-like beings that include dragons which I will talk more about later; 3) yaksas or leprechaunish dwarfs who are guardians of wealth and treasure; 4) gandharvas who are the celestial musicians who feed on fragrance; 5) asuras or titans who are a brutish, violent, and powerful lot given to jealousy and anger who were kicked out of the higher heavens for drunkenness and fighting; 6) garudas who are large bird-like beings who fight and eat the nagas; 7) kinnnara who are another type of celestial musician with horse heads and human-like bodies; and 8) serpent-like mahoragas. It would appear that some of these beings also lived on earth or were at least visible to ancient people (FIGURE 4). In Sri Lanka, they say that Shakyamuni Buddha and His disciples flew to their island several times to teach the local yaksas who were apparently more spiritually advanced at that time than the indigenous humans. Our own Western mythology is frequented by various types of spirit beings or fairy-folk who are no longer visible to most people. These beings seem to have their own evolutionary paths like humans and can be benevolent or malicious. We view them as another form of sentient being that we should help find the paths to higher levels and that we should treat them with kindness and respect. We may also seek their help or cooperation in worldly matters. We can also incarnate as these other forms of living beings from any of the five or six realms.

FIGURE 4 Guardian stone with dwarf yaksas and giant multi-headed naga towering over head of guardian deva near the Sri Maha Bodi Tree in Anuradhapura, Sri Lanka.

Nirvana: Holy Beings or Saints

It is through the understanding and practice of the Buddha Dharma that one becomes a holy person. Sainthood in Buddhism has a somewhat different meaning than that held in Christianity although both refer to people who live an exceptionally holy life, are very compassionate, and can demonstrate certain "miracles." In Buddhism it also means one who has become enlightened—been liberated from the cycle of reincarnation and all its related suffering. The Christian saint aspires to be born in the Christian heaven, but, as I said earlier, this is not the goal of a Buddhist. A Buddhist saint is one who has escaped samsara all together and gone beyond what is possible in the heavenly realms. A Buddhist saint would live in the Dharma realms or wherever he chooses to be to help living beings. A saint in Buddhism is one who, like the Buddha, has become enlightened, possessing some of the skills and wisdom of a Buddha. They have gained control over life and death and are thus liberated from the cycle of reincarnation. This is true happiness!

In Buddhism saints may not lead what is normally thought of as a conventional life. There were many examples of Buddhist saints who exhibited most unorthodox or "deliberate" behavior. Examples of these kinds of happy, crazy saints are Han-shen and Shih-te, eccentric Chan (Zen) hermit-monks from the Tang Dynasty, as well as Monk Ji-gong and Birdnest Roshi, but there are many others including the crazy yogis of Tibet like Padmasambhava, Virupa, Manjusrimitra, Tsang Nyon Heruka, and Tangtong Gyalpo. Saints can manifest in innumerable forms and may appear as humans or animals or live in any of the realms of samsara.

You must remember that ALL sentient beings are evolving toward the perfection of being a Buddha, whether they know it or not, and whether at the moment they may be very confused and behaving in foolish or even evil ways. This includes the minions of Mara and the demons of hell as well as the devas or gods in heaven.

In general, Buddhist holy beings are also known as Arhats, Bodhisattvas, or Buddhas. However, there are many levels of these beings, representing stages on the path to Buddhahood. A Bodhisattva is a being who seeks Buddhahood through the systematic practice of perfecting the six paramitas and mastering the Five Vidyas, but who renounces complete entry into nirvana until all beings are saved. A Bodhisattva is above the level of an Arhat or Lohan. Everything that Bodhisattvas do is for the benefit of sentient beings. There are also very great Bodhisattvas, like Kuan Yin Bodhisattva (also known as Avalokitesvhara Bodhisattva), who are actually ancient Buddhas who have come back to help living beings.

The six paramitas are also known as the six perfections, six perfect virtues, or six transcendent perfections. They are generosity (dana); moral discipline (sila); patience (ksanti); energy, vitality, diligence, or effort (virya); concentration (dhyana and samadhi); and wisdom (prajna). The Five Vidyas are explained in a later chapter. These represent the fundamental practices and activities of Mahayana Buddhism. They are the virtues perfected by a Bodhisattva in the course of his or her development. They are what we do to become holy beings and continue doing after we become holy beings.

Dharma Protectors or Dharmapalas

These are beings who act to protect or guard the Dharma and its adherents from all negative forces. They may be either holy "vajra beings" who are wrathful manifestations of Buddhas or Bodhisattvas or unenlightened supernatural beings from the heavenly, asura, ghost, or animal realms who are "oath bound" to protect the Dharma and those who follow the Dharma. If holy Dharma Protectors are properly evoked by one who practices the correct Dharma, they can also bestow blessings and empowerment that will enable one to quickly become an enlightened holy being.

Wondrous Strange

When we think of the many beings that exist in samsara and the Buddha Lands, we can be reminded of a famous quote from Shakespeare's Hamlet, where Hamlet talks to Horatio about talking to his father's ghost. Horatio, like Hamlet[10] a student at the University of Wittenberg and no doubt a Protestant humanist who does not believe in ghosts, then says that talking to a ghost is "wondrous strange." Hamlet responds "and therefore as a stranger give it welcome. There are more things in heaven and earth than are dreamt of in your philosophy." May you dear reader be open to this wondrous world and be able to welcome it and quickly gain access to it.

Proof that My Master Is a Buddha

While in upstate New York in 2008 on my journey to give presentations about the Buddha in all fifty states, I had the good fortune to meet the former Tibetan leader of the Nyingma sect, H.H. Penor Rinpoche (FIGURE 5). The Nyingma or "Ancient Ones" are the oldest and one of the most powerful sects within Tibetan Buddhism. After I introduced myself to the rinpoche and explained to him that I was a direct disciple of H.H. Dorje Chang Buddha III, this Bodhisattva Dharma King told me that my master was much higher than

---

10 Ibid.

he was and that it was a good thing that such a high being should incarnate in these Dharma-ending days.[11] He also said that such a being should demonstrate many miracles and supernatural powers. The rinpoche also commented "...that never before in the history of Tibetan Buddhism has anyone claimed to be Dorje Chang Buddha." Of course, the Buddha Master did not "claim" to be anyone. He was recognized as an incarnation of Dorje Chang Buddha by the greatest Dharma kings and rinpoches existing in this world (or "existing at that time" as many of them are now gone) because of His writings and other accomplishments." The late H.H. Penor Rinpoche was one of those leaders.

I will tell more about the recognitions and congratulations provided by these many Buddhist leaders and how the Jin Gang Fa Man Ze Jue Dharma Assembly confirmed the fact that H.H. dorje Chang Buddha III is a Buddha later on. I also want to share something that just happened. In 2010, H.H.

FIGURE 5: H.H. Penor Rinpoche at his Palyul Retreat Center with Kenpo Tenzin Norgay who served as our translator. Photograph taken after our audience with His Holiness at his North American headquarters and retreat near McDonough, New York.

---

11 *Shakyamuni Buddha predicted that the dharma that He brought to this world would only last for a few thousand years and there would be a "Dharma-Ending Age" where it would be difficult to find the true dharma and to practice it correctly. It was also predicted that great holy beings would incarnate to help guide living beings through these difficult times.*

Dorje Chang Buddha III received the World Peace Prize. The photograph in FIGURE 1 (page 10) was taken when He received that honor at the Capitol in Washington, DC. Ronald Reagan, Mahatma Gandhi, and others have received this award, which has been given to someone who has promoted altruism and world peace. In 2018 the group who awarded that prize and the World Peace Prize Religious Leaders Title Awarding Council officially conferred the title of Pope of Buddhism to H.H. Dorje Chang Buddha III. To their surprise His Holiness did not accept the conferment and returned the Pope of Buddhism Scepter. The Buddha Master said: **"Within the field of Buddhism, there are Buddhas and Bodhisattvas. There are titles of Dharma kings, rinpoches, Dharma masters, eminent monastics, greatly virtuous persons, and Holy Gurus. There is no need for a Pope. I am a humble cultivator. I am not able to take on such a heavy responsibility."** Most of us did not even know this had happened until we heard that the World Peace Prize organizations insisted that: "The Conferment of the Pope of Buddhism to His Holiness Dorje Chang Buddha III is unchangeable, the return of the Conferment Decree is deemed not effectible." On September 26, 2020 the Chairperson for both of the World Peace groups again presented the Pope of Buddhism Scepter to Venerable Mozhi Rinpoche, representative of the World Buddhism Association Headquarters, for the Scepter to be returned to His Holiness Dorje Chang Buddha III.

I found that my Buddha Master, His Holiness Dorje Chang Buddha III, is the highest Buddha in the universe and why He is recognized as such by so many outstanding enlightened Buddhists in Asia and the West. However, this great holy Buddha himself says that he is **"just a humble being—a most ordinary practitioner"** even though the world's most eminent monastics and Dharma kings have said that His Holiness Dorje Chang Buddha III is the greatest holy Buddha living in the world today. The most important things that I have learned, I have learned from watching and listening to my Buddha Master, seeing how the Buddha handles problems and deals with particular situations, as well as listening to the Buddha's discourses and reading His books. I am especially humbled by what I have observed about compassion. It is so much more than what I thought, and it can be "complicated," at least to us ordinary beings. I truly feel blessed.

I have seen evidence of many of the Higher Dharmas and State Practices mentioned in *The Supreme and Unsurpassable Mahamudra of Liberation* that I could write about and I personally know disciples who have received others. There are other books who tell of this. I want to limit this book to only those that I have personally experienced or have direct knowledge of and, to the extent possible, explain what I actually witnessed and experienced. Since these are inner-tantric initiations or empowerments, certain rules of secrecy prevail. I will only reveal what I believe I have permission to reveal.

one

How Did I Get Here?

How did I become a disciple of H.H. Dorje Chang Buddha III and recognized as a reincarnated rinpoche?

It took a lot of searching. Even as a young girl, growing up on White Eyes Creek in northeastern Muskingum County Ohio, I remember a thirst for understanding the nature of things and frustration over the things I could not understand—and there were many things I did not understand. I also had an unusual interest in things of a religious nature. My parents were honest, hard-working children of the Great Depression, but they managed to give my younger brother Glenn and I a good ethical foundation and what we needed to go forth into the world.

The concept of karma came to me very early in life, even though it was not part of the religious tradition I was born into. How could there be a just Creator God if good things happened to bad people and it would appear that bad things just as often happened to good people? After 9-11 when Billy Graham addressed the nation (I believe all the living presidents and their wives were there) at the National Day of Prayer and Remembrance, he asked from his heart, how could God let this happen? He also said, "I have to confess that I really do not know the answer totally, even to my own satisfaction." I am sure no Buddhist who understood the law of cause and effect would ask that question or have that confusion, although they would share the compassion and kindness expressed for those who suffered.

I received my early Christian training and learned the Lutheran Catechism under Rev. F. Martin Koepplin who returned from the heavenly realms to tell me that what he had taught me was wrong. He told me that it was as the Bible says "In my Father's house are many mansions" meaning that the heavens were not just filled with Christians (or more probably, he had taught me "were not filled just with Lutherans"). There were people in heaven from all sorts of religious faiths and backgrounds. In fact, there are many different types and levels of the heavenly realms to meet the karmic conditions of different types of beings. However, now I understand why Buddhists are not usually interested in going to any of these many heavens as an end goal. They do exist and are a sort of reward for a good life on this earth, but they are still part of samsara and thus ultimately subject to reincarnation and the cycle of birth and death and all the suffering that is associated with samsara.

Thinking of my Lutheran upbringing or I should say partial Lutheran upbringing as only my mother was a devout Lutheran, reminded me of something that I thought was most ironic. As an aside, I thought my father was the village atheist, but it was only much later that I learned that he just wanted nothing to do with organized religion. I had been very religious as a youth and would probably have gone to Wittenberg, an Evangelical Lutheran University to begin my training to become a pastor, but women were not allowed to do that sort of thing in the 50's when I started college. Every time I go to give classes or participate in ceremonies at Hua Zang Si (FIGURE 6), our temple in San Francisco, I notice the cornerstone of that temple and its German inscription: "Ev. Luth. St. Johannes Kirshe; 17 Juni 1900; Da Jesus Christum Der Eckstein Ist., Eph. 2:20. Translated into English, it means, St. John's Evangelical Lutheran Church, established June 17, 1900; Ephesians 2:20, "Ye are built upon the foundation of the apostles and prophets, Jesus Christ Himself being the chief cornerstone." I admit I sometimes smile as I am now preaching as a Buddhist in a church that would not let me preach as a Christian. All things are impermanent and subject to change.

FIGURE 6: Hua Zang Si in San Francisco, California, was originally built in 1900 as a German Evangelical Lutheran Church.

Enough of irony, my real spiritual unfolding did not begin until the mid 70's when I was around 35, although my coming-of-age years in the tumultuous 60's when I read the beat poets and Kerouac and did my own "on-the-road" adventuring did provide a crude introduction to Buddhism and were part of the quest. My karmic conditions were beginning to ripen in as much as I started to yearn for something more. I had been very career oriented and achieved success of a worldly nature in engineering, banking, and government, but that was not enough. I began having mystical experiences that I could not explain. Supernatural things happened, but I knew no one who could explain what was happening. I started my spiritual quest without a lot of clues or guidance. A dear friend in Santa Barbara tried to get me to try Transcendental Meditation and work with the spirit guides that his partner channeled. That is how I heard from Rev. Koepplin. Sam had extended an open invitation to attend their seances, but I was never that interested. One day I had a very strong urge to join them. I called Sam and asked if I could come up and he said, "Of course. Who do you think wants to talk to you?" I had no idea, but although there were five or six spirits who wanted to talk to me and all had compelling stories, it seemed like Rev. Koepplin was the most passionate about it. In fact, he got so excited, he would fade out and we had a difficult time maintaining contact.

Although the information I received from the spirits was very interesting and sometimes useful, they did not help me in my spiritual quest. For example, the spirit beings told me that I had been a weaver, and it was true I could see landscapes as weavings and when I bought a loom, I was immediately able to sit down and weave beautiful elaborate patterns without any instruction. Another one asked me if I still liked to eat pistachios and dates, which I do. He told me how much I had enjoyed them when he knew me, I believe somewhere in the Middle East. Although being in contact with this other dimension helped me realize that there was much more to the universe than my limited perspective allowed, it did not satisfy my yearnings for a deeper understanding of the mysteries of life. Spirits are, after all, merely members of the ghost realm, and although some ghosts may have greater supernatural powers than we do, they are still not enlightened beings.

On December 7, 1980 during a tropical storm in an elegant adobe hacienda at a ranch in Mexico, the first of what became a series of supernatural events occurred that I later came to know as spontaneous initiations. At that time, I was visited by rainbow lights that exploded in my body and filled me with immense bliss, but I have no words to adequately describe it. I thought of it as "rainbow dynamite." I knew I had been blessed and it was a wonderful state that I never wanted to lose. This experience happened 5 or 6 times over a period of five years. In the other experiences, I was visited by a light being as before, only the other times the light was pure white and sometimes there were beautiful rainbow jewels in the light. The feeling of bliss was incredible. Something was happening to me. Some of my negative karma was being washed away and at least for those moments I had clarity. Some of the empowerments I received from my Buddha Master later in my life were like that, too. I received incredible clarity and, at least for the moment, felt a whole other level of existence, but it was up to me to practice what I was taught to actually achieve that level. I am afraid that too often I failed. I was more chicken than phoenix. I resisted.

On the journey taken across America to promote my Buddha Master, I met several people who told me of also having such life-changing experiences and wanting to continue in that state, but not being able to do so. Perhaps gaining this insight into the true nature of how things are is not so rare but being able to understand what is happening and abide in such a state is certainly not possible for most people. It is only through learning and practicing the correct Buddha Dharma that one can obtain and abide in such holy states. How can people who have never even heard of Buddhism experience such states—if even only momentarily? I can only think that this is the maturing of good karma earned in previous lives. The Buddha Master often talks of being a "causal Bodhisattva." I think that means that at a given moment you have created the causes to be a bodhisattva. The transformation can be that immediate, however most of us do not have the training, discipline, or ability to stay in that state. You merely get a glimpse of what this wondrous state is like, but you may never be the same.

The last time these light beings came, I was staying at the San Francisco Zen Center and was clearly told that they were finished and now I was on my own to continue my work. They would not be back, and they have not been. Not remembering anything about these sorts of experiences from my past lives, I wanted to share the experiences with everyone. I did not know that you do not do this.

You do not tell others about supernormal states and experiences for many reasons. One is that they will not believe you and think you most strange or even crazy. Some may even think you to be an alien. I could understand that. I remember a comment made by someone criticizing what I had said about my guru that I "…must have been off my meds." I know I run that risk in writing this book and describing my experiences. I could not believe what had happened and I had experienced it. How could I expect someone else to believe me? Another reason is that other people will cause you to doubt what happened. The shamans warn that evil sorcerers or demons will steal your powers, or try to, and there is always the risk of generating pride and self-attachment. But by studying this sort of thing under my Buddha Master, the great Holy Dorje

31

Chang Buddha III, I now know that it is just not in accord with the principles of the Buddha Dharma.

In Buddhism you must be very careful not to do, say, or think negative things that will generate negative karma, and you must also not do anything that will cause others to do so either. Those who have not had such experiences may generate negative responses, either doubting their own worth because they have never experienced such states, or they may become jealous and envy you because of your experiences. They may want to discredit you or harm you to make themselves feel more secure. I understand that.

How can I talk about my supernormal experiences in this book? I am doing so to help others have faith in the powers of the Buddha Dharma and know that there is another world or realm that is much different from what we normally experience, and that we can access that world. Because of this, my Buddha Master has often told me that I could tell my story, so that others may also believe and develop faith in the true Buddha Dharma. I humbly pray that any merit that I may have received from these events may be shared with all living beings, including those who may malign me.

I searched for answers in many of the traditional world religions that would explain what I was experiencing. I converted to Judaism when I married my second husband. The rabbi who I then studied with was helpful. I became active in the Church of Religious Science and the Unitarian Universalist Church and studied yoga with a disciple of the great swami Yogananda. I had many, many questions. I even went back to my Native American roots to gain an understanding of what was happening to me. Although the religious leaders and medicine men or shamans to whom I told of my experiences were very understanding, they could not help me or explain why I had these experiences. I was having periods of extraordinary insight and bliss, but the rest of my life seemed to be unraveling and coming apart. I was drinking and compulsively engaged in my work and other unwholesome activities while still trying to practice Zen Buddhism. It almost killed me. I could not reconcile what was happening in my inner state with what I was doing in my outer life. This struggle has continued even as I found the answers I sought. Knowing or finding the truth was one thing. Actually, doing what was correct was another matter.

I had begun my spiritual quest to seek an end to the suffering that I was experiencing and saw in others, but I could not find any answers. Someone told me that only within the correct Buddha Dharma would I find the answers I was looking for. This proved to be true, but where would I find it?

On a business trip to Asia while working for Bank of America, I had found the path of the Buddha in the ancient and magnificent temples of Kyoto and began my search for a master who practiced and taught the true Buddha Dharma of Shakyamuni Buddha. I became convinced this was the only system that worked. At least it had worked in earlier times, but what I found seemed so different from when Shakyamuni Buddha taught the Dharma.

I sat with Jack Kornfield and other Theravada practitioners in Marin County and with Zen masters in San Francisco and Berkeley. In 1985, I took refuge and received my first Buddhist precepts from Roshi Jinyu-Kennett at Shasta Abbey in northern California. In 1987, I left my job in international banking with full intention to become a nun. I practiced at many monasteries in America and in Japan with several wonderful Japanese, Korean, and American Masters. However, no matter how hard I tried to practice within these traditions, I could not find what I was looking for or the answers to my questions.

Zen Buddhism gave me glimpses of the Dharmakaya state through meditation practice, but it did not help me with my self-cultivation to become a holy person. I learned from my Buddha Master that training the mind was not enough. You had to train all aspects of your life to be able to become truly enlightened. Your three karmas—your actions, speech and thoughts—had to become like a holy person for you to become a holy person. You needed to transform your worldly consciousnesses into the transcendental wisdom of a Buddha. You had to cultivate all three bodies of a Buddha--the Nirmanakaya, the Samboghakaya, and the Dharmakaya. Most of what I knew and read about Buddhism was merely so-called "popular Buddhism" that was helpful and nice, but I did not think it was the essence of what Shakyamuni Buddha had taught. I found that this was so.

The Supreme and Unsurpassable Mahamudra of Liberation, which I will discuss later, contains specific and detailed instructions on how to do this cultivation, transforming your mindset into action. It teaches you how to practice enlightenment based on truly great compassion and the correct timing of this activity in relationship to your meditation. For example, you will not be able to realize the Nirmanakaya and Samboghakaya that you must have to become a Buddha if you practice entering emptiness prematurely. Accomplishment in the Dharma depends on very careful attention to these things. These are teachings that I had never even heard of in my years of Zen practice. Zen and other meditative techniques may be good for certain phases in your development, but they are just not complete. I know that one of my students who was a former serious Zen practitioner for years, came to this practice because she realized that the self-cultivation aspect of Zen practice was missing. One needs to develop one's morality, concentration, and wisdom and do so in the proper sequence for this practice to become effective. Here I am referring to Zen as taught in the modern Zen schools and not zen as a state of mind that is common to all forms of Buddhism and many other religions including in the teachings of H.H. Dorje Chang Buddha III. Zen is a Japanese term but is transliterated from the Chinese chan or ch'an, which, in turn, came from channa which was the Chinese transliteration of the Sanskrit dhyana. Dhyana or its Pali equivalent of jhana was a term for training the mind or meditation.

A good friend and Zen priest at the San Francisco Zen Center suggested I become a shaman and learn how to journey to different realms and meet spiritual guides in these places, which I did. He knew I had many questions and that I had not met anyone who could answer my questions. Once while traveling in the upper realms, I did encounter the same phenomena of the great white light beings with their sparkling jewels, but I was not able to enter the light or experience the bliss as before when they visited me. I could see and momentarily experience higher states of consciousness, but not stay or abide in those places. I was still a long way from my goal. I am grateful that I did that shamanic work. I doubt if I would have been prepared for many of the experiences I have had following my Buddha Master, if I had not been made aware of other dimensions and worlds beyond what we think of as ordinary reality.

I had already been introduced to the esoteric Dharma when I met my true Buddha Master, His Holiness Dorje Chang Buddha III. I knew enough about the esoteric tradition that I knew I had finally found the perfect guru who could answer all my questions, even though I did not at first know His true identity. At that time, He was known to be a Dharma King by the name of Master Wan Ko Yee. All I knew was that my ultimate Buddha Master could communicate directly with the Buddhas and Bodhisattvas and had the full power of the true Buddha Dharma just like Shakyamuni Buddha! I had the extremely good fortune to train intensely and directly with this Buddha Master and receive many initiations and empowerments from the Buddha. At various times in my practice I was even able to stay and travel with this Buddha and His family. At one point in my training I was able to ask my guru anything and He was always able to give a satisfactory answer. I remember that at one time I had a list of almost six hundred questions.

I lived for many years with Great Rinpoche Akou Lamo, who came from Tibet. Ven. Akou Lamo is very kind and compassionate and her state of realization is very high. Akou Lamo spent most of her time in the hermitage that we shared practicing Dharma. I am sure she is still like that. She is most remarkable and her accomplishments in the Dharma are very great. I am convinced, although she fiercely denies it, that she is a great Bodhisattva. Her supernormal powers are also very great. Although she was mostly able to conceal her abilities, every so often she would do something amazing or know something that was about to happen that could only have been the case if she had supernormal powers. I can still see her lifting the two-ton pool of water at the Ultimate Bathing the Buddha Ceremony held in 2004 (FIGURE 7) and more recently, I watched her body temperature soar to over 140 degrees Fahrenheit when she practiced tummo. I was very fortunate to have been able to spend so much time with her. I will describe these events in more detail later.

We were both sent to study with His Holiness Dorje Chang Buddha III so that we might learn the highest Dharma. It was on my way to study with the Buddha that I encountered the magnificent Buddha Light shown in FIGURE 8. On looking closely at the photo I took of that Buddha Light, you can see the Buddha sitting in a bright red robe. There were other auspicious signs in the sky that day. A bright rainbow cloud appeared early in the morning and Sanskrit seed syllables appeared in the sky with the rainbow. Sure enough, these were but portents of things to come. The next day there was a very special ceremony in which I encountered my first red Holy Vajra Pill. At that time several pills were placed in my hand. A certain Dharma was performed and one of them flew out of my hand to a holy land in a flash of brightly colored (red) light. It was incredible! I have since learned exactly where that holy pill went and understand the prophecy that was made at that time. Since then, I have had many encounters with these magical holy pills.

A certain Dharma King had recognized me as a rinpoche. The Buddha also told me that I was a rinpoche when He tonsured me (see FIGURE 9). I have not yet been enthroned as a specific reincarnation nor do I know who it is. The karmic conditions have not yet matured for that to happen. Perhaps it is something I simply do not need to know in this lifetime. When I became able to "awaken" the vajra pill and cause it to do a vajra dance telekinetically I realized that I had begun my process of awakening. I have a theory, but it is only my own and not at all verified, that anyone who is a serious student of H.H. Dorje Chang Buddha III is probably a reincarnated Buddhist of some sort as you would need the good fortune from past lives of training in Buddhism to have the karmic affinity to be able to do so today. When I took the exam in the holy realm a few years ago, I was able to pass the test at the three blue button plus level and was able to venture into the next level, only I did not have the ability to stay there and earn a gold button. My practice needs much work and I still feel like I am just starting.

I was also given the Tibetan name Zhaxi Zhuoma (Tashi Drolma). "Zhaxi" means auspicious while "Zhuoma" means either Tara or holy (celestial) woman. However, I know that I must continue to practice and cultivate myself to become greatly accomplished. The dharma that I have learned is the dharma of

FIGURE 7: Disciples Lifting Pool of Water weighing over two tons at the Ultimate Bathing of the Buddha Ceremony in the Los Angeles area.

cultivation—self-cultivation. Although there are specific dharmas and practices that we learn to help us on the path, the real work or effort must be reflecting on and changing our daily behavior. We change our lives by changing our karma. We only do that which will create good karma and avoid that which is evil. We build a retaining wall of good karma that will protect us from the maturation of evil karma. We become Buddhas by following the Dharma and learning to act, think, and speak like Buddhas. Only a Buddha can know the mind of another Buddha, but we can follow the Dharma that the Buddha taught that corresponds with us and eventually we will also become a Buddha.

I not only found answers to my earlier questions, but being a rinpoche, I know that I need to benefit all living beings, friends and foes alike, with the Dharma I have learned and received. My job is to benefit living beings and propagate the true Dharma, which I have devoted my life to doing. I dedicate any merit accrued from publishing this book to living beings everywhere so that they may quickly gain enlightenment.

FIGURE 8: Great Buddha Light as it appeared over Interstate 5 near Bakersfield, California. Looking closely, you may be able to see a red-robed figure sitting on the bottom of the rainbow. Not everybody can see it. The tiny objects at the bottom left are parking lot lights providing some sense of scale.

two

Thus Have I Seen

Ultimate Bathing the Buddha Dharma Assembly

In order to study and learn the Dharma with H.H. Dorje Chang Buddha III, I moved back to California from North Carolina. The first extraordinary large-scale Dharma assembly I attended after moving was the Ultimate Bathing the Buddha Dharma Assembly held in May 2004. My roommate Akou Lamo Rinpoche and I lived near where this grand assembly was to take place. As usual, I did not have a clue as to what was going on or what to expect. Elaborate procedures were in place to create the special mandala and a very large, mysterious, and beautiful box was being prepared to serve as a pool to hold the water that

FIGURE 9: H.H. Dorje Chang Buddha III tonsuring me.

would be used to bathe the baby Buddha. As I became aware of what was to happen, I learned that whenever the true Dharma goes to a new country, this Ultimate Bathing the Buddha ceremony must be performed. It was only performed once in any given country. The day arrived for this most special dharma assembly. I think about 70 or 80 people attended from all over the world. Some I knew, but many I did not. We clustered together in great anticipation. Since conditions must be absolutely right, there can be delays. Finally, the Buddha Master was ready to perform the necessary rituals and we were admitted to the actual elaborate mandala area.

The giant box was filled with special scented water to create the pool to bathe the Buddha. I believe it weighed over two tons. Ropes were under the box and the strongest disciples tried to lift it but could not even budge it, even when many of them tried together to do so. Then two disciples stepped forth and announced they would lift it. The Dharma for this ritual required that once the bathing of the Buddha was completed by all present, the water in the large pool needed to be poured into a smaller basin. These two, my young roommate and an elderly almost frail gentleman, proceeded to begin chanting and were able to lift it using the power of their mantras. We were all amazed. The super-human ability to lift this pool depended upon the level of realization of those who tried, and both of these disciples were quite accomplished. This accomplishment was necessary for the event to be a successful ceremony (FIGURE 7 page 36).

Many other awesome things happened during that Dharma Assembly including a sudden powerful wind that had been predicted beforehand and a mysterious cloud that remained in place to serve as a parasol that always shaded the statue of the Baby Buddha used in the ceremony. The roar of dragons was heard like thunder in the sunny sky. This was also my first glimpse of the Buddha Master's Vajra Dharma Wheel that transformed into Dharma Protectors in the pool and was later used to remove karmic hindrances from a certain lama who was present. I will tell you later about my experience with that Vajra Dharma Wheel when I received the same empowerment.

Diamond Blessing

Once, while staying in a small boutique hotel with the Buddha Master and His family in San Francisco, I received a special blessing that caused a diamond-shaped mark to form on my forehead and the top of my head. It was about 3 to 4-inches on each side. The point was in the center of my forehead toward my nose. I think it happened after I brought the Buddha Master some water. Normally, I would not be the one to do that, but on that occasion everyone else was laying low and hiding in the kitchen. Something had happened, but, as is often the case, I was clueless, because I do not understand Chinese. The Buddha Master was not happy and sitting alone and, not knowing any better, I offered him some water. He blessed me at that time and touched my head. Later in that trip I remember him looking at me in a funny way and smiling. When I finally saw this blotch on my forehead, I pointed to it and asked in sign language if this was His handiwork, and He laughed again. This mark would turn bright red and pulsate from time to time. This often happened when I read English translations of the Buddha Master's discourses to my students, but other times as well. Many of my students saw it. I understood this was done to help rid me of karmic obstructions.

Daily Life with a Buddha

It seemed something miraculous happened almost every day, especially when we traveled together. I was living practically next door to the Buddha Master. I think the backyard fence at the place where I was living touched the backyard of the Buddha Master's home. We needed to be quite discreet. The Buddha Master actually lived in several places at that time. He needed to be protected from both his loyal disciples and people who wished Him harm. I will talk a little about how He had been and continued to be persecuted by corrupt officials in China later. My day consisted of morning chores and practice and then going to the Buddha's home to see what was needed or happening, and there was always something going on. Perhaps I received a teaching. This would continue until sometimes quite late at night. Those of us who had the good fortune to be in the inner circle or mandala and could visit at almost any time, were expected to stay until dismissed for the day.

My training was different as it usually depended on there being a willing and capable translator present. Many of the Chinese students who could speak acceptable and understandable English would not translate anything Dharma related. They did not have that special language of Buddhist terms and they did not want to risk mistranslating Dharma, and the Buddha understood when I was not getting it and would use His vajra voice to call them on it. I felt very bad for them as it may well have been my stupidity and not their lack of translating skills that were the problem. That is still the state. There are only about three or four people who are able to translate anything for me about Dharma practice. They are all very generous and helpful, but they are not always at the Buddha's side and they are very, very busy. Because the Buddha Master was so generous with the time He spent trying to teach me, I did often receive mini-discourses. The other students knew that, so whenever I tried to tell my guru about my practice, an audience would suddenly appear. It was like trying to practice in a goldfish bowl. And I also had the sometimes annoying Western habit of always asking questions. If I did not understand something, and that was often the case, I would ask about it. I was not concerned about saving face like my more

40

cautious and probably more respectful Chinese counterparts, but that was how "What Is Cultivation?" and other teachings came into being.

Rainbow Crystal Lights and Earthen Mandala with Auspicious Grass of the Four Jewels

There were many wonderful sights and events that just spontaneously happened while being with the Buddha Master. Magical rainbow lights appeared on the special grass at the mandala where the Buddha performed many of the empowerments that I had witnessed and received. You can see them in FIGURES 10 and 11. They were like tiny red, yellow, green, and blue jewels that sparkled independently of any external light source. Some were clear like large diamonds. The only time I had seen that sort of phenomenon was when the light beings had visited me twenty years earlier. Again, we heard the sound of heavenly dragons roaring like thunder across a clear blue sky. The sparkling lights changed color and glittered on and between the blades of grass. It was amazing! This was no ordinary site. Earlier, a special kind of grass grew there on a mound that spontaneously formed into a sacred mandala. This grass mandala naturally grew where the Ultimate Bathing the Buddha Ceremony was held.

We were told that the flowers we saw there were called "Auspicious Grass of the Four Jewels." The flowers had four distinct very thin parts or leaves. They grew in a particular pattern and formed a perfect circle. Prior to the ceremony the area had been perfectly flat. After the ceremony, the ground became slightly elevated, forming a mound upon which these special flowers grew. These flowers grew no other place in the yard. H.H. Dorje Chang Buddha III explained that this was an offering from the Dharma Protecting Deities. Now three or four years later the magical jewels could be seen on this distinctive grass.

This had been the site of the Ultimate Bathing of the Buddha Dharma Assembly that I discussed earlier. This was also the site of one of the Buddhas Bestow Nectar ceremonies performed in 2000, before I met His Holiness.

Vajra Dharma Wheel Empowerment

I received a special Vajra Dharma Wheel Empowerment at this same site similar to what another rinpoche had experienced during the Ultimate Bathing of the Buddha ceremony. His experience is described in the Big Blue Treasure Book with a photo of the mark left by the initiation. Although this was a high level inner-tantric initiation and as such cannot be publicly discussed or shared with others in detail, I am able to briefly tell others of my experience so that they can learn of the true power of the magnificent Buddha Dharma. The Buddha performed this ritual for me to remove certain negative karma that was an obsta-

FIGURE 10: The Jewel Grass Mandala. In 2004, a few months after the amazing Ultimate Bathing the Buddha Dharma Assembly was held, the previously flat ground used for the ceremony raised up naturally and became a mandala of Auspicious Grass of the Four Treasures. This was the site where many powerful empowerments and initiations were given by H.H. Dorje Chang Buddha III. Several years later that same spot exhibited various colored jewels as shown here This phenomenon lasted for several days. Finally, the jewels coalesced into a rainbow and flew away with many disciples watching.

FIGURE 11: Details of Jewels on Grass Mandala.

cle to my becoming a holy person and the achievement of liberation. After the Dharma protecting deities arrived, the Buddha practiced the Buddha Dharma and placed the Dharma Wheel on my body. The Buddha's Vajra Dharma Wheel quickly exhibited samadhi fire. I screamed. The impact was very intense, but in that moment, I also realized the truth of the Buddha Dharma. Although there was intense feeling—greater than anything I had ever experienced before—there was also no feeling. I realized the emptiness of that magical experience while at the same time experiencing it. It was the pain of "no-pain." The Buddha explained to me that this experience was a precursor to the realization of the Dharmakaya.

I actually understood a little of how my Buddha Master and other enlightened beings could accomplish their amazing feats. Although there are no words to adequately describe this experience and it would be presumptuous for me to assume I understood the mind of a Buddha, it was a glimpse of the Dharmakaya—the truth of the universe! This is what is meant by "form is emptiness, and emptiness is form." Living in this pure state, if only for a moment and through the power of my Buddha Master, I understood that the Dharmakaya is everywhere. There was no place that is not the Dharmakaya. This is what enlightened beings experience or realize at all times and They can therefore do anything! All things are inherently empty and at the same time contain the potentiality of all things! This reality exists while living in this mundane world... and, it exists for all sentient beings! We all have the inherent nature of a Buddha. We just have to awaken to that nature.

The initiation caused me to not only eliminate certain obstacles but reinforced my resolve to practice and help others learn the true Buddha Dharma. I also understood the necessity of obtaining inner-tantric initiations from a true holy vajra master if one wants to achieve enlightenment in this lifetime! Only a true holy vajra master can summon the Dharma protecting deities and communicate directly with the Buddhas and Bodhisattvas to perform this sort of powerful ritual! Only a true holy vajra master can manifest the awesome power of the true Buddha Dharma. My Buddha Master, H.H. Dorje Chang Buddha III, is such a master!

Nectar from the Buddha Lands, Shariras, Varja Pills, and Nectar Rain

I missed the grand nectar ceremonies in Los Angeles that happened right after the Buddha Master came to America and before I arrived in Pasadena. Much has already been written about them. However, I did attend another Dharma assembly held a year or so after those grand Dharma assemblies when the elderly Dharma King Wan Ko Yee, wearing red robes and having long grey hair and beard, presided over the manifestation of innumerable multicolored shariras[12] appearing in a cloud of nectar. I cannot tell you I saw this, because my eyes were closed through the entire ceremony, but I have seen a photo of this happening with me sitting with Akou Lamo Rinpoche before Him, and I have seen a display of various colored shariras that I believe were from nectar ceremonies like this. After the ceremony we went to a secret location and I met this same Dharma King sitting with another Dharma King, my Buddha Master, Who I knew then also as Master Wan Ko Yee, but know now as H.H. Dorje Chang Buddha III. It was very strange. Some say these were the same person, but I saw with my own two eyes, these two great holy beings sitting together side by side. My understanding is that they had studied together with the same master. I do not know whether or not they might also be the same person. I also saw several beautiful glowing round shariras that appeared in hair clippings that another disciple had been collecting from when the Buddha Master had His hair cut (FIGURE 12). The disciple was organizing the various packets of hair she had collected after she had taken the Buddha Master to have His hair cut when she noticed three shiny red "beads." She thought this was most unusual and that she should report this to the Buddha Master. I just happened to be with the Buddha Master and His wife, the Buddha Mother, when she brought them into their kitchen to ask what the ruby-like beads were. The Buddha Master announced that they were, in fact, shariras and proceeded to practice Dharma to prove it.

Later the Buddha Master gave a special discourse on this matter, stating that "**This happened because of conditions and the level of fortune of all sentient beings. It does not matter where they come from. Perhaps they originated from the empowerment of the Buddhas and Bodhisattvas. It actually does not matter what the disciples think concerning how or where they come from. If they can appear out of nothing, then they can disappear out of nothing. The important thing is the cultivation of each one of us and the need to live in accordance with the teachings and abide by the principles of Buddhism.**"

One of these shariras was placed in a crystal stupa and placed on an altar where we often held ceremonies and I believe the others were returned to the disciple who discovered them. She told me that one disappeared. Her account of this matter was publicly reported in the Big Blue Treasure Book.

---

12 *Shariras are holy objects in Buddhism usually left in the cremated remains of holy beings. They are proof that the being has attained enlightenment. They may appear as precious jewels or in other forms including a net-like form. They may also appear in holy nectar or be left by living holy beings as shown in FIGURE 12. See FIGURES 83, 84, and 92 for examples of shariras left by disciples of the Buddha Master that I have personal knowledge of.*

Nectar has miraculously manifested during Holy Buddhas Bestowing Nectar Ceremonies conducted by H.H. Dorje Chang Buddha III. This nectar was not like anything in this world. It was truly from another realm. The Buddha Master was able to have different Buddhas bestow different types of nectar on different occasions that could be used in various ceremonies and initiations. I

FIGURE 12: Perfect red shariras that grew out of the hair of H.H. Dorje Chang Buddha III.

personally attended one such ceremony with another rinpoche where we saw the nectar manifest in a bowl that we had washed just before the ceremony. We were able to taste this nectar, albeit in a diluted form. This is the same type of nectar that is used to make the nectar and vajra pills we use in many of our higher empowerments and initiations. The tiny blue Vajra Bodhi pills I have given to many living beings (human and other) also contained nectar.

One night we made bright red nectar pills that were used the next day when the Buddha practiced the Torma[13] Offering Dharma. These nectar pills

13 Objects or cakes used as offerings in tantric rituals, usually hand-molded and traditionally make from yak butter and roasted barley flour. Often, they are cone shaped and may be painted or dyed

were made from holy nectar bestowed by the Buddhas at the invocation of H.H. Dorje Chang Buddha III and mixed with barley flour and butter. This nectar came from the Buddha Lands, it was not of this world. These pills were placed inside a jade bowl in the middle of the offering tables along with an array of many brilliant fresh flowers, rare fruit, and other offerings. The Buddha empowered all of us by giving us a portion of those pills leaving the jade bowl partially empty. However, when the offering ceremony was completed, we all noticed that the pills had increased so that the jade bowl was again full of pills and had formed a dome that rose above the brim of the bowl (FIGURE 13). How could this be? We also heard the laughter of Dharma protecting deities at the end of this Dharma assembly.

Other rinpoches talk of producing a type of nectar pill, but these are not made from true nectar nor do they have the power of nectar that comes directly from the Buddha realms. This is worldly nectar made from certain mundane ingredients, such as betel nuts and saffron to which five different types of substances are added. After all of these ingredients are combined, the nectar mantra, as well as other mantras, are recited. The Dharma is practiced to empower these kinds of nectar pills. Sometimes shariras or clothing or other artifacts from holy beings or fine medicinal herbs are added. They are not at all like the holy nectar pills made from true nectar bestowed from the land of the Buddhas. These pills produced by other rinpoches are called nectar because ordinary people have labeled them as such. They are merely pills made from medicinal herbs, things from a human body, things from an animal's body, etc. Sometimes there is reference to the essence of ancient nectar pills being added to these pills. These might have been made from true nectar, but rarely can you find evidence that true nectar is being manifested in modern times except by H.H. Dorje Chang Buddha III. When people speak of nectar or nectar pills, they are generally referring to this type of man-made worldly nectar pill and not the holy nectar pills made with nectar from the lands of the Buddhas.

I once heard a vajra pill chant and dance. I later participated in a number of ceremonies involving these vajra pills. I was also able to use my practice of the Buddha Dharma to cause a Vajra Pill to move and do a little vajra dance inside a clear transparent container on several occasions.

I remember when I first saw a video of the Buddha requesting and receiving such holy nectar, I could hardly believe it. That was before I had met the Buddha. The Buddha was on a dais some distance from where the nectar was to descend. Everyone chanted mantras and beseeched the Buddhas to bestow the nectar. Suddenly, a red flash of light appeared and penetrated the crystal bowl

different colors and richly adorned.

that contained the special nectar bowl. When the crystal lid was removed there was shimmering white nectar inside. This time it was the Nectar of Long Life from Amitayus, the Buddha of Longevity, but there are other examples from other Buddhas. The video was filmed in southern California in the year 2000 right after the Buddha first came to America. You can see this video at most of our Dharma centers and temples. FIGURE 14 shows a photograph of this nectar. It is not of this world.[14]

FIGURE 13: Jade Bowl containing Holy Red Nectar Pills that miraculously multiplied during a Torma Offering Ceremony after some of the pills were distributed to disciples.

I have seen two kinds of nectar manifest: the rare magnificent holy nectar bestowed in a bowl from a Buddha Land mentioned above and the substance that rains from the heavens when there are no clouds in sight. The first time I experienced the raining of nectar was when I was living with Dorje PaMu in Southern California.

I remember the event quite vividly. H.H. Dorje Chang Buddha III had been visiting us and was sitting quietly beneath a tree in a wicker chair when

14 *There are more examples of holy nectar in* True Stories About a Holy Monk, *a book about El-der Dharma King Dorje Losang, a disciple of H.H. Dorje Chang Buddha III, that was published in English in 2000.*

we noticed that although the sky was perfectly cloudless and it had not rained for some time, there was something raining through the tree. It was sweet to the taste and did not touch the tree but came from above the tree. However, it did not rain anywhere else. It also did not rain on the Buddha. Some of those present could smell a beautiful fragrance as well. People came from Taiwan and

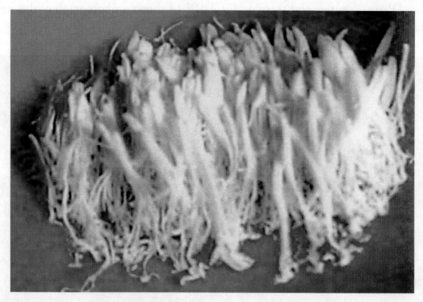

FIGURE 14: Detail of the Long-Life Nectar from Amitayus Buddha from Los Angeles Nectar Dharma Assembly held in 2000.

other places to witness this miracle. In fact, so many people came to this private location that those of us who lived there had to leave in order to have some privacy. Since where we lived was a closely guarded secret, people had to be blindfolded and brought there by bus and caravan to assure our privacy. Many people wanted to preserve the tree and move it to a place where it could be adored by everyone and enable anyone to receive the blessings from this holy event. The large tree was pruned, its roots carefully boxed, and with a tall crane, lifted over the house onto a large truck to be taken over four hundred miles to the temple courtyard of Hua Zang Si in San Francisco. It rained nectar just before we started the Dharma Propagation Tour under that same magnolia tree after it had been moved to San Francisco. (FIGURE 25 page 71)

The following year, as students performed skits and other shows in honor of H.H. Dorje Chang Buddha III's birthday, the beautiful jacaranda tree over the veranda where the Buddha and the Buddha's family and several of us rinpoches were sitting began raining nectar as well. The nectar continued to be visible for many days. Many of us watched the nectar as it fell in front of the large thangka of the Thousand-armed Kuan Yin Bodhisattva that was hanging in the jacaranda tree. Sometimes the nectar would appear as needle-like streaks, sometimes like fluffy snowflakes. Sometimes, you could feel it, sometimes you could not. It was very mysterious. A still camera cannot capture this heavenly substance. I asked for permission to photograph it with my digital camera and was told I could, but it would be a waste of time. It was. Only the video cameras could record this miraculous event. Many of our Dharma centers and temples have a video of this event. Of course, this is no ordinary place. His Holiness has practiced the Dharma at this site many times. Many disciples have witnessed holy states there.

It has also rained nectar at the H.H. Dorje Chang Buddha III Cultural and Art Museum when the Buddha Master conducted Dharma Assemblies there as well as at the Holy Heavenly Lake site. The disciples love it and try to capture as much as they can—on their tongues, bodies, clothing, whatever. It is always magical, no matter how many times I see and taste it. I finally got to smell it the last time. As for so many of these manifestations, different people experience them differently and some never see, smell, taste, or feel anything. There are also written accounts of nectar raining in China at the dedication of an art museum devoted to the work of the Buddha Master.

There were many other strange and mysterious events that I was able to experience that have been written about elsewhere, so I will not describe them here. The nun Shi Zheng Hui who lived at the same place as my Buddha Master has documented some of them in her autobiography *Revealing the Truth*[15].

---

15 *Shi Zheng Hui*, Revealing the Truth, *Great River Books 2016*

three

The Big Blue Treasure Book and Recognition of my Buddha Master

Sometime during 2004 or 2005, I came up with the idea of visiting every state in the union and introducing my Buddha Master, H.H. Dorje Chang Buddha III to the people there. I wanted to do that out of devotion to my magnificent Buddha Master and to introduce the correct Dharma to Americans who might have the karmic affinity to learn it. I wanted to do this so that they might acquire good fortune and wisdom and be liberated from suffering. At the time we had no books about the Buddha in English. We had nothing in English that we could use to introduce this Buddha to non-Chinese speaking people. We also didn't know yet that our Buddha Master was in fact an incarnation of Dorje Chang Buddha. At that time, my plan was to find the major temples, retreat centers, Dharma centers, and/or other suitable locations and visit them and tell them about my holy Master. When I first presented the idea of trying this out at the local Unitarian church in Pasadena where I used to be a member, my Buddha Master supported the idea. The new director of religious education at that church was also supportive.

First, however, we needed a biography or something that could be translated into English that would explain just who my Master is. There had been a biography written in China by Zi-Gong Zhuang that I hoped we could have translated. However, it was felt that this book was out-of-date and would not do. The very night I introduced the idea, the Buddha called Magnolia, a young talented woman who had been a newscaster in China, to join us and began to dictate an autobiography. On another front, the Master Wan Ko Yee International Cultural Institute was planning an exhibition of a few of the accomplishments of the Buddha for the annual Chinese New Year Celebration. I forget the timing of these two events and which came first. The New Year's celebration was held on January 22, 2006 in San Gabriel, California. I gave the opening comments at that event, telling the crowd that the exhibition was not the work of an ordinary person.[16] I did not know just how prophetic that remark was. I already knew my master was no ordinary master and that He had to be a very high holy being, but I had no idea that He was an incarnation of the supreme Buddha—Dorje Chang Buddha—even though my Buddha Master kept chiding me and telling me, "You don't know who I am, do you?"

Indeed, I did not, but I was quite concerned over that remark. Earlier my Buddha Master had told us a story about His master, Great Dharma King Zun Sheng, who was a manifestation of Mahavairocana Buddha. His master had once told His disciples the same thing, "You don't know who I am, do you?" Only, after saying that, Great Dharma King Zun Sheng turned into a rainbow and flew away. Although the Great Dharma King would return in his rainbow body form to teach his fortunate students from time to time, he never lived with them after that. I hoped that we would not lose our beloved Buddha Master.

The exhibition was so well received, that immediately the exhibition was expanded and taken to what had been a historic Catholic church in San Francisco that was being remodeled and scheduled to open in March of that year as Fu Hui Si--the Temple of Good Fortune and Wisdom (now known as the Macang Monastery). That exhibition was widely publicized and introduced the Buddha to the people of San Francisco. Billboards were posted on city buses and all over the city inviting everyone to come and experience art and other exhibits from another dimension.

It was then decided to further expand the exhibition, now having twenty-one categories of achievement in honor of the twenty-one Taras, and move it to Hua Zang Si, our coral-red gothic-style temple in the Mission District of San Francisco that had opened on December 26, 2004 (FIGURE 6 page 29). That exhibit lasted until November 9, 2006 and was viewed by many. I moved to San Francisco to live at Hua Zang Si and help the many English-speaking visitors experience these two exhibitions. Two publishing companies decided they wanted to publish a book documenting the accomplishments of the Buddha and further expanded the scope to include 30 categories of accomplishments. I was so moved by all of these events and the things I had seen and experienced that while I was staying at Hua Zang Si, I wrote my humble "Hymn of Praise to my Buddha Master" included as Appendix C. I wanted all Americans to see what was possible for someone who truly had the power and wisdom of the Buddha Dharma: what it was like to be a Buddha.

While work on this publication was under way, I asked the Buddha how we should explain the Buddha Dharma that we were being taught to Westerners. The result was the now famous discourse "What Is Cultivation (Xiux-

16 *See page 215 for more on this speech.*

ing)?" that was carefully translated into English and included in this book of accomplishments. Xiuxing is a marvelous Chinese term that means to cultivate or improve oneself by reflection and correcting one's behavior. It is the foundation of our practice. The Buddha also imparted the *Sutra on Understanding Definitive Truth* that was included in the treasure book in Chinese. A series of discourses that further explain the *Sutra on Understanding Definitive Truth* was given late in 2008 by the Buddha while the Buddha and the Buddha's entourage traveled across the USA. The Buddha would often give discourses while traveling with small groups of close disciples in various parts of the world.

"What Is Cultivation?" (also called "The Dharma of Cultivation") is such a special discourse that holy beings came to the mandala where it was given and made themselves known to a number of us by flashing dazzling colored lights. At first, I thought someone was using a flash camera, only that seemed very disrespectful and this was much brighter and more dazzling and had a more golden color than that of a camera. I very rudely looked around. There was no camera nor apparent source. My second thought was that I was just imagining it. Of course, no one else was showing any signs of seeing anything— they were all so engrossed in the Buddha's discourse, and much too well behaved to respond. The lights came again many times—I lost count after the third, but I know it was more than three times. They were very bright and quite distinct. No sooner had the Buddha ended the discourse and we had paid our respects, than everyone began talking at once. Even though it was in Chinese I could gather from the hand gestures and excitement that they had seen the same thing I saw. Ven. Gadu Rinpoche of Taiwan, whose English is quite good, explained what he had seen as did several others. It appeared that everyone present had seen something, but we did not all see the same thing or the same colors. This was often the case when supernormal events occurred. There was no doubt that holy beings had come to listen to this very important discourse, and they were very pleased and showed their joy by blessing us with their presence.

For a short period of time after that, these lights would miraculously appear. Once I saw them flash most auspiciously when the Buddha was talking to Ven. Gadu Rinpoche. At that time the Holy Beings were indicating approval of the design proposed for the cover of *A Treasury of True Buddha Dharma* (the draft version of the book *H.H. Dorje Chang Buddha III*). The sparkling lights showed up right after the Buddha agreed to the design composed by the rinpoche. I just happened to be standing near the Buddha when this happened. They also flashed one Sunday morning at the hermitage where I lived when I was reading one of the Buddha's discourses in preparation for a class that would be taught later on that day. They came at another time when the Buddha was giving a discourse, but this time I was told to not be distracted and pay attention to the Buddha, but I must confess that before I was reprimanded, I searched the mandala thoroughly for any possible sources of light. There were none. These were truly blessings from another dimension. These were the manifestation of the Buddhas and Bodhisattvas who came to show their respect to our great Buddha Master!

After a preliminary draft of this book was compiled, it was sent to high level, Buddhist leaders—some who were world renowned Dharma kings and some not, but all of very high spiritual esteem. Eventually more than one hundred wrote back to either recognize the Buddha Master as an incarnation of Dorje Chang Buddha, corroborate the recognition, or offer congratulations on the magnificent achievements of the Buddha.

Five Vidyas

Sound
Art & Craftsmanship
Healing
Causal or Logic
Inner Realization

H.H. Dorje Chang Buddha III

Now, how did these incarnated holy beings know that Master Wan Ko Yee, as this Buddha was previously known, is an incarnation of Dorje Chang Buddha? When they were sent this earlier draft version of the treasure book, they were asked to read it. That book contained over thirty categories of accomplishments that indicated the Buddha's achievements in the Five Vidyas and His mastery of both exoteric and esoteric Buddhism.[17]

So, these accomplished Buddhist leaders looked at the evidence of what Master Wan Ko Yee had done in regard to craftsmanship—creating beauty and joy in the arts and the area of technology. His paintings sell for millions of dollars. A recent auction sale of one painting sold for the highest price per square foot of any Chinese painting in history. There have been several museums constructed to showcase His work in both China and now in the United States. They looked at what the Buddha had done in regard to healing—both humans and non-humans as well as fixing broken, inanimate objects. They looked at what the Buddha had done in regard to sound, both in music and debate as well as all forms of communication in the human and in other realms. They looked at the Buddha's understanding

---

17 *Exoteric and esoteric Buddhism: The exoteric includes the open or public teachings of Shakyamuni Buddha that serve as the foundation or fundamentals of all forms of Buddhism, while the esoteric includes everything in the exoteric plus certain secret practices that are usually only transmitted orally from master to disciple. Theravada, Zen, and Pure Land traditions are examples of the exoteric while the various Tibetan and Chinese Vajrayana sects and the Shingon tradition in Japan are examples of the esoteric.*

of cause and effect or Buddhist logic. Finally, they looked at the Buddha's level of inner realization as expressed through His demonstration of supernormal powers and the supernatural events that occurred in His presence. The latter include manifestations of beautiful rainbow "Buddha Lights" around the sun and moon or on the clouds after or while the Buddha expounded the Dharma or in conjunction with events associated with the Buddha. It also includes having the Buddhas bestow nectar from the sky into a bowl in front of disciples.

These same Buddhist leaders also investigated Master Wan Ko Yee's understanding of the principles of exoteric and esoteric Buddhism. Some determined on the spot that this had to be the work of a Buddha. No ordinary being could accomplish what was shown in that book. Other more highly realized ones actually went further and used their own supernormal powers to determine just who this magnificent holy one was by entering into a deep samadhi

FIGURE 15: H.H. Dodrupchen Dharma King (1927--), of the Nyingma Sect, sole holder of the complete Great Perfection Longchen Nying-thik, the highest dharma for transforming into the rainbow body.

state and traveling to the Dharma realms to investigate. They determined this holy being was the third incarnation of Dorje Chang Buddha. H.H. Dodrup-chen Rinpoche, (FIGURE 15) H.H. Penor Rinpoche, (FIGURE 5 page 26) and H.H. Omniscience Jamyang Lungdok Gyaltsen who was also known as Lama Achuk (FIGURE 36 page 97)—all Dharma Kings of the Nyingmapa Sect; H.H. Jigme Dorje, Dharma King of the Jonang Sect (FIGURE 16); H.E. Chogye Trichen (FIGURE 17), Dharma King of the Sakya sect; and H.E. Shamarpa Rinpoche, (FIGURE 18) Dharma King of the Kagyu sect were among the Buddhist leaders who recognized H.H. Dorje Chang Buddha III.

FIGURE 16: H.H. Jigme Dorje Dharma King (1944--), Supreme Leader of the Jonang Sect.

Some years later as confusion arose over whether or not H.H. Dorje Chang Buddha was actually a Buddha, Great Holy Wangzha Shangzun conducted a Jin Gang Fa Man Ze Jue Dharma Assembly to perform a Dharma of Selection to also verify His status. This astounding event is described in detail later in this book. This is one of the highest holy inner-tantric "selection" Dharmas used to determine correct results among alternative outcomes and is used to determine the true or false status of any holy being.

Of course, no one in this world truly has the ability to recognize a Buddha,

55

nor is it necessary for them to do so. H.H. Dorje Chang Buddha III is a Buddha because of His level of realization and not because He has been designated so by anyone's recognition.

FIGURE 17: H.E. Chogye Trichen Dharma King (1920-2007), of the Tsharpa Branch of the Sakya Sect.

FIGURE 18: H.E. Shamarpa (1952-2014), of the Kagyu Sect.

four

Who Is Dorje Chang Buddha?

Let us start by looking at just who Dorje Chang Buddha is. In the beginning of beginningless time, there was only the primordial Adharma Buddha[18] or Dharmakaya Buddha. Everything was boundless and everything was silent. The great world religions have this concept but call it by different names. It can only be referred to as a concept since it is beyond our feeble ability to comprehend or understand it completely. Some call it the Absolute or Universal Truth—which is expressed in Buddhism as infinite wisdom and compassion, while others refer to the Void, "All-That-Is," and so forth. Some Native Americans refer to it as the Great Mystery. Some Buddhists refer to this primordial Buddha as Samantabhadra, but the naked bright blue Buddha personified on some Tibetan lineage trees whom they call Samantabhadra Buddha or the red sun and the yellow crescent moon shown on our lineage chart are only symbols for that which cannot be seen or heard. The Dharmakaya or Adharma Buddha has no form. The Dharmakaya Buddha cannot speak or save living beings.

So, out of infinite love and compassion, the sambhogakaya[19] form was manifested and that being was known as Dorje Chang Buddha (Tibetan) or

---

18 *Adharma Buddha is also referred to as the Adi-Buddha and represents the dharmakaya. This aspect of a Buddha represents the truth of the universe and is experienced by those who obtain the direct realization of emptiness. It has no form, does not come or go, is boundless. It is sometimes also called the Truth Body. It is synonymous with "ultimate enlightenment" or "original nature," or "Buddha-nature. The dharmakaya is sometimes referred to as the mind or wisdom of a Buddha, but that is not quite correct. The Buddha's mind or wisdom is the use of the dharmakaya, but not the same as the dharmakaya.*

19 *Sambhogakaya: The subtle body of a Buddha that is only visible to great adepts (Bodhisattvas) and sometimes referred to as the bliss or reward body. The various Buddhas use their sambhogakaya form to communicate the dharma to select audiences of Bodhisattvas and celestial beings. The sambhogakaya beings do have form, but of a different type than of the nirmanakaya that is visible to most humans.*

Buddha Vajradhara (Sanskrit), a bright blue holy being Who is usually portrayed dressed in elaborate silks and adorned with jewels. It was Dorje Chang Buddha who began transmitting Dharma and saving living beings in the universe. As a result, Buddhism was born, and the Buddha Dharma began spreading in the world of living beings. Without Dorje Chang Buddha, there would be no Buddhism in the universe. H.H. Dorje Chang Buddha III's Lineage Tree (FIGURE 19) shows the original Dharmakaya Buddha as symbolized by the sun and the moon followed by the primordial Sambhogakaya Buddha, Dorje Chang Buddha. Next is H.H. Dorje Chang Buddha II, Venerable Vimalakirti, followed by our current manifestation, H.H. Dorje Chang Buddha III. The Lineage Tree also shows the ten Dharmapalas or Dharma Protectors of our lineage.

Dorje Chang Buddha is the master and teacher of all the Buddhas and Bodhisattvas including the five different colored Buddhas of the five directions[20] plus Shakyamuni Buddha and Vajrasattva Mahasattva. Of course, there are many, many more Buddhas in the universe.

The Buddhist Lineage Refuge Tree in Appendix D shows the three emanations of Dorje Chang Buddha radiating out in rainbows from the original, central form. On the left is Ven. Vimalakirti, a great layman who incarnated in this world to help Shakyamuni Buddha over 2,500 years ago. Many people are familiar with His

> *"One Buddha is all Buddhas."*
>
> *All Buddhas are one Buddha."*
>
> — *H.H. Dorje Chang Buddha III*
> *The Definitive Truth Sutra*

famous sutra where He performs all sorts of supernormal manifestations to convince Shakyamuni's disciples of the true nature of reality and why they should follow the Mahayana path to become Bodhisattvas. Many Buddhists never thought Ven. Vimalakirti[21] actually existed and felt that His miracles were merely metaphors. Well, He did exist and, as the first incarnation of Dorje Chang Buddha, He was, of course, able to do all the miraculous things reported in His sutra. Now, He has come back again as the second incarnation of Dorje Chang Buddha in the form of H.H. Dorje Chang Buddha III, who is shown on the far-right side of our lineage charts. There is also Dipamkara Buddha, sometimes referred to as the "Lamp Bearer Buddha," who was the master and teacher of Shakyamuni

---

20 *The Five Buddhas of the Five Directions are Amitabha of the west, Amoghasiddhi of the north, Akshobhya of the east, Ratnasambhava of the south, and Mahavairocana of the center.*

21 *H.H. Dudjom Jigdral Yeshe Dorje, the first dharma king of that lineage after the Tibetan diaspora, discusses Venerable Vimalakirti in his monumental treatises on the history of the Nyingma sect.*

Buddha. Dipamkara Buddha was also an emanation or manifestation of Dorje Chang Buddha, but in another world system—not on this earth. Appendix D graphically portrays these Buddhas and how they have transmitted Dharma to this world system with the founders, patriarchs, and matriarchs of the major exoteric and esoteric schools that are still existing in our world today. Three of the existing Tibetan sects were founded by holy beings who were advanced enough to be able to receive teachings directly from Dorje Chang Buddha although they also follow the teachings transmitted by the Buddha who is in charge of our current era on this earth, the World-Honored Shakyamuni Buddha.

FIGURE 19: The Lineage Tree of H.H. Dorje Chang Buddha III. The BUDDHAS listed from top to bottom—The Original Dharmakaya Buddha as symbolized by the sun and the moon; The Primordial Sambhogakaya Buddha, Dorje Chang Buddha; H.H. Dorje Chang Buddha II, Venerable Vimalakirti; and H.H. Dorje Chang Buddha III. The Dharma Protectors from left to right are Yama, Hayagriva, Yamataka, Ekajati, Lion Vajra, Kalachakra, Vajrakilaya, Chakrasam-vara, Maha-kala, and Guhyasamaja.

Shakyamuni Buddha (FIGURE 20), the historical Buddha for this era and the first to teach what we know as Buddhism in this world, was a nirmanakaya[22]

22 *Nirmanakaya: The form a Buddha takes that is visible to most humans. It is also called the trans-formation or emanation body. A Buddha can appear in many forms to save living beings, both human*

FIGURE 20: Shakyamuni Buddha as painted by H.H. Dorje Chang Buddha III.

Buddha when he walked on this earth 2,500 years ago. His Holiness Dorje Chang Buddha III is also a nirmanakaya Buddha. Shakyamuni Buddha was not the first buddha in this world, only the first to teach the holy Dharma. Prior to that time, living beings had not evolved to a point where they could receive the Dharma.

However, H.H. Dorje Chang Buddha III is not the only current manifestation of a great holy being. There are Bodhisattvas or Bodhisattvas who are even equal to a Buddha who have also incarnated in recent times. Examples of this

and non-human, and even as inanimate objects like a bridge or a tree.

60

include H.H. Dodrupchen Rinpoche (FIGURE 15 page 54), a manifestation of Guru Padmasambhava; the other Nyingma Dharma Kings H.H. Penor Rinpoche (FIGURE 5 page 26), mentioned earlier who was a manifestation of Vajrapani Bodhisattva and H.H. Trulshik Rinpoche, a manifestation of Maitreya Bodhisattva; and the Kagyu Dharma King H.E. Shamarpa Rinpoche (FIGURE 18 page 56), who was a manifestation of Kuan Yin Bodhisattva, just to name a few. They were among the many Buddhist leaders who recognized Master Wan Ko Yee as the true incarnation of Dorje Chang Buddha, the highest Buddha in the universe.

Why Did H.H. Dorje Chang Buddha III Come to America?

Now, why did my Buddha Master, H.H. Dorje Chang Buddha III, come to this world and why is He living in America? There is a prophecy that is often quoted in Buddhist circles. Guru Padmasambhava, a great Bodhisattva who brought Buddhism to Tibet in the 7th-8th century, predicted that when "iron birds fly and horses run on wheels, the Tibetan people will be scattered like ants across the face of the earth and the teachings of the Buddha or Dharma will go to the land of the red man." That prophecy refers to the Western world and that time has come. We have seen increasing interest in Buddhism in America partly due to the Tibetan diaspora of Buddhist leaders and practitioners leaving Tibet and many Tibetans settling in America; partly due to the tremendous immigration of people to the U.S. from other Buddhist countries, especially Southeast Asia, China, Korea, and Japan; and partly due to the many Americans living here who were searching for something more than what their culture and traditions provided them and who went to Asia and found the path of the Buddha. I was such a person.

We know that over the centuries many errors have been perpetuated within the various lineages of Buddhism. Anyone who has studied Buddhism knows that we are living in the Dharma ending age whereby it is becoming increasingly difficult for us to hear, understand, and practice the true Dharma. His Holiness Dorje Chang Buddha III came to correct these errors and to transmit Dharmas that are appropriate for this age. It is true that most of what is being presented as the teachings of the Buddha today in America is but a dim shadow of what Shakyamuni Buddha taught and His disciples practiced 2,500 years ago in India and even later in China, Japan, Tibet and elsewhere. Many no longer believe that enlightenment is possible in this lifetime or at all, yet that was not the Buddha's original message.

There are also many erroneous views and practices that have crept into Buddhist practice that are not only not helpful, but some are even harmful.

Several years ago, I was able to go to Thailand and participate in an ordination ceremony for several young women. It was an illegal ceremony held in secret some distance from Bangkok. We had to be careful going to this site as women are not allowed to be ordained in Thailand, or at least not at that time. I will never forget how happy these women were and one in particular, who spent the entire trip singing the most beautiful chants. It was heavenly music. When I asked about her, I was told her sad story. She was Thai but her husband was Chinese. Her in-laws had forced her to sell her daughter so as to have the money to send her son to a monastery to become a monk. Apparently, there is a belief that having a son who is a monk can help you get into the Buddha Lands. This seemed unbelievable to me. Later I learned that the little temple where these nuns lived was burned down by local monks.

In just the past 50 years much of the true Buddha Dharma has been lost. Almost no masters currently exist who possess the power of the Buddha Dharma that can liberate living beings in their current lifetime. It is as was also prophesized by Shakyamuni Buddha and mentioned earlier that the true Buddha Dharma would only last a short time on this earth and after several thousand years we would enter the "Dharma Ending Age" where the remaining practitioners would be of limited or low capacity, the Dharma would not be transmitted correctly, and the world would be beset with so many problems that it would be impossible to practice. Master Jamgon Ju Mipham Gyatso (1846 -1912), a famous master and Dharma King of the Nyingma sect from the Derge region of Kham in Eastern Tibet, also warned us that "…as sutras and tantras prophesy, there are many who, having abandoned the profound meaning through dry analysis…distribute quasi-doctrine for material gain, leading those of low merit and small intelligence on a perverse path at this time of the end of the era."

Just by looking around us, it can be seen that we have entered this "Dharma-Ending Age." However, Shakyamuni Buddha, having foreseen this dark age, provided for teachings that were appropriate for the different ages and predicted that great Holy Ones would incarnate at appropriate times and places to revitalize and teach the Dharma that was appropriate for that period of time and place. This happened in India with the incarnation of Master Nagarjuna, Master Asanga, Master Vasubandhu, and others; and again in Tibet with the incarnation of Guru Padmasambhava, Master Marpa, Lord Tsongkhapa, and Master Longchenpa; and it happened elsewhere. It is because of these conditions that His Holiness Dorje Chang Buddha III came to this world to demonstrate that the true Buddha Dharma does still exist and to offer us a "quick path" to liberation.[23] I believe that is why H.H. Penor Rinpoche told us that H.H. Dorje

---

23 *The term liberation is used to mean enlightened or free from the cycle of birth and death. It can be thought of as the ultimate accomplishment.*

Chang Buddha III should demonstrate many miracles and supernatural powers. My Buddha Master has told us that today people will only believe in the power of the Buddha Dharma if they see miraculous things. Dry analysis and theories are not enough. Theories alone do not lead to liberation. Only a holy being can liberate other beings and a holy being must be able to demonstrate miracles.

It is to help propagate the true Buddha Dharma and to help others have faith in these teachings that I am writing this book about my own unbelievable experiences and teachings that I have received, as well as sharing evidence of the appearance in the West of a Holy Vajra Throne that can provide the portal and connection to holy beings to help others become enlightened.

The Good News!

Although H.H. Dorje Chang Buddha III promotes and teaches from all the great traditions and "yanas"[24] of Buddhism, the Buddha has also given us a simpler and, for those who have the karmic affinity to follow it, a quicker path to liberation from the suffering and worries of this world. That path is introduced in a discourse given by the Buddha entitled "What Is Cultivation?" and is expounded further in *The Supreme and Unsurpassable Mahamudra of Liberation* and other teachings by the Buddha Master. The *Mahamudra of Liberation* is the highest Buddha Dharma that Dorje Chang Buddha transmitted to Amitabha Buddha and all the other Buddhas and Great Bodhisattvas in the ten directions during their cultivation stage. The Buddha tells us that it is a wonderful treasure that leads to the fastest attainment of happiness and benefits if practiced by any cultivator. No matter what sect or school you belong to and no matter whether you have received an initiation or not, as long as you are one who cultivates yourself according to the Dharma and who practices according to the Dharma set forth in *The Supreme and Unsurpassable Mahamudra of Liberation,* you can become perfectly accomplished in either the Blessings, Longevity, and Wealth Accomplishment Dharma or the Ascendance to the Stage of a Great Bodhisattva Accomplishment Dharma. "**The Xiaman Most Excellent Oceanic Mind Essence**" and "**The Ultimate Bodhicitta for Attaining Dharma-Nature True-Suchness Oceanic Mind Essence**" from *The Supreme and Unsurpassable Mahamudra of Liberation* have been made publicly available to all who want to learn and practice in order to obtain perfect good fortune and wisdom and to become accomplished. It does not matter what sect of Buddhism you follow or even if you are a Buddhist! A person who practices this Dharma

24 Yanas: *Most commonly referred to as the "triyana" or three yanas of the traditional or fundamental hinayana, the exoteric mahayana, and the esoteric or secret teachings of the vajrayana. All of these traditions are now well represented in America.*

does not need a guru or to recognize H.H. Dorje Chang Buddha III as his or her master to be able to successfully follow this Dharma. The Dharma practice of *The Supreme and Unsurpassable Mahamudra of Liberation* is divided into the complete practice, the simple and easy practice, and the supreme practice of essence within essence. It is also classified into seven types of Dharma practices at different levels according to the level of the master giving the initiation: Jingxing Practice, holy inner-tantric, inner-tantric, or outer-tantric initiation; practice without any initiation; practice based on one's own reading of the rituals without being taught by a master, and even practice by one who has not taken refuge and does not consider himself a Buddhist.

When asked what sect He represented, H.H. Dorje Chang Buddha III said He represents the Buddha Sect or the sect of Shakyamuni Buddha. The Buddha has also been very careful to explain that it is not His intent nor should anyone attempt to consolidate all the sects into one giant mega sect. That would be very much against the teachings of the Buddha. Each sect or school represents a particular method or system of methods that is appropriate for the karmic conditions of a particular group of followers. Shakyamuni Buddha taught 84,000 methods to help living beings on the path. The Buddha also told us that Shakyamuni Buddha only taught about 30% of the Dharma He had learned from Dipamkara Buddha (Dorje Chang Buddha) while on this earth because that was all those living at that time were ready to hear.

All these different methods evolved into particular schools or sects. The Buddha further told us that no matter what the school may be, we do not dismiss it. The Buddha emphasized that the various Buddhist schools must not be lessened. If Buddhist schools decrease in number, then living beings will not be able to correspond with them. That is because each living being has his or her own karmic conditions. The Buddha further told His disciples that whether they were of the Nyingma, Kagyu, Sakya, Geluk, Jonang, Pure Land, Zen, exoteric or esoteric school, each of them should diligently establish the teachings and precepts of their school and carry out the teachings of Shakyamuni Buddha. The bibliography at the end of this book provides more on the major sects or schools that still exist, especially in America.

Appendix D shows the genesis and evolution of the major sects. The chart is no indication of the level of realization of the Dharma kings, rinpoches, and Dharma teachers shown there, but it does attempt to show the major schools that are still in existence and are active in America. All of the schools can trace their roots back to the original Dorje Chang Buddha and some had matriarchs and patriarchs like Lady Niguma and Master Tilopa who were evolved to the point that they were able to receive Dharma transmissions directly from Dorje

Chang Buddha in the Sambhogakaya realms. This chart represents a greatly simplified overview of the major sects of Buddhism. Roughly, the sects can be grouped according to one of four major lineage traditions.

The first three are all within the exoteric part of Buddhism:

1) "The Lineage of the Elders" is the first. It is based on the fundamental teachings that Shakyamuni Buddha taught while he lived in India over 2,500 years ago and is recorded in the hinayana version of the *Tripitaka*. It is known as the First Turning of the Wheel of Dharma and was taught at the beginning of Shakyamuni Buddha's career. It is the form of Buddhism that was exported very early to Sri Lanka, Burma, Thailand, Cambodia, Laos, and southern Vietnam and is still practiced in those countries. It is practiced in this country by the people who immigrated here from those countries and by Western students who often refer to it as "Insight Meditation." It also forms the foundation for all the other lineages.

2) "The Profound or Wisdom Lineage" of the Madhyamaka School is the second great lineage tradition. It is primarily based on the *Prajnaparamita Sutras* from the Second Turning of the Wheel of Dharma. These were teachings given by Shakyamuni Buddha later on in his career but were not accepted or understood by most humans living at that time. Shakyamuni Buddha predicted that the world would be ready for them about 500 years after He left this world and entrusted the teachings with the Naga kings and certain Bodhisattvas, especially Manjurshri Bodhisattva. Around the time of Christ, Master Nagarjuna developed and taught this Dharma. It formed the foundation for the Pure Land and Chan schools that later developed in China and spread into Vietnam, Korea, and Japan and from those countries into the West.

3) The third is "The Method Lineage." It included the teachings of the Mind Only or Yogachara School that are based on the Buddha's teachings on Buddha-nature from the Third Turning of the Wheel of Dharma, also using the Prajnaparamita Sutras, along with the *Lotus Sutra* and others as its foundation and forming the basis for the T'ian T'ai and Fa-Hsiang Schools in China and later the Tendai and Nichiren sects in Japan. In the fourth century of the current era, Master Asanga was able to go to the Dharma realms and receive the teachings of this tradition directly from Maitreya Bodhisattva including the *Uttaratantra Shastra* and others listed in the Bibliography. Except for Soka Gakkai International (SGI), a branch on the Nichiren sect, this school is not as popular in the United States. The Yogachara texts have not been translated as widely as others.

However, these were still but a small part of the Dharma that Shakyamuni had learned from Dipamkara (Dorje Chang) Buddha. While alive, the Buddha taught additional secret teachings to His son Rahula, but before He left this world, He also entrusted them to His assistant, Ananda, with instructions to teach them to Padmasambhava, who was born a few years later in what is now known as the Swat Region of Pakistan in the fifth century BCE. The early Dharma kings and adepts in India received and practiced these esoteric teachings and were able to evolve to a level that some could even directly access the Dharma from Dorje Chang Buddha. Padmasambhava and his disciple Yeshe Tsogyal also left behind many hidden Dharmas known as "termas" that were discovered by their evolved disciples when the time was right.

All these secret esoteric practices or tantra became known as:

4) "The Practices and Blessings Lineages" that were exported into Tibet and Mongolia starting around the seventh century of this era. Although they reached China, where they formed the basis for the Chen-Yen sect, they were deemed too powerful for the masses and only practiced secretly by elites. They were, however, exported to Japan where they became known as the Shingon sect. This esoteric branch of the Mahayana became known as the Vajrayana.

While living in India, Shakyamuni Buddha also taught the Kalachakra Tantra to King Suchandra. This advanced form of tantra practice eventually found its way to India and then Tibet to become the foundation for the Jonang sect, although it is also popular in the other Tibetan sects. I will write more about this great dharma later.

Appendix D shows how the five or six major sects evolved in Tibet but does not show many other important linkages. The Vajrayana or esoteric schools require strict adherence to secret practices and depend on the blessings and help of Buddhas, Bodhisattvas, and Dharma Protectors from other realms in order to more quickly achieve liberation—even in one lifetime, which is something not possible in the exoteric traditions.

five

The Big Blue Treasure Book Tour of America

I again broached the subject of making a tour of the USA to introduce the Buddha to the American people, only this time it would be with the big blue treasure book *H.H. Dorje Chang Buddha III* (FIGURE 21). There was a lot of support for the idea and the Dharma Propagation Tour was begun. Many wanted to participate, contributing funding, books, silk khatas,[25] and other things to make the trip possible. A team that included monastics and lay people was assembled. With the help of students in different parts of the country, we compiled a list of over 2,500 Dharma-related locations in every state and representative of all the major sects. We first sent a letter to these places telling them that we would either be sending them a copy of the treasure book or we would be visiting them while on the tour and giving them a copy at that time. We arranged to visit all fifty states to make public presentations at over seventy locations.

I had another motivation for the trip and criteria for selecting certain stops on the trip. Ever since I had learned that my Buddha Master was a Buddha, I felt we should erect a stupa to commemorate that fact and His coming to America. Unfortunately, I knew very little about stupas. In fact, I had never even seen a stupa. So, I researched where there were stupas in America and plotted our tour to be able to visit and pay our respects at as many as possible.

The Dharma Propagation Tour of the USA unofficially began in March 2008 when Bodi Wentu Rinpoche and I first went to the nation's capitol to brief certain congressional staff members on the treasure book and introduce them to the Buddha. I knew this would be an auspicious event when I saw a great Dharma protector watching us as we prepared to leave the condo where

---

25 *A kharta or khata is a gossamer thin silk scarf that is ceremoniously offered as a sign of respect in Tibet. Most of the books that were distributed were wrapped in a pure white kharta, which was then presented to the recipient when the books were delivered by hand.*

FIGURE 21: H.H. Dorje Chang Buddha III: A Treasury of True Buddha-Dharma, a book that explains who has recognized this holy being as the supreme Buddha and why, establishes thirty categories of accomplishments in the Five Vidyas, and includes two sutras on cultivation and realizing definitive truth.

we were staying in Maryland to go on to Capitol Hill and do our work explaining how an ancient Buddha had come from another realm—another dimension—to help relieve the suffering of living beings. Earlier that morning there had been bright lights flashing in my room, just like I reported earlier when "What Is Cultivation?" was first transmitted by the Buddha Master. Now there was a large red transparent figure moving through the trees in the wooded area across from the condo. We were being watched and protected so that we could carry out this important mission. I kept thinking that

FIGURE 22: Congresswoman Ileana Ros-Lehtinen, who spoke at the Library of Congress ceremony, talks to Disciple Denma Tsemang II Longzhi Tanpe Nyima Rinpoche, Washington, D.C.

this was such an auspicious start for our effort to let America know that we have a very great holy one living in our midst.

Honorable Tom Lantos, California Congressman and the late chairman of the House Foreign Relations Committee, had sponsored a tribute to Master Wan Ko Yee in the House of Representatives in September 2007 and arranged for us to use the formal and elegant member's meeting room at the Library of Congress for our presentation to members of Congress, the Diplomatic Corps, Dharma kings and rinpoches from around the world, and other monastic and lay Buddhists. We unveiled the treasure book *H.H. Dorje Chang Buddha III* and told those present about the accomplishments of this holy Buddha and how the Buddha had been recognized by the leading Buddhists in the world at a presentation at the Library in April 2008. Disciple Denma Tsemang II Longzhi Tanpe Nyima Rinpoche, secretary to the Buddha, and Ven. Long Hui Shi, Chairperson of the International Buddhism Sangha Association, formally presented the book to Dr. Judy S. Lu, Chief of the Asian Division of the Library of Congress of the United States. Congresswoman Ileana Ros-Lehtinen of Florida and other dignitaries spoke at the ceremony (FIGURE 22).

The Dharma Propagation Tour to all fifty U.S. States formally began on June 21, 2008 at Hua Zang Si, a Buddhist Temple located in San Francisco, California, with a Grand Assembly honoring the treasure book, *H.H. Dorje Chang Buddha III*. When the banner announcing the event was erected over the entrance to the temple, beautiful Buddha-lights could be seen all over the city, across the bay, and even as far away as Davis, California. This beautiful rainbow encircling the sun was visible in a clear sky with no sign of rain or rain clouds. These Buddha-lights are often visible around the sun or moon whenever there are events associated with H.H. Dorje Chang Buddha III and other holy beings. This was but the beginning of the auspicious signs and events that accompanied us on the tour.

I have seen these Buddha lights so frequently that they do not seem unusual, but I am still in awe of their beauty. These magical lights can appear around either the sun or the moon or sometimes on clouds. In the entire sixty years before I met my Buddha Master, I saw what is commonly referred to as "sun dogs" or parhelia three times. Two were just auspicious occasions and one was when the body of a Tibetan Rinpoche was cremated under the watchful eye of H.H. Dilgo Khyentse. Since I have been following H.H. Dorje Chang Buddha III, I have seen dozens of these rainbows. Furthermore, none of the earlier events were as vast or as colorful as the ones I have seen since following my Buddha Master. The Buddha-light shown in FIGURE 8 was the biggest I had seen up to that time and it lasted for many hours. I must admit I did not notice the red robed being sitting in the halo of that Buddha-light until my Buddha Master pointed

FIGURE 23   Snow Lions and Dragons came to dance in the street in front of the temple at the auspicious Grand Assembly to honor the release of the Big Blue Treasure Book at Hua Zang Si in San Francisco, California.

it out. Of course, I could see Him then, although sometimes He appears to be visible and sometimes, He does not appear to be there. Also, some people can see Him and some cannot. This phenomenon was part of an even more mysterious series of events that I will explain later.

Before the tour could begin, however, the treasure book had to be officially presented at this Grand Assembly at Hua Zang Si, our main temple in San Francisco. Prior to the start of the Grand Assembly, Chinese music was played in the barricaded street and snow lions danced to welcome the official arrival of the treasure book at the temple (FIGURE 23). Flowers from well-wishers lined the street outside the temple for the Grand Assembly to honor the release of this book. (FIGURE 24) Many Dharma kings, venerable ones, rinpoches, Dharma masters

FIGURE 24: Flowers from well-wishers lined the street outside the temple for the Grand Assembly to honor the treasure book.

FIGURE 25: Magnolia Tree that rained Holy Nectar at Hua Zang Si in San Francisco after the Grand Assembly. Nectar has rained through that tree both when it had leaves and before its leaves came out. The rain does not come from or even touch the tree.

and lay men and women attended the dignified formal ceremony that followed. After the treasure book was received and congratulatory speeches given by temple officials and local dignitaries, I addressed the group and told them of the forthcoming Dharma Propagation Tour to introduce the book to all fifty states.

No sooner had I finished talking and the group started to assemble outdoors in the courtyard of the temple, when I heard much shouting and could make out the words, "It's raining nectar!" Sure enough, fragrant and sweet holy nectar could be seen, felt, smelled, and tasted under the holy magnolia tree in the courtyard (FIGURE 25).

Now the magnolia tree from southern California was the site of nectar rain again in San Francisco and this time on many people. There was a jubilant commotion in the courtyard with hundreds of excited people trying to get a taste of the nectar when it was then announced that it was also raining nectar under the tree in front of the temple. It was as if the Buddhas and Bodhisattvas wanted even more of us to partake in the blessings. The crowded courtyard could not hold the thousand or so people who had attended that Grand Assembly.

Sunday, the next day after the Grand Assembly at Hua Zang Si, we met in the temple to complete our plans for the tour. When we left, someone noticed that nectar was once again raining under the tree in front of the temple. Hands went up to catch the precious dew. I am not certain if it was also raining in the courtyard or not, but I understood it continued to rain the blessed nectar for some time. There is also a film documenting this whole event. Everyone was happy to receive so many blessings and experience the blessings of the true Buddha Dharma.

However, Sunday afternoon, immediately following this joyous event, I became quite ill. It is not uncommon for karmic conditions to ripen or demonic obstructions to arise when one is taking on a major Dharma activity. I knew something serious was happening and wanted to get back to southern California as soon as possible.

Several of my students volunteered to drive me back. I did not let them know just how bad I was feeling because I did not want them to worry and if they had driven me to Pasadena, they would need to turn around and make the return trip, yet that night, in order to be at their jobs the following Monday morning. I asked them to just put me on a plane, but secretly I was very glad for their support and presence.

When I got up the next morning in Pasadena, I had major problems. The right side of my body was numb, and my voice was slurred. It was difficult to even put a sentence together. When I tried to walk, I found myself staggering. My dear roommate, Akou Lamo Rinpoche, and another vajra sister drove me to the emergency room. It looked like a stroke and the good folks at the hospital responded accordingly. However, they could find nothing. When my Buddha Master, H.H. Dorje Chang Buddha III, heard I was in the hospital, the Buddha told my vajra brothers and sisters that I had indeed had a stroke and also that the medical doctors would not be able to find anything, which was indeed exactly what happened. The Buddha also told them to get me to the Buddha's mandala as soon as possible. Jue Hui Fa Shih, one of the abbots at Hua Zang Si, came and got me as I wasn't able to drive. Once there, my compassionate Buddha Master performed certain rituals whereby the Buddha transferred a little of the Buddha's energy to me and gave me a longevity empowerment. I could tell I was healed, but I was still pretty weak. After a couple of days of rest, I felt fine. The Buddha had saved my life one other time before, so I was quite certain that this problem would be solved, and this would not delay the tour.

On the other occasion I found that I was losing my life force. I was slowly becoming weaker and weaker and my body was growing colder and colder. The Buddha had promised to cure me so that I was not too worried, but I did find it increasingly difficult to even function. I knew that my Buddha Master was very busy, so I did not want to bother the Buddha by reminding the Buddha of His promise. One night when I reported that I needed to go home to rest, the Buddha looked up at me and told me to stay. I did, while my Buddha Master went into the next room. When the Buddha returned, He told the group who then gathered around me something in Chinese that caused them to be very serious. Since I did not understand what was said, I was not concerned as the Buddha was quite jovial and laughing. He then performed the ritual that saved my life. What the Buddha had told the others was that my chakras were shutting down and unless He intervened, I was a goner. They should be prepared to notify my next of kin and arrange for my funeral. After I received a little of His energy I recovered, but it took several days to do so. My body felt as if I had been run over by a semi. Every cell in my body ached. The shock of all that energy was so intense, but it did the job and my body temperature returned to normal and I was okay. Once again, I was intimately aware of just how magnificent my Buddha Master is.

The treasure book *H.H. Dorje Chang Buddha III* could now officially be distributed. Copies were both hand-delivered and mailed to temples and Dharma centers, public libraries, and other locations. The Dharma Propagation Team would distribute other copies as we did presentations across the country. The team started in southern California since our first presentations would be in that area. Thousands of copies were distributed with copies being hand delivered or mailed to the governors and state libraries of all fifty states. Our first presentation was at the annex of the Bodhi Tree Bookstore on Melrose in West Hollywood on July 6, 2008. This was an auspicious place to begin in as much as there was a large Bodhi tree behind the bookstore, just like the one that Shakyamuni Buddha had sat beneath over 2,500 years ago. I had been a little apprehensive about following the formal protocols of the Dharma at the beginning and end of these presentations like I normally do when conducting Dharma classes. After all, there would be all types of people there. Some who understood what bowing meant and why we always dedicated the merit of what we did, but there would be some who would find this quite strange and foreign. If it seemed necessary, I explained why we did those things. I am ashamed to admit these doubts, because my fears were unfounded. Oh, there were a few who couldn't bring themselves to bow or dedicate merit, but I honestly believe that most of those present were very comfortable with the concepts. Perhaps it was because they realized what an extraordinary event this was. A Buddha really had come to this earth and they just intuitively knew what to do to show the proper respect, no matter what they thought of the religion. There were even participants who went up to the altar after the presentation and did more prostrations and offered prayers.

Eight Fundamental Right Views of Cultivation

1. Impermanence
2. Firm Belief
3. Renunciation
4. True Vows
5. Diligence
6. Precepts
7. Meditation
8. Bodhicitta

— "What Is Cultivation?"

In addition to introducing the Buddha, I also introduced His Dharma by presenting the principles and concepts contained in the treasure book as "What Is Cultivation?" I explained the Eight Fundamental Right Views that were required and the order in which they needed to be practiced. You needed to understand impermanence to have correct motivation; develop a firm belief to have sufficient determination; follow with renunciation that forms the causes of liberation; thus enabling you to take true vows that ensure correct action; with the diligence that guarantees success; take precepts to provide correct direction; practice meditation to achieve wisdom and insight; and finally develop the bodhichitta that enables you to become a holy person or Bodhisattva and eventually a Buddha.

The original schedule was to continue to San Diego and then go up the coast to Santa Barbara and through central and northern California and on to the Pacific Northwest and down through Idaho and Utah to the Rocky Mountains and then head east. We would come back through the south in late October, November, and December. I wanted to be in the mountains during the heat of summer and make New England in time for fall. I did not want us to take our fifteen-passenger van through the mountain passes in the snow. We had delayed the trip almost a month to allow for the June ceremony at Hua Zang Si, but with this schedule there was still time to complete the tour this season.

However, after only two presentations and those from my home base in Pasadena, I was exhausted. Obviously, I was doing something wrong. I would like to tell you that I followed the advice I gave everyone else and changed my ways and was wonderful and on my way, but it was more difficult than that. Hearing the Dharma, understanding the Dharma, and even bringing others to the Dharma are one thing, but actually practicing the Dharma yourself is not so easy. Things were wonderful and many marvelous blessings happened, but that was due to the blessings of my Buddha Master and the importance of this mission, not my leadership. The Buddhas and Bodhisattvas were with us in spite of my negativity and poor self-cultivation. What made this trip so successful was attributable to the incredible compassion and kindness of many people and the blessings of holy beings. It was certainly no reflection on my abilities or accomplishments. In fact, my karmic obstacles continued through most of the tour and they continue to plague me. Life in samsara still bears the suffering of illness, pain, and death. Only when we can escape this realm can we be free.

I was very worried about going on what I was certain would be a stressful trip, traveling to so many states and giving so many talks over a short period of time. It would be intense! I was also uncomfortable with the entourage that was to accompany me. There was a lot acrimony and hard feelings and mistrust between several of the team members that I anticipated would make the trip even more stressful. Unfortunately, I was right.

More than once there were team members who wanted to leave the tour because they could not take the stress or endure the perceived insults. Each time they were told they could go, but that the person whom they did not get along with would have to leave as well. That was pretty much a bluff on my part because I knew we needed everyone, but it worked for most of the trip. All of the team were dedicated to propagating the Dharma and absolutely loyal to the Buddha. The thought that the trip might be jeopardized by their inability to cope helped them to try harder. Individuals brought their own personal problems with them and that contributed to the stress as well. However, this had to be a most awesome opportunity for practice. I needed to be very grateful first to my Buddha Master for blessing us and giving us the reason for taking the trip in the first place, then to all the individuals and groups who helped underwrite the cost of the trip and supported us in so many ways, and finally to the other team members who were going to give me so many opportunities to practice the Dharma.

Now I was having serious and sudden pains in my chest. Being close to seventy years old, I paid attention to them. As the chest pains got worse, I was uncertain if I could or should take this trip after all. My doctor wanted me to go back into the hospital for a complete cardiac check out. Additionally, because of my health problems, there were many things that I had not been able to do to prepare for the trip that still needed to be done. Frankly, some of the members of the team were not much help—or at least I was not able to get them to help. Several of the team seemed to have their own agendas and were pretty clueless about taking on responsibility for what I had hoped would be their portion of the tour. Perhaps I just didn't have the energy to give them clearer instructions and they lacked the ability to know what to do on their own. Other team members were great and handled their assigned areas very well. At the last minute there were two more people added to the team who were invaluable. That made a big difference, but I still had the chest pains to deal with. So, the weekend before we were to leave the following week, I checked in at the palatial Huntington Hospital in Pasadena—the second time in a little over a month—and not at all sure that the trip would proceed.

Just before I went back to the hospital, I learned that there would be a very high-level initiation, a Vajra-Bodhi Seed Empowerment for which I would need to prepare. My roommate came to the hospital to help me prepare. On Sunday I was released with a clean bill of health. My heart was just fine—better than normal even. A few of the Buddha's more senior disciples gathered to receive the first phase of the Vajra-Bodhi Seed Empowerment. It was a very special initiation that would plant the holy seed that guarantees one's accomplishment if, and only if, one keeps the vajra precepts. In strictest secrecy, we each selected either a vajra seed or a bodhi seed from a concealed container. There were an equal number of each type of seed. What was so amazing about this ceremony was the fact that the Buddha correctly predicted who had received which type of seed even though there was no way that the Buddha could have known that by ordinary means. This is one of the great Dharmas from *The Supreme and Unsurpassable Mahamudra of Liberation.* We not only received the empowerment, but also received a supply of precious and holy pills made from those used in the ceremony that we could pass on to those with whom we had a special karmic affinity. Once living beings (not just human beings) received such a pill, it was guaranteed that they would become an accomplished Buddhist in this life or at least have the opportunity to do so in their next life. I distributed several of these bright blue pills to not only my students, but others whom I met on the trip including a few members of the animal realm. I have continued to give these tiny pills to all who want them and more for their animal friends.

It had been predicted that a memorable event would occur during this ceremony. Sure enough, just before we gathered to enter the mandala of the Buddha there was such an event. It was just as the Buddha said it would be. A powerful earthquake struck to the east of where we were, and we felt it.

The empowerment gave me the energy to begin and we were on our way to Las Vegas as called for in our revised plans. We would need to postpone the North-West part of our trip, but we could still make New England by Fall and return through the south before the end of the year.

Deserts and Mountains

I remembered passing through the desert twenty-five or so years earlier and stopping near the Mojave National Preserve on I-40 on my way to Questa, New Mexico. I pulled into a roadside rest stop and took a brief nap under a pepper tree. I always traveled with a pillow and blanket as I had become increasingly prone to stop for naps when I drove. As I woke up from my nap, the light beings revisited me as before in Mexico, only this time I was able to communicate with the pepper tree I had been sleeping under. In fact, I could communicate with anyone, anywhere in the universe, or so it seemed. It was part of the initiation process and a very special sort of supernatural state. I was aware of the possibility of such altered states of consciousness and that other states of existence or realms actually existed and I could go there. At that time, I had no idea how you achieve that state or that this was one of the six supernormal powers that holy beings have. These supernormal experiences appeared to be random occurrences and, I found out, the result of spiritual work I had done in learning and practicing the Dharma in past lives. It had to be. I certainly was not living in accord with the Dharma at that time. But my good karma was maturing.

> "These eight fundamental right views are the foundation of cultivation, liberation, and accomplishment in the Dharma."
>
> H.H. Dorje Chang Buddha III
> What Is Cultivation?

We were anticipating hot weather—really, really hot weather for this part of the tour. When I had been in Las Vegas in March for a weekend intensive, I was told horror stories about Las Vegas in the summer—steering wheels so hot you had to wear gloves to drive; people sleeping during the day and doing their shopping and errands at night when it was cooler; and so forth. This was mid-August. But we were lucky. Or was it something else? We had near perfect weather for the entire trip. Except when we got the tail end of a couple of hurricanes, a tornado that missed us, and some dramatic hail and thunderstorms that were more drama than inconvenience, the weather could not have been better. We were truly blessed.

While in Las Vegas, I explained at a public meeting the importance of

Dorje Chang Buddha in all the various traditions of Buddhism and answered questions about esoteric Buddhism to representatives of many of the local Buddhist groups and others. I stressed the importance of learning the fundamental teachings of the Buddha that are common to all forms of practice prior to receiving the secret esoteric practices. I also talked about how when one follows the correct Dharma one receives the blessings of holy beings who will guide one in one's practice. When the photos of the pictures of the event were reviewed, there were mandalas or orbs everywhere. It was as if holy beings from another realm had come to listen to the Dharma and bless those present. This phenomenon continued to appear at many of the places where we presented the treasure book or when I gave a presentation about H.H. Dorje Chang Buddha III and His teachings.

This was the fourth or fifth time I had seen such phenomena. The first time was a few years earlier in San Diego when a large mandala appeared over my head and a smaller one over my left hand which I use in healing and where I always wear my rosary or mala. This was in a photo taken while I was having dinner with other healers. The second time I actually saw them while in the mountains back of Pasadena. I had taken a short nap in my car prior to driving home and as I woke up, I saw two of them in the car. The third time they appeared in photos taken by one of my students. I had asked my Buddha Master about this. The Buddha seemed pleased to hear of them and said that some of them were probably Dharma Wheel Mandalas, the Buddha also told me that they were just phenomena and not to give them too much consideration or become attached to them. Another vajra brother said this sort of phenomenon was really quite common. I'd forgotten, I had also seen many of these magical orbs on photos of rinpoches in Tibet. Another of my students told me later on the trip that when he was visiting the holy pilgrimage sites in India and Nepal, many of his photos exhibited these phenomena as well.

"Bodhicitta is actual conduct based upon great compassion that aids living beings in becoming Buddhas or Bodhisattvas. It is the mind of love in the holy sense that the enlightened and the unenlightened or the holy and the ordinary both have."

What Is Cultivation?

For my visit to Colorado, I had the International Buddhist Sangha Association send a copy of the book *H.H. Dorje Chang Buddha III* to the USAF Academy Cadet Chapel. I wanted to see if they had received the book and what sort of Buddhist program they had at the Academy and how we might fit into that program. When we visited the Academy, we were also able—quite by accident— to present a copy of the treasure book to the wing commander of the Community Chapel for their interfaith library. This was one of the many serendipitous events whereby we set out to do one thing, got lost and found something quite wonderful in the process. The campus of the Academy is quite extensive and although the Cadet Chapel is visible from many vantage points and quite unique, it is not so easy to access. Many of the original roads had been blocked and the maps had not been changed to reflect these adjustments. So, we were hopelessly lost and when we asked a jogging officer, he sent us to the wrong chapel, the Community Chapel for the officers and staff and not the famous Cadet Chapel that we were looking for. Once there we were most fortunate to meet Assistant Chaplain Matthew Jones who just happened to be a very fine young Buddhist from Texas. He knew all about the Buddhist program at the academy and wanted us to meet his commanding officer to whom we gave a second copy of the treasure book. In fact, Chaplain Jones wanted us to stay and attend the service that they were having that evening at 6:30. We declined as we were on a tight schedule and needed to reach the Unitarian Church in Colorado Springs to make arrangements for the next night's presentation. We did visit the famous Cadet Chapel before we left for our next stop (FIGURE 26).

FIGURE 26: Tour Team leaving the famous Cadet's Chapel at the USAF Academy.

In Colorado, some of the team visited the Great Stupa of Dharmakaya at the Shambhala Mountain Center near Red Feather. The 108-foot monument to the late Chogyam Trungpa Rinpoche was the largest stupa that the group visited (FIGURE 27). Chogyam Trungpa Rinpoche was one of the first lamas to popularize the Tibetan form of vajrayana teachings in America. The nun Zhengxiang Shi had a bright pink pillar of light appear intermittently in a video she took of this stupa that was similar to those we saw at the Xuanfa Institute and elsewhere.

FIGURE 27: The Great Stupa of Dharmakaya at the Shambhala Mountain Center. This bright neon pink pillar of light appeared intermittently in a video taken of this stupa at Red Feather, Colorado by the nun Zhengxiang Shi. Similar phenomena were also seen at the Xuanfa Institute when I returned to California from the Book Tour and also at gatherings at the home of my Buddha Master.

The Dharma Propagation Tour had crossed the desert and the continental divide and been blessed with many auspicious signs. We had visited three state capitols—Salt Lake City, Denver, and Cheyenne—and the major cities in the region like Las Vegas. It was now time to follow the scenic Arkansas River into the wilderness and cross the spectacular Sangre de Cristo Mountains into the headwaters of the Rio Grande. This was believed to be one of the most spiritual places in America. It is said that dragons still roam freely in these mountains and earth spirits can sometimes be seen even by ordinary people. How would the local earth spirits, dragons, and devas respond to the good news that H.H. Dorje Chang Buddha III had incarnated to help living beings in their evolution to higher levels of existence and in the elimination of their suffering? Afterall, earth spirits, dragons, and devas were living beings and spiritually evolving, too.

The Rio Grande Valley

One of the most intensely spiritual areas that we encountered on the tour was along the Rio Grande River in Colorado and New Mexico. More than a third of the major stupas that we visited in America were in that area. We experienced more supernormal phenomena in that area than anywhere else and had some of our best responses to the teachings. Some traveled several hours to hear the presentation a second time. There were those who immediately felt the karmic affinity to the practice and wanted to take refuge. Out of this leg of the tour the Taos Xiuxing Institute took form and came into being as a Dharma center to help others learn about the practice and to start their cultivation according to the teachings of H.H. Dorje Chang Buddha III.

We entered the headwaters of the Rio Grande located in the San Luis Valley, an area between the Continental Divide and the Sangre de Cristo Mountains in southern Colorado, at the beginning of our tour and came back up the Rio Grande River several months later when we returned to the west coast through El Paso, Texas, and Albuquerque and Santa Fe, New Mexico.

It should not be surprising that this area was so special. Crestone, Colorado, is after all one of the most sacred settings in America. The Hopi, the Navajo, the Ute, the Apache, the Pueblo Indians, and other native tribes have all considered the San Luis Valley, where Crestone is located, as holy land. Buddhist leaders have likewise recognized the spiritual power of this place and erected stupas and built retreat centers here. The San Luis Valley sitting at a little over 7,000 feet elevation and surrounded by over 12,000-foot peaks serves as the beginning of the Rio Grande River that flows south through New Mexico and forms the southern border of Texas and the US as it meanders eastward to the Gulf of Mexico. We stayed at the White Eagle Village just outside of the tiny village of Crestone where the clouds were so close you could almost touch them. The clouds did touch the mountaintops and often obscured the Sangre de Cristo peaks. It snowed in the mountains while we were there in August.

An old self-proclaimed Druid, looking as old as the hills and just as tough, whom we met at a local coffeehouse over breakfast, told us that there would be months of temperatures in the double digits below zero. This same wizened character and the entourage that seemed to gather for his sage advice also told us about a local dragon and other earth spirits who could often be seen around 4:00 am dancing in the mountains. Suspecting that this just might be tales fabricated for naive tourists, some of us were still curious enough to get up early and go up on the roof of the lodge to meditate and wait for a glimpse. The energy was so intense and the place so magical that anything seemed possible. I don't think any of us saw a dragon, but there were some pretty mysterious lights that appeared about that time of day that didn't seem to have any "normal" cause. I saw both red and yellow lights and another team member saw other lights from a different location that could not be explained by anything we understood. Perhaps it was the dancing dragon.

There are many types of dragons, such as heavenly dragons, water dragons, spirit dragons, etc. They are all called dragons. They are different from humans in as much as dragons, unlike most humans, can exist in different realms. Heavenly or celestial dragons belong to the heaven realm, while spirit dragons (nagas) belong to the Naga Palace located under the ocean. There are also Dharma protecting dragon spirit-beings. Dragons are divided into beneficent and malicious types. The beneficent type is a spirit-being. The malicious type is an evil spirit. This is how they are primarily categorized. Those dragons who are at a lower level, for example, have just started to practice. They are not developed yet. These are the evil ones. Actually, some dragons can also be categorized as part of the animal realm.

It was to the nagas or spirit dragons that Shakyamuni Buddha entrusted the great prajnaparamita teachings when he gave them on Vulture Peak and predicted that Nagarjuna would incarnate to retrieve these teachings about five hundred years after the Buddha left this world. Nagarjuna was a famous Indian Dharma king from the first or second to third centuries. He founded the Madhyamaka School. He was one of the "seventeen great panditas" of ancient India. He wrote the *Fundamental Wisdom of the Middle Way* that is still one of the classic commentaries studied in Buddhist monasteries. He is often portrayed with a halo of snakes, symbolizing the nagas from whom he obtained the great *Prajnaparamita Sutras*. There are other accounts in the sutras and literature of the East where nagas are mentioned as protectors of the Dharma or the Buddha. For example, the naga king, Mucalinda, came and protected the Buddha by spreading his body over the Buddha's head when a thunderstorm broke out while the Buddha was meditating in Bodhgaya. The statues and paintings that show what appears to be a giant cobra poised over the Buddha are actually of Mucalinda. The Buddhist temples of Cambodia and Thailand are filled with statues and images of guardian nagas. We visited such a statue at a Cambodian temple in Fresno later in the trip. FIGURE

4 (page 23) is a photo of a guardian stone at the entrance to the famous Sri Maha Bodhi Tree in Sri Lanka that contains an image of a naga protecting a devic being.

Many of my students and other vajra brothers and sisters once boarded two large boats and went out to sea off the coast of southern California to witness a ceremony performed for a certain disciple to beseech the blessings and assistance of the nagas to raise the consciousness of the disciple's parents. At that time a request printed on yellow cloth was lowered into the ocean and, after the appropriate chanting and rituals, was raised back up with a message from the nagas granting part of the request. The printing on the cloth had actually changed while it was underwater. I remember that this rinpoche carried this request with her for several days. I was told she even slept with it, never being separated from its message.

Many of the close disciples of the Buddha were able to have the consciousness or souls of family members raised to higher levels. The Buddha did this for my parents who had passed on some years earlier and for an aunt and uncle who left this world while I was with the Buddha. So much of our practice involves developing deep compassion for all living beings. We start seeing everyone as our mother or our parents and contemplating how they sacrificed their lives for us, loved us, worked long hours and very hard to support us and take care of us. Then we consider the fact that all beings have at some time been our parents. Thinking in this way, we develop our bodhichitta and intense motivation to quickly become enlightened so that we can help them. We really do want to help all our relatives—all living beings. [26]

Mountain-range dragon spirit-beings, like the one here in the Sangre de Cristo range belong to the ghost realms, but they belong to a higher rank within the ghost realms than what we normally think of as ghosts. I had encountered such a being once before when I was living at a retreat center in the Appalachian Mountains. This dragon told me she was a female dragon and that I could call her Happy since she lived on Hap Mountain, but that wasn't her real name. I could not see her at her home, but a clairvoyant friend whom I took to the site where Happy lived could. You could certainly feel her presence and I was able to communicate with her in my shamanic journeys. I was drawn to the place because there were ancient ruins of mounds constructed on the site by indigenous people who were no doubt aware of the dragon. In fact, my clairvoyant friend also saw the spirits of ancient Native Americans guarding the site and when I was able to communicate with them, I learned that they were from a pre-Cherokee tribe that had lived in the area a very long time ago. The site was near where

26 *I think of the term "Mitakuye Oyasin," a phrase meaning "all my relatives' in the Lakota language used to reflect the world view of all living beings (not just humans) being interconnected.*

a co-worker lived. He was part Cherokee and completely freaked out about the site and would not venture near it because of its intense spiritual energy.

In the West, we felt we needed to slay our dragons and are thus deprived of their power, but in these remote areas they do still exist. In China they were revered and thought to hold both great celestial and earthly power. Only the emperor could wear images of the five-clawed imperial dragon. Anyone else would be put to death. Perhaps as Buddhism takes root in the West, we will find ways to elicit the support and blessings of these powerful beings. Dreamwork's movie "How to Train Your Dragon" is a start in popular culture. Perhaps this wish is part of the reason the dragon Dharma Protectors later came to the Xuan-fa Institute and participated in the filming of the video about the Institute. We have heard their roar at ceremonies and empowerments many times and I heard them when I attended a sweat lodge with my father, except, the Native Americans present called them Thunder Beings.

FIGURE 28: Column of rain and hail that preceded us to Crestone, Colorado. Maybe it was sent by the Dakinis?

Throughout this trip, we encountered representatives from other realms that wanted to hear the Dharma. When we first came to Crestone we were dramatically greeted by a pillar of rain and hail that preceded us to White Eagle Village (FIGURE 28). We could see the rain and hail in the distance, but it moved with us and was always just ahead of us, like it was leading us to our destination. It was very strange and awesome. When we arrived at the lodge there were hailstones piled up everywhere. The owner of the lodge told us that this was the dakinis[27] welcoming us and that

27 *Dakinis are celestial wisdom beings who may either be a human being who has attained high realizations of the fully enlightened mind or a non-human manifestation of the enlightened mind of a meditational deity such as a female dharma protector. They are usually depicted as a wrathful or semi-wrathful form, but sometimes they appear as very beautiful women.*

the dakinis had been dancing for joy over the news that we were bringing.

These powerful beings knew how magnificent my Buddha Master was and how wonderful it was for all of us that He had returned to this earth. Now, if I could only convey that joy and excitement to others.

Although the spiritual energies and powers were immense, the human interventions in this area certainly exhibited signs of impermanence. In fact, it felt as though the primary energy of the area was not intended for human beings— at least not ordinary human beings. I felt we were impinging on another world and one where we might not be welcomed. It was a "wild" or untamed place. Although many may come here for retreats and/or empowerments, this was not the sort of place where most ordinary people could live year-round. We made offerings to the Buddhas and Bodhisattvas at many of the local stupas.

When I explained how and why H.H. Dorje Chang Buddha III had come to America to a group at the White Eagle Village, many more of the magical dharma wheel mandalas appeared. A particularly large pink and green mandala appeared over the altar and another in the crowd. Why was this happening? It is true that these colored lights, commonly referred to as "orbs," do appear on all sorts of photographs in all sorts of situations, but not as frequently or in such vivid colors as we were seeing. Can it be that these are some form of life from another realm that wanted to hear the Dharma and manifested when we were presenting the treasure book *H.H. Dorje Chang Buddha III*? Were they the souls or consciousness of departed beings from the ghost realm as some thought? Some of these brightly colored lights were no doubt dharma wheel mandalas. However, we knew that we should not pay that much attention to them in as much as they were just another form of illusory phenomena, but their appearance in such frequency and intensity was quite astounding.

FIGURE 29: Tornado on drive from Crestone to Questa, New Mexico. Could this be the Dakinis sending us off?

Thunderclouds, giant hailstones, and tornados accompanied us on the scenic drive from Crestone, Colorado, to Questa, New Mexico (FIGURE 29). Could this have been the work of the local dakinis again? It was certainly spectacular. The first stop was at the beautiful 38-foot Kagyu Mila Guru Stupa just north of Questa. This was one of my favorite stupas that we visited and made offerings to on the trip (FIGURE 30). An amazing red transparent light form appeared on one photograph of the stupa that was actually visible to several of our team members (FIGURE 31). The nun thought she saw a red flag waving when she took the photo, but there was no earthly object anywhere near her at the time. Another team member also saw the red light but was not able to photograph it. The Buddha Master later told us that this was a Dharma shield erected by local Dharma protecting deities. We felt that this was just another example of beings from other dimensions blessing the dissemination of the treasure book and the tour and expressing their joy that H.H. Dorje Chang Buddha III has come to this world and is living in America. It was similar to what I had seen dashing through the trees outside of Washington, DC. Later that night, I explained the genesis of H.H. Dorje Chang Buddha III and how this Buddha has come to America to a gathering of local residents and visitors at the Taos Jewish Center. During the opening ritual for the presentation, a giant dharma wheel mandala appeared on my robe. We showed the group the pictures of some of the nectar that has miraculously manifested during Holy Buddhas Bestowing Nectar Ceremonies conducted by H.H. Dorje Chang Buddha III.

FIGURE 30: Making offerings inside the Kagyu Mila Guru Stupa in Questa, New Mexico.

FIGURE 31: Red Dharma Protector Shield at Kagyu Mila Guru Stupa, Questa, New Mexico.

We visited a stupa that was thought to be the first stupa constructed in America. The Khang Tsag Chorten (Stacked House Stupa) is an eight-foot tall, square monument that was built to commemorate the 1972 visit to Santa Fe of H.H. Dudjom Rinpoche (1904-1987) and consecrated in October 1973 by H.H. Drodrupchen Rinpoche (1927-), who is the sole holder of the complete Longchen Nying-thik. Translated as the "Heart Essence of the Vast Expanse," it represents the highest teachings of the Nyingma sect. In Dodrupchen Rinpoche's (FIGURE 15 page 54) letter of congratulations to H.H. Dorje Chang Buddha III about the treasure book he said, "I found the book wonderful and amazing and totally inspiring... [It is a] truly miraculous and extraordinary expression of truth expressed and unexpressed beyond words in Buddha Dharma". The building was locked when the team arrived, so we were only able to see the stupa from a ladder that was conveniently located on the side of the courtyard containing the stupa.

It is said that this stupa marks the establishment of Tibetan Buddhism in America. An ancient prophecy by Guru Padmasambhava that I quoted earlier predicted that the Dharma would go to the land of the redman when "iron birds fly and horses run on wheels." Moreover that prophecy also predicted where the Dharma would first be established by the Tibetans: "There would be a round turtle-shaped mountain to the north, high snow-capped mountains to the east (the Sangre de Cristo Range), a stream flowing down a valley to the south (the Rio Grande), and a wide view with red cliffs in the west." This site fulfilled all those requirements. The turtle mountain is located to the north behind the light beige courtyard and temple that surrounds the stupa. Although the Tibetan Dharma represented the highest teachings that came out of India, they, too, were not complete. As I noted earlier, Shakyamuni Buddha did not transmit all of the Buddha Dharma that He had received because of the karmic conditions of living beings at that time. By the time the Dharma was transmitted to Tibet it already contained some erroneous views and corruption. Even Atisha, Marpa and the other patriarchs of the great Tibetan traditions did not have all the Dharmas or hold entirely correct views.

I knew this, as I had heard the story of how these noble Tibetan Dharma Kings had carried the ancient prophecy concerning the Dharma coming to America. I wondered how we would mark the transmissions that H.H. Dorje Chang Buddha III would bring. We needed to build a stupa to mark this great event. Perhaps the retreat I was building at Sanger would be the place.

FIGURE 32: Presentation at a former Catholic retreat center in Albuquerque, New Mexico.

In Albuquerque we were delighted to see the book *H.H. Dorje Chang Buddha III* prominently displayed at Wat Buddhamongkolnmit, a Thai temple. Several of the monks from that temple came to the public presentation and asked very useful questions. The presentation was held at a former Catholic retreat center. Several people came from Taos to Albuquerque to hear the presentation again. There was an amazing display of dharma wheel mandalas in several of the pictures taken at this presentation (FIGURE 32).

Now it was time to leave the more exotic landscape of the wild west and head toward the Heartland of Middle America. When I had last lived in the Midwest over twenty years earlier, it was still very difficult to find any traces of Buddhism. What would we find now?

The Heartland

We left New Mexico early in the morning and headed east crossing the Texas panhandle and on to Oklahoma City. This was a long driving day. We stopped in Amarillo, Texas, to give a copy of the treasure book *H.H. Dorje Chang Buddha III* to the local public library and went somewhere nearby for lunch. I'm not sure of the town, but I remember us going to a Dairy Queen sort of place that had probably been built as something else. All I really remember was that the place had large plate glass windows. There was a loud thud and suddenly one of the monks ran outside to pick up a small sparrow that had mistaken the window for open space and collided with the glass. The very large lama picked up the tiny dazed bird and held it gently and warmed its limp body until it recovered and flew away.

Oklahoma City has several Buddhist temples that serve the families who have come here from the Southeast Asian countries of Laos, Cambodia, Thailand, and Vietnam. When we visited Wat Lao Buddharam, a Laotian temple, we again found the book, *H.H. Dorje Chang Buddha III* displayed on the main altar of the temple. The abbot of that temple came to the presentation with a translator.

During my presentation at the Wichita Public Library, several residents from Wichita reported seeing beautiful, multicolored rainbows around the full moon for three consecutive nights just prior to our arrival. They had never seen anything like this before. When they heard of the other miraculous events that had accompanied the arrival of the treasure book *H.H. Dorje Chang Buddha III,* they wondered if there might be a connection. I explained just who H.H. Dorje Chang Buddha III is and why He has come to America and why this is such a most wonderful event for all living beings and, yes, there might be a connection. These sorts of lights have appeared before in conjunction with activities related to H.H. Dorje Chang Buddha III.

We visited several Buddhist temples that serve the residents of Wichita, Kansas, including Buu Quang and Chua Phap Hoa from Vietnam, as well as other temples from Cambodia and Laos. Seeing these beautiful temples in the heartland of America and knowing that there were many devout followers of the Blessed Buddha in the middle of America in states like Kansas and Oklahoma made me think how fortunate we were to have His Holiness Dorje Chang Buddha III living with us. I became even more determined to find ways to spread the good news that the Buddha had brought us on how we can end our suffering and obtain freedom from the pains of birth, sickness, and death. No matter where we went there were people who wanted to learn about the path of the Buddha and how they could follow it.

At our presentations, we showed the group examples of supernatural events that are documented in the book *H.H. Dorje Chang Buddha III*. I also explained how the book provides evidence of some of the accomplishments of the Buddha in the Five Vidyas and that an earlier manuscript version of the book was sent to the world's leading Buddhists. It was these holy Dharma kings and patriarchs who identified Master Wan Ko Yee as the third incarnation of Dorje Chang Buddha. Biographies of these Buddhist leaders along with their letters of recognition and certification are all included in the treasure book.

Later that day, many dharma wheel mandalas appeared on photos of the train station in Creston, Iowa as one of the monastic team members left to return to San Francisco to prepare for her ordination ceremony. Earlier another lay team member had left to take care of personal business and because of the acrimonious environment that was developing within our team. We were down to a four-member team and there was still some bad blood between certain of the team members. The presence of the other two female members, who had just left, had tended to soften the grumbling and hard feelings. Now, they were gone.

Sure enough, at our next stop in Cedar Rapids, Iowa an explosion occurred. The fighting was so loud and violent, I was afraid we would be thrown out of the motel where we were staying. I think it was something really silly over what TV program they could watch that triggered it, but this was certainly not the behavior of cultivators or what we wanted to project to the world. The venom and hatred were there, no matter how sweet a smile the team members tried to put on. People could feel it. It had to stop. I decided the fighting members had to leave the group. There was no wrong or right in the matter. If they could not get along and behave like vajra brothers, then they had no right to be on the tour and they could not propagate the Dharma. One of the warring parties was so fed up he was ready to leave, but I told him he had to take his brother with him. This was not a fight they could win by usual means or by running away from the problem. I printed copies of the discourse "What Is Cultivation?" and told them to read it and reflect on their own behavior. They did, decided to do better, and we were back on track for a while. I believe there were some genuine feelings of remorse and regret.

However, the bigger interpersonal conflicts between other members were still brewing. No matter who we are or how long we follow the Buddha, if we do not practice the way of the Buddha and cultivate ourselves, we will not progress, and we will have problems. The way of the Buddha is through self-cultivation—xiuxing—a Chinese term that means "to cultivate or improve oneself by reflection and correcting one's behavior." We were certainly not exempt from doing this just because we were on a holy mission.

I felt deeply ashamed that I was not better able to handle the situation. I had to ponder my own cultivation. What could I do differently to make this situation work? How could I change my behavior so as to set a better example for my brothers? Buddhism offers the methods to obtain good fortune and happiness in this life as well as a way to escape the cycle of reincarnation and the suffering of continual rebirth and death—BUT, you must follow the teachings. No matter your status or how long you are on the path, you must follow the system of self-cultivation and Dharma expounded by the Buddha. I knew I had much work to do.

FIGURE 33: Memorial to Katagiri Roshi (1928-1990) at Hokyoji, New Albin, Iowa.

We drove through the cornfields and pastures of eastern Iowa to the Mississippi River where we stopped for lunch at a sleepy river town. We then headed into Minnesota to visit Hokyoji, a Soto Zen Monastery. We visited the memorial to Dainin Katagiri Roshi (1928-1990), one of my early Zen teachers and the founder of Hokyoji and Ganshoji, a temple in Minneapolis (FIGURE 33). I offered prayers for the well-being of all at the memorial site and expressed my gratitude to Katagiri Roshi for his teachings. Joen Snyder O'Neal and Michael O'Neal, the guiding teachers of the Compassionate Ocean Dharma Center in Minneapolis, were conducting a weeklong silent retreat there, but welcomed us as did the abbot of the monastery, Dokai Georgesen, a Zen monk.

Both the monastery and the Dharma center in Minneapolis had received copies of the book *H.H. Dorje Chang Buddha III*. I had attended the last practice period given by Katagiri Roshi at Hokyoji with Joen and received a special Dharma transmission at that time.

While I lived in Kansas, I had painted a picture of Katagiri Roshi standing in the Konza Prairie that I knew he loved, and I heard it was still in his home or where his wife was now living. I was able to visit with Tomoe-san when I stopped at Ganshoji in Minneapolis on a later trip and asked if I could take a picture of that painting. Later Tamoe-san sent me that painting that I keep in my Dharma room (FIGURE 34).

FIGURE 34: My painting of Zen Master Katagiri Roshi on the Konza Prairie in Kansas.

While in South Dakota, I visited Bear Butte (called Mato Paha by the Lakota Sioux and Noavosse by the Cheyenne) near Sturgis to make offerings and pray for world peace. This mountain is sacred to many Native American tribes. This was a place where native people were able to communicate with holy beings and where they left brightly colored prayer flags and tobacco ties as offerings. The Cheyenne prophet, Sweet Medicine, received the four sacred arrows, the four commandments, and a moral code for his people here from such holy beings. Many years before, on my first visit to this special place, I had climbed the mountain and left my own offerings for the local spirits (FIGURE 35).

In North Dakota, I gave a presentation at the Fargo Public Library. Those attending were interested in the miracles that H. H. Dorje Chang Buddha III and the Buddha's disciples had exhibited and asked many questions about how

FIGURE 35: Bear Butte, a sacred mountain near Sturgis, South Dakota. A Bodhisattva-like being had presented teachings to the Cheyenne on this mountain. I stopped to make offerings and pray for peace.

the teachings of the Buddha related to the teachings of other world religions. I remembered an amazing story told by my vajra brothers and sisters from China. When the Master Museum was being built near the Buddha's hometown in western China, there was much concern that it would not be finished in time for the opening ceremonies. It was the rainy season and rain was forecasted for the limited time remaining. They knew that one of our brothers was able to forecast the weather and sometimes could even influence it. He was able to go to the heavenly realm and communicate directly with the Emperor of Heaven, the Jade Emperor who could control the weather. The brother did not want to do this as you do not casually make such requests, but he did. He was able to get a guarantee that there would be good weather to enable the work to continue. He wrote down his predictions and they were posted at the construction site. Although it continued to rain at night and in the surrounding areas, the site of the Master Museum was dry during working hours and the museum was finished on time. His predictions were 100% accurate. A patch of cloudless, sunny sky blessed the site for a month. We also distributed copies of the Big Blue Book to local officials, including the State Librarian.

In Wisconsin, the team paid their respects to the Kalachakra Stupa at the Deer Park Buddhist Center and monastery. The stupa was built in 1982 to commemorate the site of the first Kalachakra initiation in the western hemisphere, which was bestowed in July 1981 by H.H. Tenzin Gyatso, the fourteenth Dalai Lama. We encountered two other Kalachakra style stupas on the tour—in Indiana and again in Hawaii. Both had been sites of Kalachakra initiations. Many Westerners have participated in the large-scale Kalachakra empowerments and initiations that have been given in the United States by a number of Tibetan masters. In the U.S., it is probably the best known of all the tantric Dharmas.

However, many do not know that this is a Dharma that was transmitted by Shakyamuni Buddha while He lived on this earth. At the same time Shakyamuni Buddha was imparting the *Prajnaparamita Sutras* at Vulture Peak (Mount Grdhrakuta) near Rajagrha, Shakyamuni Buddha manifested his wrathful twenty-four-armed form as the Kalachakra Buddha and gave the Heart Essence form of the Kalachakra Tantra teachings at Dhanyakataka to King Suchandra and his retinue of ninety-six minor kings and emissaries from Shambhala. Certain advanced practitioners in India knew of the existence of these teachings. In the tenth century Venerable Kalachakrapada Jamyang Dorje of India tried to journey to Shambhala to receive them. Shambhala is actually a sort of "pure land" that is part of our world system, but not visible or accessible to most humans. It can be considered part of the Samboghakaya realm. It exists on a different plane or dimension than what human beings can normally experience.

The eleventh Kalkin King of Shambhala realized what this Indian adept was about to do and how difficult it would be for this venerable one to make such a journey and took pity on him. With great compassion the Shambhala King met the venerable one on his journey and transmitted the Kalachakra Dharma to him. This Dharma was then transmitted throughout India and later to Tibet. Somantha, the Kashmiri Kalachakra master, transmitted the Heart Essence Kalachakra Dharma to the Tibetan translator Dro Lotsawa Sherab Drak and another Tibetan disciple, Yumo Mikyo Dorje around the eleventh century. They formed the foundation of the Jonang sect, which has maintained the lineage to this day.

Kalachakra literally means the cycles of time. It addresses the astrological cycles of the physical world as well as the cycles of human existence. The popular concept of "as above, so below" applies as the tantra emphasizes the similarities and correspondence between human beings and the cosmos. It teaches the practices of working with the most subtle energies within the human body as the path to enlightenment. It has been considered the most advanced of all the Buddhist teachings in the world today. However, at best this has only been an outer tantra transmission in modern times and, in fact, few receiving these teachings are able to actually practice them. It could be said that what we have generally seen as the Kalachakra is but the shell or a mere semblance of the original Dharma and lacks certain special powers of the true Buddha Dharma that Shakyamuni taught. It is given as a sort of empowerment for world peace and blessing that makes people feel good. This is why it is not easy to understand people's level of practice based on their reputation or the Dharmas they transmit and receive. Some have great accomplishment and some—even some in very high positions—are quite ordinary. We must look and see evidence of realization to understand who they really are and whether they have the true Buddha Dharma that can liberate living beings in their current lifetime.

This Heart Essence form of the Kalachakra is not the highest form. However, Shakyamuni Buddha never taught the higher form, even though he himself had the Dharma and practiced it. The higher form is known as the Holiest and Most Secret Kalachakra Dharma. The Vajra Substitution Body Meditation is part of this Dharma whereby the crown of the disciple is opened within two hours of receiving the initiation so that the disciple's consciousness can freely move about. The great holy being and patriarch of the Kagyu sect, Tilopa, was able to learn this Dharma directly from Dorje Chang Buddha in the Samboghakaya realms but did not transmit this Dharma to his disciples as he was not yet a Buddha and only Buddhas can transmit this dharma. The true phenomenon of the opening of the crown is simply not found elsewhere in the world today. Those claiming to have such Dharma have not received the Vajra Substitution Body Meditation Dharma.

Because we are living in the Dharma Ending Age, Dorje Chang Buddha has incarnated again to teach us this highest form of tantra, known as the Holiest and Most Secret Kalachakra Dharma, from *The Supreme and Unsurpassable Mahamudra of Liberation* as well as other very high Dharmas. This may well be what the late Penor Rinpoche meant when he told me that "because this is the Dharma Ending Age, it is good that such a high being has incarnated." Penor Rinpoche was considered a master of the Kalachakra Dharma, but I believe he only had the Heart Essence form.

The treasure book *H.H. Dorje Chang Buddha III* includes testimonials of two advanced disciples who received the Xian Liang Great Perfection Dharma. This is also Buddha Dharma from the *Supreme and Unsurpassable Mahamudra of Liberation.* Those fortunate enough to receive this Dharma can enter the rainbow body state after only practicing the Dharma for a few hours. These two disciples also received the Vajra Body Substitution Dharma whereby their crowns were opened so that they could manifest another vajra body that could freely come and go anywhere, including other realms of existence. This is not the same dharma as the phowa dharma that is commonly given to the dying to release their consciousness. With the various forms of phowa dharma, like the Kuan

Yin Phowa, when the consciousness leaves the body, it does not come back, but that is not the case with this form of the Holiest and Most Secret Kalachakra Dharma. The practice of this Dharma enables one to be in more than one location at the same time. Before and after MRI images of the skulls of those who received this Dharma clearly reveal an opening in the crown, big enough to insert several fingers. When I started this book, there were only 10 or so people in the world who had received this Dharma and only one, H.H. Dorje Chang Buddha III, who can transmit it.

In case you are wondering why opening the crown is so important, we know that the crown must be opened for consciousness (or the soul or spirit) to ascend to the higher realms when one is finished with this life. Consciousness will leave through a particular place in the body and where it leaves will determine where it goes next. I will write more about this later when I tell of my own crown opening. There are many dharmas that one can practice to open the crown or one can have the crown opened by a Vajra Master.

In Wisconsin, I lectured to a primarily non-Buddhist group at the Madison Public Library one night. The audience had very many questions, some relating to comparisons between Buddhism and Christianity and how one can know what is the truth and find the correct path. This was a particularly diverse and challenging audience. I tried to explain that it is because individuals have differing karmic affinities for different dharma (teachings) and that one path may be correct for one person and not another. Shakyamuni Buddha taught 84,000 different paths to help those with different karmic conditions. Also, you may find you need different dharmas at different times in your evolution. It is just like finding the correct medicine to cure a particular disease. You may start with one medicine and end up with something quite different as the disease progresses. I also told how in the *Dhammapada* or *Sayings of the Buddha*, Shakyamuni Buddha tells his followers: "Do not believe in anything simply because you have heard it. Do not believe in anything simply because it is spoken and rumored by many. Do not believe in anything simply because it is found written in your religious books. Do not believe in anything merely on the authority of your teachers and elders. Do not believe in traditions because they have been handed down for many generations. But after observation and analysis, when you find that anything agrees with reason and is conducive to the good and benefit of one and all, then accept it and live up to it." I went on to tell the group that you need to test the various teachings to see if they work. Do they enable you and others to have good fortune and be happy? Do you continue to suffer? Do people who follow these teachings become liberated and are they able to escape the suffering of earthly existence? I spoke of how, in the past, over 100,000 practitioners from just one temple in Tibet at Kathok were able to attain the rainbow body and ascend like Jesus. There were other temples like that as well. Even today people are achieving that level of realization in their current lifetimes, but it is now extremely rare. For example, the rainbow body Dharma has not been transmitted at Kathok in Tibet for several generations.

FIGURE 36: H.H. Jamyang Lungdok Gyaltsen Rinpoche (Lama Achuk (1927-2011) signs his congratulation letter after reviewing the manuscript version of the Big Blue Treasure Book, H.H. Dorje Chang Buddha III.

Father Francis Tiso, who was with the U.S. Conference of Catholic Bishops and taught Tibetan Buddhism at the Pontifical Gregorian University in Rome, heard of the rainbow body[28] and went to Eastern Tibet to investigate a claim that an obscure lama had achieved this state whereby his body transformed into rainbow light and disappeared. He interviewed H.H. Jamyang Lungdok Gyaltsen, also known as Lama Achuk, and became convinced that attainment of the rainbow body was possible. He also found that Lama Achuk already exhibited this state.[29] Lama Achuk is one of the holy beings who recognized H.H. Dorje Chang Buddha III as an incarnation of Ven. Vimalakirti and Dorje Chang

28 *Father Tiso published* Liberation in One Lifetime: Biographies and Teachings of Milarepa *in 2014 and* Rainbow Body and Resurrection: Spiritual Attainment, the Dissolution of the Material Body, *and the Case of Khenpo A Chö in 2016.*
29 *After departing this world, the body of Lama Achuk shrunk from a height of almost six feet (1.8 meters) to about 18 inches tall, a sign of very high realization. From the time of Lama Achuk's paranirvana to the cremation, many auspicious signs appeared, five colored rainbows were often sighted in the sky and five colored pure lights often appeared in the area surrounding Lama Achuk's body.*

Buddha. The book *H.H. Dorje Chang Buddha III* includes Lama Achuk's letter of recognition along with a photo of the lama signing the letter (FIGURE 36). The book also includes testimonials of those who have already achieved the rainbow state of awareness by practicing Dharma from *The Supreme and Unsurpassable Mahamudra of Liberation.*

> # "Not all Bodhisattvas are Buddhist."
> H.H. Dorje Chang Buddha III

It was in Madison that I met a very kind and impressive young Christian mystic who reminded me of something my Buddha Master had taught me some time before: "Not all Bodhisattvas are Buddhist." Surely, I could embrace and honor the compassionate teachings of Jesus as dharma that helps people on the path to becoming holy beings, even though that may not be the stated goal of most Christians. This same young man visited me later on the trip while we were both in New York City and we continued to correspond. Why couldn't Jesus, Saint Francis, and other Christian saints who lived to help living beings be Bodhisattvas? Bodhisattvas appear to living-beings (not just humans) in ways that those beings can understand and relate to. I remembered a story that I am fond of telling about Dr. John Blofeld (1913-1987), a professor of religion at Berkeley, who was traveling in China with a Jesuit priest. Both men saw a shining white apparition, however, the Jesuit saw the Virgin Mary and Dr. Blofeld, a Buddhist, saw Kuan Yin Bodhisattva.

We stopped in Milwaukee and gave two public presentations in downtown Chicago. I talked about the teachings contained in the book *H.H. Dorje Chang Buddha III* including the two methods taught in the discourse "What Is Cultivation?" on how to develop bodhichitta: the practice of seeing all living beings as your mother and the practice of having your behavior correspond to that of the Bodhisattvas whereby you actually put the well-being of others ahead of your own selfish interests. When one participant from a farm in Iowa heard this, she stated that she did not think she would be able to kill any more of her chickens if she saw them all as her mother. She figured she was going to have some pretty old chickens around and not have any more chicken dinners on Sunday.

From Chicago, we traveled down to southern Indiana to visit the Kumbum Chamtse Ling Monastery at Bloomington, Indiana. This was one of the very few times we encountered inclement weather, probably the tail end of Hurricane Gustav.

We drove by, but did not have time to stop at Sanshinji, the Sanshin Zen Community, founded in 1996 by Shohaku Okumura, (1948--) a Soto Zen

Priest and renowned translator of Japanese Buddhist texts. Shohaku had been one of my teachers as he had taken over the Minnesota Zen Meditation Center in Minneapolis after Katagiri Roshi left this world. He was the disciple of Kosho Uchiyama Roshi (1912-1998), the abbot of Antaiji, a monastery and temple located in Kyoto, Japan.

In Fort Wayne, Indiana, I once more gave a talk on who H.H. Dorje Chang Buddha III is and why this great Buddha has come to America. It was a very diverse crowd that included nine monastics from local monasteries and temples. Venerable Sundima from the Vihara Mon Monastery (Burmese) in Fort Wayne came early along with a member of the Library staff to help translate for the various monastics. The crowd asked many questions concerning the status of H.H. Dorje Chang Buddha III and who has recognized Him as well as questions concerning the basic doctrines of Buddhism.

We visited many of the Buddhist temples in Fort Wayne. Fort Wayne is another Midwestern city where a large number of recent immigrants from southeast Asia have settled. These new settlers had brought with them their monks and established their own temples. The Burmese monks at Wat Laosamakky wanted to be photographed with the book *H.H. Dorje Chang Buddha III*.

The Team visited several Buddhist temples and Dharma centers in Ohio including the Wat Lao Buddhamamakaram and Karma Thegsum Choling, a Tibetan temple near downtown Columbus, Ohio. A thangka in this Kagyu temple of their lineage tree had a bright blue Dorje Chang Buddha as the central Holy Being.

The first patriarch of the Karma Kagyu Tradition, Master Tilopa, received tantric teachings directly from Dorje Chang Buddha as did the matriarchs of the Shangpa Kagyu sect, Lady Niguma and Lady Sukhasiddhi. Both women achieved very high levels of realization in a very short period of time. They both were very compassionate and had very deep roots of kindness. Lady Sukhasiddhi was an elderly and poor housewife who was kicked out of her home by her six children and husband for her generosity and who went on to become an enlightened being. She learned how to support herself by selling beer. She continued her generous ways and gave the beer away to a holy man who taught her the Dharma. Her level of realization was such that she was able then to learn directly from Dorje Chang Buddha in the Samboghakaya realms. Her physical appearance became as that of a beautiful 16-year-old fair-skinned girl. She was one of the major root gurus of Khyungpo Naljor, the founder of the Shangpa Kagyu sect as was Lady Niguma who also was able to learn directly from Dorje Chang Buddha. Both women mastered the Dharma taught by Dorje Chang Buddha and reached an enlightened state in only a few days. It is said that Lady

Niguma was the sister of Naropa, the abbot of Nalanda who had spent many years and much difficulty in learning the Dharma from his guru Tilopa. As mentioned earlier, Tilopa was also able to learn the Dharma directly from Dorje Chang Buddha. Most of these holy beings are shown in the Buddhist Lineage Tree included as Appendix D.

The East Coast

We left Columbus and headed toward the Great Lakes, stopping in Erie, Pennsylvania for an al fresco lunch on the lake. The mid-September weather was perfect, and all was well. One of the team members had lived there as a boy and wanted to see his old hometown. It was quite late in the afternoon when we got to Buffalo, but we decided to take a short side trip to Niagara Falls since several of the team members had not seen this natural wonder. Although the park was just closing as we arrived and it was getting dark, we managed to see this power-ful show of Mother Nature and the sacred site of the Haudenosaunee (Iroquois) Confederacy whom we later visited.

The Dharma Propagation Team visited a number of monasteries, temples, and Dharma centers in upstate New York including the Palyul Retreat Center near McDonough, New York, the North American headquarters and principle retreat center for H.H. Penor Rinpoche, the former head of the Nyingma sect. We were fortunate to catch His Holiness before he returned to India after his summer teaching at the center. Khenpo Tenzin Norgey Rinpoche, the resident rinpoche at the retreat center, translated for us as we explained the purpose of our visit and journey. FIGURE 5 (page 26) shows a photograph from this meeting. His Holiness Penor Rinpoche was one of the Dharma kings who had written a letter of recognition for our Buddha Master that was included in the treasure book. The rinpoche expressed his awe and admiration for H.H. Dorje Chang Buddha III. He wrote the following in a letter to rinpoches: "H.H. Dor-je Chang Buddha III Yangwo Wan Ko Yeshe Norbu... has been recognized by numerous greatly virtuous and eminent monastics... A Treasury of True Buddha Dharma... will provide the karmic conditions for living beings to... attain the ultimate state of Buddhahood."

We could tell that the rinpoche was not in good health, so we felt very hon-ored to have been able to meet him. Unfortunately for living beings, this kind rin-poche passed on the next spring at his Namdroling Monastery in southern India.

We had arrived in New England for the first frost of the season and in time to see the beginning of the spectacular fall color that the region is famous for. It was September 21. After giving a presentation at the historic Friends Meet-ing House in Cambridge, Massachusetts, we visited the Providence Zen Center and Diamond Hill Monastery founded by Seung Sahn Soen (1927-2004). Seung Sahn Soen had been one of my teachers and I wanted to go back to his home base to pay my respects. Although its foundation was in place, the master's stupa had not yet been built. A 65-foot World Peace Pagoda is located just outside the Zen Center (FIGURE 37). Skanda Bodhisattva stands guard outside the zendo (meditation hall) located inside the center while Shakyamuni Buddha can be found in the zendo itself. The Diamond Hill Monastery contains a beautiful traditional blue-tiled Korean temple. It is located on the grounds of the Providence Zen Center. Turtles sun themselves on the pond in front of the temple while squirrels and other wildlife play in the woods surrounding this peaceful setting.

FIGURE 37: World Peace Pagoda at Diamond Hill Monastery near Province, Rhode Island; founded by Seung Sahn-sa (1927-2004). His memorial had not yet been erected when I visited the site.

On the way to the Catskills, we stopped in Connecticut and then proceeded to the Chuang Yen Monastery near Carmel, New York to pay our respects to the largest indoor Buddha in the western hemisphere. The 37-foot statue of Buddha Vairocana sits in the 84-feet tall Great Buddha Hall surrounded by ten thousand small Buddha statues. The Buddha Hall itself as well as the nearby Kuan-Yin Hall were built in the style of the Tang Dynasty (618-907 CE) without any internal pillars supporting the ceilings. The entire project was constructed under the guidance of the renowned architect, I. M. Pei. A bas-relief sculpture of Skanda Bodhisattva, the great Dharma protector, guards the Buddha's left while Guan Yu with his magnificent beard stands on the Buddha's right.

After visiting the major retreat centers in the Catskill mountains of New York State, we proceeded southward to New York City. We did experience some challenging weather entering the city. Again, we were getting the onslaught from one of the season's hurricanes as it dissipated its fury across the Northeast coast and drenched us in the process. The New York disciples were very kind and generous. We were able to stay in Manhattan near the United Nations and only minutes away from everything.

I read a preliminary English translation of one of the Buddha's discourses to the New York disciples. This was one that had been given for the benefit of the Western students and I do not believe had been made available to the Chinese students. A student had raised the point that it was very hard for Westerners to practice the Dharma as many of the Dharmas are contrary to the concepts that we hold dear in the West, but the Buddha took issue with that point. The Buddha noted that it is true that there are cultural differences, but there are strengths and weaknesses in both cultures that need to be considered. The Buddha said that in the West, the self is valued and very much respected in such concepts as individual privacy and human rights, noting that these concepts are regarded as very important. However, the Buddha Dharma demands that we cut off attachment to self and that we always be patient under insult. Thus, in the mundane sense, these two perspectives are contradictory. However, in the absolute sense, these two perspectives are consistent. The Buddha continued to tell the Western students that this did not mean that just because the Westerner values the individual it means that the Westerner wants to harm that individual but will use his regard for individual rights to help other people. In fact, Western people are very kind to others. There must first be the existence of this sense of self to believe in oneself, learn well, or become a talented and outstanding person and be able to help others. This is correct. This confidence and sincere belief in oneself is especially important in Vajrayana practice when one practices actually visualizing one's self as a Buddha. The Buddha said that Western culture is very excellent and Eastern culture is also very excellent. It is just that their ways are expressed differently. If Westerners are temporarily unable to accept the Buddha Dharma, then this is a matter of cause and effect. That is, the karmic conditions for them to accept the Buddha Dharma have not matured. The time for the bearing of fruit has not yet come, which requires the planting of seeds, time, sunshine, rain or watering, fertilizer, and gradual growth. Success will come when the karmic conditions have matured. So, as we propagate the Buddha Dharma in the West we must learn to be expert gardeners and know how to make the garden grow.

John M. Lundquist, the Chief Librarian of the Asian and Middle Eastern

FIGURE 38: Librarian at the New York Public Library receiving the treasure book in New York City.

Division of the New York Public Library was very happy to receive the book *H.H. Dorje Chang Buddha III* for the library's research division. He also wanted a copy for the library's branch system that will be available for circulation. Dr. Lundquist kindly showed us the hand-printed volumes of the Tibetan Canon that the library had recently acquired. This particular text that he showed us was a terma that had been printed from wood blocks at the famous printing center in Derge in eastern Tibet. The New York Public Library is one of the five largest libraries in the world and one of the first in the West to acquire the entire Tibetan Canon. Now it also had the treasure book *H.H. Dorje Chang Buddha III* (FIGURE 38).

I was also able to present the treasure book to a very eager group at East-West Living on Fifth Avenue. Many dharma wheel mandalas and other magical lights appeared at this presentation (FIGURE 39). After New York we headed south to Washington and the District of Columbia, stopping in Trenton, New Jersey, and places in Pennsylvania, including Philadelphia.

We then continued south to the beach communities in Delaware. We held an impromptu ceremony at Pickering Beach near Dover for the thousands of horseshoe crabs

FIGURE 39: Dharma Wheel Mandalas (orbs) appear at presentation on the treasure book in New York City.

who perish there every year in their annual breeding cycle. Pickering Beach is one of the most productive horseshoe crab spawning areas in the world (FIGURE 40).

FIGURE 40: Disciple flipping Horseshoe Crabs at Pickerington Beach near Dover, Delaware.

Buddhists not only vow to not kill living beings, but also vow to rescue captive or endangered animals and people. Every year the disciples of H.H. Dorje Chang Buddha III gather from all over the world in Marina Del Rey, California, to hold a Dharma Assembly to release captive fish in honor of the Buddha's birthday. They sometimes do this more often. The Buddha requested that given the economic conditions caused by the unprecedented financial crisis of 2008 and various natural disasters and diseases in so many parts of the world that year, the disciples should save the transportation and lodging expense of attending the Fish Release Dharma Assembly, and instead hold life-saving activities locally; and that is what we did.

Every year hundreds of thousands of adult American Horseshoe Crabs die as they are stranded on the beaches of Delaware as well as other East Coast shoreline locations during their annual mating ritual. They come to shore to lay and fertilize their eggs and often end up on their backs and are unable to turn over by themselves so as to return to their aquatic homes. The churning surf will also expose their fertilized eggs to predators and combined with the burning sun results in the death of millions more baby horseshoe crabs. Although death is a natural part of the cycle of life, we nevertheless compassionately acknowledge their presence and contribution to the lives of other living beings. They have been featured recently in national media, as the blue blood of the horseshoe crab is essential in testing many medical vaccines that are now being developed to combat the dreaded Covid-19 virus. Unfortunately, the number of horseshoe crabs is declining.

One of the monks, went back to the Migyur Dorje Stupa in Maryland to sit and pray for people he knew with incurable diseases while the rest of us went to the Smithsonian Institution in Washington, DC. That stupa is dedicated to the eradication of diseases for which there is no known cure. When he came back, he found that a healing had taken place for himself as well. There had been a troublesome growth on his right arm for some time. He had been worried that it might be cancerous as it had been growing and had some dangerous signs. After praying at this stupa, the growth just fell off, left a red mark for a day or so, and now there was no sign of it. These things happen when one practices the correct Dharma and develops one's bodhichitta. We all experience healings and blessings from the Buddhas and Bodhisattvas as we progress on the path.

The South

In North Carolina we stayed with disciples. It was hard to find their home in the mountains even with our trusty GPS and it was quite late that night when we finally were able to settle in. Our host in Arden, also had an interesting story to tell about how the Buddha had impacted his life. In 2005 I received a phone call from this disciple informing me that his mother in Montana was very ill and would probably not make it. He was on his way to visit her and wondered what he should do to help her make the transition. I reported the matter to our Buddha Master and was given some Dharma that I was to teach this disciple and he in turn could teach his mother. The Buddha told me to tell the disciple not to worry and that the Buddha would personally arrange for an angel to take her to heaven or a Bodhisattva to take her to a Pure Land in the Buddha Realms. He couldn't believe his ears and was awestruck that his Buddha Master would do this for someone who had not even practiced Buddhism before.

Now although his mother was not a Buddhist, she was a very compassionate and spiritual person who was open to what her son had to say. She continued to practice this Dharma after he returned to North Carolina. Shortly before his mother passed on, a neighbor called to tell her that she had seen heavenly beings around her house. Earlier, his sister, who is also not a Buddhist, said she had felt H.H. Dorje Chang Buddha's presence outside her mother's room. The night before her passing, his sister said she "saw" the Buddha holding her mother's hand and walking away with her. As this happened, she said, "I felt so much love, gentleness, and compassion from His Holiness Wan Ko Yeshe Norbu (The Buddha had not yet been recognized as H.H. Dorje Chang Buddha III when this happened) that I wanted to put my head down and cry. It was beautiful. I could hardly believe what I felt and saw." How could it be that the Buddha would appear over 1,000 miles from where the Buddha was staying to help this woman make the transition? However, it is true. Such is the nature and compassion of the Buddha.

I had planned on stopping a few days to give the refuge vows to several who had requested them and to continue reading various discourses by His Holiness Dorje Chang Buddha III at the Embracing Simplicity Hermitage and Center for Contemplation near Hendersonville. One of the discourses was entitled "Does the Attainment of Supernatural Powers Enable One to End the Cycle of Birth and Death?" or "Qigong Is Not the Same as Buddhism." In this discourse the Buddha explains what must be used to end the cycle of birth and death—the power of the Buddha Dharma. The Buddha goes on to say that this power must be something that can be seen or measured. It cannot just be empty words or theories.

As in Asheville and elsewhere on the tour many colorful dharma wheel mandalas were recorded at these presentations and many beings from other realms manifested in the surrounding enchanted forest. I saw bright flashing red and yellow lights on the leaves and branches of the shrubs and trees, which sometimes looked like Christmas lights. One of the abbots at the Hermitage, Venerable Pannavati, told us that sometimes she was able to communicate with these earth spirits or devas. At one point in the development of the retreat center, they strongly objected to a construction project that was planned and started. They created so much havoc that the project had to be moved to another location that was acceptable to them. Now the abbot knows to contact these spirits and include them in plans for the area. Several people have seen the black local guardian dragon who sometimes stays in a corner in the back of the meditation hall. I did not see this dragon, but I did encounter another red and gold female dragon on another mountain north of Asheville, North Carolina that I already told you about. I was told that she was the local guardian spirit for that mountain. These woods are truly magical and alive with all sorts of beings. I gave a lot of thought to how to include these beings in my efforts to propagate the Dharma. After all, the Dharma is not just for human beings.

On our way to Atlanta we stopped in Waynesville, North Carolina where I read a discourse by H.H. Dorje Chang Buddha III on "What Is My Sect?" The Buddha has stated that the Buddha practices the true Buddha Dharma of all the legitimate sects of Buddhism whether they represent the Theravada, Mahayana, or Vajrayana systems. This includes the Pure Land Schools that chant the name of Amitabha Buddha, the Vinaya School that emphasizes the precepts and disciplines, the various Zen sects that stress meditation, or the shamatha and vipashyana meditation of the Theravada schools as well as the practices of the Fa-Hsiang, Consciousness-only and other schools of exoteric Buddhism and also the various Dharmas of the esoteric or secret traditions. If they were not part of the Buddha's sect, Shakyamuni would not have spread such Buddha Dharma in this world. If only one sect could be relied upon to save living beings, then that one sect would be taught.

In that discourse, the Buddha also asked us what is the function of the Buddha Dharma? It is to liberate and save living beings. How are living beings liberated and saved? They are liberated and saved by adjusting and changing their karma, or their causes and effects. Living beings are saved in this way. This is the reason that we stress cultivation and understanding the principles of cultivation and this is the reason that it is extremely absurd and wrong to insist that everyone can become liberated through practicing a particular dharma or the teachings of a particular sect.

This does not mean that the teachings of a particular sect are wrong, only that they cannot be exclusively right, either—not for everyone. This is the danger of sectarianism, one of the great destructive forces that was pervasive in Tibet as well as other parts of the Buddhist world. The great non-sectarian thinkers in Tibet of recent times were not trying to create a "Master sect" of only the best of each sect but trying to preserve the diversity and richness of what had evolved in all the lineages, some of which were on the brink of extinction. This was so that the myriad types of individuals with varied sets of karmic conditions could find a path that was right for them. An earlier teacher of mine often talked of the "different birds in the forest" in reference to this diversity of karmic affinity and conditions in people. It is because of all these "different birds" that Shakyamuni Buddha taught so many Dharma methods and that so many different sects evolved based on these methods. Everything is the dharma of correspondence, the dharma of cause and effect. However, a living being can only obtain liberation by relying upon his or her own cultivation. Only when a living being corresponds to a particular dharma of a certain school within the Mahayana, Hinayana, or Vajrayana can that living being attain success in accordance with the Dharma.

Originally, we had planned on giving a presentation in Atlanta and again in Savannah, Georgia, but changed our plans so as to spend more time in North Carolina and be able to read more discourses to the eager students there. We visited places in Mississippi, Florida, Alabama, and Louisiana in the South. We didn't stop in Arkansas, but almost a year later, I did go there. One night in Little Rock I was awakened at 4:00 am by a mockingbird outside my motel room that was singing its heart out. It was still dark outside. I remembered my favorite poem by the great Indian poet Rabindranath Tagore: "Faith is a bird that feels the light and sings while the dawn is still dark." It was my total faith in my Buddha Master and the teachings of the Buddhas that enabled me to make this trip. I felt like that bird and wanted to sing my heart out as well, no matter how exhausted I felt.

This phase of the trip was coming to an end. We left the deep south for Texas, which is a region in itself, and the Southwest and headed back home toward California, Hawaii, and the Pacific Northwest.

Maybe we were just tired, but it did not go well in Texas. We had driven only 550 miles the day before from New Orleans, but it was a hard drive under difficult conditions. The road to Baton Rouge was being rebuilt and was slow and scary. We had all had issues with the driving style of the primary driver, but that was getting better. Even so, much of the trip had been a white-knuckle ordeal. There had been a couple of scenes over this issue. The van was not so comfortable and after 25,000 miles it was getting to us. Everyone was exhausted. What had been, at least to me, more-or-less a truce between the monastics was wearing thin. What I found out was that although they were not quarreling in front of me as much as when we started, the tensions and bitterness were still there and wearing on everyone else. In Texas this all exploded. One of the team members frankly declared he was going home. He didn't care if it meant he had to leave the practice and the monastery; he simply could not endure these conditions anymore.

I agreed he could go, but as when this had happened a couple of times before, I told him that the person with whom he could not get along had to leave too. I had no idea how we would continue the tour or if we could, but this seemed like the only way to handle the matter. I did not want to take sides as I felt they were both equally contributing to the problem. Neither one respected the other one. I told them they were vajra brothers and how serious it was to fight with a vajra brother especially one who had received empowerment from the Buddha in the same mandala. On several occasions, the Buddha had warned us that this was the work of demons. The brother who was determined to leave denied that this was any brother of his, but when he realized I would be left with the van and have to drive home as the remaining team members could not drive, he reconsidered and said he would stay.

This truce lasted less than 24 hours. I wanted them to go out to hand out flyers as they had done in the other cities. The monastic who wanted to leave became quite irrational. He revealed he had mace on him and would use it on the other monastic if need be. It also came out that the other monastic had been secretly recording the conversations of the other team members so as to prove their misdeeds. The hatred and poison were so strong that I called them both in and seeing there was no way I could resolve their conflicts, I told them both they had to leave the tour. The toxicity was too great. We had only one person show up at the previous night's presentation. Who would want to attend anything with this kind of energy around? I did need them to drive and help with the presentations, but this was just not working and I lacked the ability to solve the problem. I have thought a lot about what I might have done differently to make the group work as a team, but still can see no better solution. I simply lacked the wisdom to resolve the issues involved.

So, one monastic was sent home immediately and the other would leave as soon as replacement drivers would join us in El Paso. It turned out that the best air travel connections were out of Albuquerque so the second monastic left then. But that was not the end. The other remaining team member was now very sick and his doctor had ordered him to go home and enter the hospital. I knew he would not do this and leave me without some support, so we asked one of the monastics to return to help drive the van back to San Francisco. This whole matter would be sorted out when we all reconvened in San Francisco to continue the tour. Albuquerque was the last presentation on this part of the tour.

I also became very ill. I had gone to Washington, DC from Phoenix and caught some sort of virus that put me in bed for almost a week. I flew back to San Francisco as planned and my dear kind students drove me to Los Angeles. The trip north to Eureka, Seattle, and Portland had to be cancelled. It was the Thanksgiving season and it had been very difficult to find suitable venues anyhow. I was really sorry to cancel our stop in Eureka, California as this was the second time and there had been considerable interest there. We would start again in Sacramento the first of December. That gave us some time to rest and heal on many fronts.

I wasn't certain the monks would join us the last leg of our journey. When I talked to one, he was still blaming the other one and me for all that had happened and was not able to take any responsibility for what had happened himself. I had told them both that they needed to reflect and repent, but this wasn't happening. So, I sent them both a long e-mail reminding them to read and reread "What Is Cultivation?" and study the words of our Buddha Master. What I asked was that they reflect on what happened and what they did to create that environment, not what the rest of us did—that was our business and work—and truly repent of their misdeeds.

It seemed to work. I received positive communications from both of them and they did rejoin the tour with much better attitudes. Maybe they got it.

We all learned from this. I know I did. You must show respect for other living beings. Whether you like them or not is not important. Not liking anything or anyone is your problem and merely a sign of your attachment to your own petty self. The Buddha's great teaching in "What Is Cultivation?" about it all being so simple if we could only let go of that attachment to self is so true.

My Buddha Master had been after me for my judgmental mind concerning those whose behavior or means of livelihood or whatever were not to my liking. I could see myself in these conflicts and vowed to be more tolerant and compassionate. Developing our bodhichitta is the most important job we have, and it does not mean just being kind to soft fluffy animals and people we like. I remembered the words of Shakyamuni Buddha and the fact that all living beings had been my mother at some time in my evolution:

Verses of Drumsong, King of the Serpentines:

The sea is not my problem,

My task is not the mountains,

My job is not the earth;

My calling's rather to attend That I should never fail

Repaying kindness granted me.

Even with all this drama, we did hold three public meetings in Texas. In discussing the book *H.H. Dorje Chang Buddha III* at the Unitarian-Universalist Church in San Antonio, I described the three bodies of a Buddha; the vast form-less mind of a Buddha, the Dharmakaya, that we symbolized by the red sun and the yellow crescent moon; the Sambhogakaya or bliss body of a Buddha that is only visible to holy ones; and the Nirmanakaya or transformation body that is visible to most people. Shakyamuni Buddha and H.H. Dorje Chang Buddha III are both examples of Nirmanakaya Buddhas who incarnate into this world to help living beings.

When I was asked during my presentation at Casa de Luz in Austin, Texas about the significance of the lineage chart used in the presentations, I told the assembled group that it not only shows the lineages of the major sects of Buddhism, but it also shows that all the sects, whether they be of the Theravada, Mahayana, or Vajrayana tradition, originated with Dorje Chang Buddha.

In Sedona, Arizona, I explained why and how H.H. Dorje Chang Buddha had been recognized by the world's major Dharma kings including the former head of the Nyingma sect, H.H. Penor Rinpoche, H.H. Dodrupchen Rinpoche, and others. When asked about others who claim to be incarnations of great Buddhas or Bodhisattvas, I said that there are certain criteria given in the book *H.H. Dorje Chang Buddha III* for such recognition. For example, a true holy one should be able to perform authentic inner-tantric initiations and empowerments whereby the Buddhas and Bodhisattvas actually come to the mandala and make their presence known. The person receiving such an initiation actually experiences a holy state. A true holy one should be able to have the Buddhas bestow sacred nectar in front of witnesses and be able to use that nectar to help living beings. A true holy one excels in all five of the vidyas and has mastered the sutras and secret tantric teachings of the Buddhas. H.H. Penor Rinpoche also said that such a holy being should manifest many magical and miraculous attributes. These qualities of the Buddha are all well documented in the book *H.H. Dorje Chang Buddha III*. In fact, for anyone even to be considered a holy being or saint, they must both have an exceptional level of realization and manifest the great bodhichitta and compassionate state whereby everything they do is for other living beings AND they must demonstrate a physical body that is different from that of an ordinary person. No matter what else they may say or do, if they cannot meet these two criteria, they cannot be considered a holy being, let alone the ultimate holy being of a Buddha or Bodhisattva. As an aside, in February 2020, H.H. Dorje Chang Buddha III lifted a 420 pound vajra pestle using a hook and only one hand at a dharma assembly held at the Holy Miracles Temple in Pasadena, California after no one else could do so.

Tribal Visits

The team had been warmly welcomed by Governor Paul T. Martinez and Lt. Governor Tom Lujan, Jr. of the Taos Pueblo when we visited the Rio Grande Valley. When told about the book and the fact that H.H. Dorje Chang Buddha III had come to America, the Lt. Governor became very excited and told the team that when he was very young he knew that there was a young boy from Tibet (China) who was "the one who is the root of Buddhism." He said, "I think he would be in his early fifties now and that he would be the highest leader of Buddhism." The team members explained that H.H. Dorje Chang Buddha III was indeed the highest Buddhist in the universe and the root source of all Buddhism and would fit that description. The pueblos are considered to be the oldest continuously inhabited communities in the USA, having been built over 1,000 years ago. Blue Lake (Ba Whyea) and its related mountains are the most sacred lands of the Taos Pueblo, but are off-limits to all but members of the Pueblo.

My brother, Glenn Welker, who at that time was doing volunteer work at the Smithsonian's National Museum of the American Indian gave us a tour of the facility while we were in the Washington, DC area (FIGURE 41). I wanted to see this museum as I had been formulating an expanded vision of the Bodhisattva that I thought might help explain a major Buddhist concept to the West.

FIGURE 41: My brother, Glenn Welker at the Smithsonian's National Museum of the American Indian in Washington, District of Columbia.

My Buddha Master had told me on several occasions that not all Bodhisattvas were Buddhists so I wanted to look at how they might have presented themselves in other cultures. What better place to look than within our own native cultures? I thought this beautiful museum should hold many clues. I believed the Peacemaker or Deganawida and his follower the Mohawk Hiawatha of the Haudenosaunee (Iroquois) Confederacy might just be Bodhisattvas. I found that my own native ancestors, the Ashinabe or Ojibway told of the Little Boy who received the spiritual teachings of his tribe from the seven grandfathers after a long and difficult journey across the land. Were these actually Bodhisattvas giving these people the teachings they needed to develop a basic moral code and way of life? Later when we visited the Hopi, I came to think of the Kachinas as a type of Bodhisattva as well. They were, after all, spirit beings from another realm that came to help living beings. Wasn't that a definition of a Bodhisattva? How can we tell just who is or is not a Bodhisattva? And what about the White Buffalo Calf Woman (Pte Ska Win) who brought spiritual teachings to the Lakotas? She was considered a sacred woman of supernatural origins who gave the Lakota their "Seven Sacred Rituals." Was that another Bodhisattva who came in a form that the Lakotas would appreciate? When I visited the Dakotas in September of 2009, I spent some time sitting on Bear Butte (Mato Paha or Noahvose), a mountain located in the Black Hills near Sturgis, South Dakota, that is sacred to many native tribes (FIGURE 35 page 93). It was here that over 4,000 years before, a Cheyenne man named Sweetwater had received guidance and gifts for his people. Was Sweetwater another Bodhisattva, or was he able to communicate with them? "Not all Bodhisattvas are Buddhist" my Buddha Master had told me.

After we left Texas and the Rio Grande, we headed into Indian Country, stopping first at the Acoma Pueblo in New Mexico to deliver a book to their tribal council. I had spent considerable time at that pueblo while traveling in that area with Dorje PaMu a few years earlier.

From there we went to Window Rock, Arizona but were too late to find anyone who could take the precious treasure book to the Navaho leaders. It was the weekend, so we knew this would be difficult and we had stayed too long on the mesa at the Acoma Pueblo. We planned on staying longer at the Cultural Center of the Hopi at Kykotsmovi and hopefully being able to meet with some of their elders. On Sunday I stayed at their Cultural Center and enjoyed my native hominy stew (nok qui vi) and caught up on the internet postings of the tour while the rest of the delegation went further west to visit the Grand Canyon.

The Hopi Nation does not allow photos to be taken on the reservation, but the tribal leaders did consent to have their pictures taken at the tribal office where they received the treasure book. (FIGURE 42). They were especially interested in the photo of the Buddha's Yun sculpture "Mysterious Boulder with

FIGURE 42: Hopi Tribal officers receive treasure book, Kykotsmovi Village, Arizona

Mist" shown in FIGURE 43. In this work of art, the Buddha had crafted two grottos in a sculpture of a rock, only in one side there was a heavy mist and in the other it was quite clear. It is truly a miraculous phenomenon. Everyone who sees this yun sculpture[30] is amazed. How can someone carve mist from the air and place it inside a rock? This work of art was part of an exhibition given at the Rayburn Building in Washington, DC for members of Congress in 2003. This sculpture is now part of the permanent collection on display at the International Art Museum of America in San Francisco. The Vice Chairman of the Hopi Nation requested additional copies of the book for their libraries and school. Shrouded in clouds, the sacred San Francisco Peaks, home of the Hopi Kachinas, could be seen on the way from the Hopi Nation to Flagstaff.

The West Coast, Hawaii, and The Pacific Northwest

It was December 1, 2008 when we started the next leg of the journey in our home state of California. Our first stop was in Sacramento where I gave a presentation at the Belle Cooledge Branch of the Public Library.

FIGURE 43: The Hopi elders were interested in the Yun Sculpture "Mysterious Boulder with Mist" hand sculpted by H.H. Dorje Chang Buddha III.

Although the tour was supposed to continue to Reno, Nevada and the Nevada State Capitol in Carson City, we cancelled those presentations and headed back to San Francisco. One morning, as soon as I felt one of the drivers was up, I asked to be taken to the hospital. Something was not right and without help, I

---

30 *Yun Sculpture is a highly innovative form of art invented by H.H. Dorje Chang Buddha III. Disciples of the Buddha have offered a $12-million-dollar reward to anyone who could reproduce these masterpieces, but to date no one has come close.*

knew I would not be able to make any more presentations. The kind emergency room doctor told me I had a form of pneumonia and sent me to bed with antibiotics and other drugs. I was exhausted, but I knew I could muster the strength to give the presentation in Sacramento that night. Those presentations tended to energize me. I am sure I had the blessings and power of my Master and the Buddhas and Bodhisattvas whenever I talked to groups about the treasure book and how blessed we were to have the Buddha living amongst us. As the tour had progressed, I found myself often besieged with violent fits of coughing. I started asking my yidam for help to deliver the presentation and sure enough I did not cough while I was presenting. However, if I was not clever enough to ask for help during the question and answer period that followed, I would then begin coughing again. You do have to be careful what you ask for.

As soon as we were finished in Sacramento, we headed back to San Francisco where the nuns again helped nurse me back to health. Between the miracle of modern drugs and the kindness of the nuns and a lot of rest, I was able to give a powerful presentation to a large group at Hua Zang Si, their temple in San Francisco. (FIGURE 44)

FIGURE 44: Mountain of treasure books at my return presentation in Hua Zang Si.

We had come full circle back to Hua Zang Si, where the tour had begun, almost six months before. My presentation at Hua Zang Si was preceded by a video of that June assembly so that those present could witness the ceremony and experience the nectar rain that had manifested outside the temple after the event. When I was challenged by an attendee who insisted that the Buddha was only a prophet and not divine, I explained how becoming a god was not the goal of Buddhists. I further told how Shakyamuni Buddha had responded to someone who questioned just who He was when He walked on this earth over 2,500 years ago. When asked if He was a god, He said "No." "Was He a man?" Again, the Buddha answered "No." "Then what are you?" He was asked. The Buddha replied, "I am awake." And that is the goal of all Buddhists—to become awakened to who they really are and to be able to leave samsara or the suffering of earthly existence. Actually, the goal is much broader. For Mahayana Buddhists the goal is to save all living beings—we only seek enlightenment so that we can help other beings—all our relatives from all the realms of existence.

One night I gave a presentation on why and how H.H. Dorje Chang Buddha III has come to America at the Martin Luther King, Jr., Branch of the San Jose Public Library next door to San Jose State University. There were many questions, especially from the college and high school students who attended. I am often asked what it is like to be a close disciple of H.H. Dorje Chang Buddha III. I sometimes just smile and tell them to read *The Life of Milarepa* to see how Marpa taught his most famous disciple. We are all tested, but rarely asked to build and tear down stone towers—at least not in a physical sense. Sometimes I see it, but most of the time I have only realized that I was being tested a long time after the test was given and it was too late. It seems I catch my mistake sooner, but I still miss a lot.

One thing I have observed is that the Buddha never gives a test that is too difficult for the student, although it may be quite a stretch and not anything that you could have possibly anticipated or would ever have done otherwise. I have seen students tested in front of their peers in a formal way, but most of the time it is just part of ordinary events and can be done anywhere and anytime and when you least expect it. Actually, the Buddha Master did not need to test me. As a Buddha, I am sure He knew what my level of realization was. These tests were to enable me to see how I was or was not progressing.

One of the realizations that I have recently gained is how the Buddha has been training me to let go of my judgmental mind. Sometimes the lessons have been subtle and sometimes I have been called on something in front of hundreds of my peers, but I am getting it. Am I perfect in this regard? No, but I am infinitely better than when I started to practice with my Buddha Master, and I can see the fruits of my transformation. This is the way it works whereby we use our cultivation to transform our ordinary consciousness into wisdom. The Christian use of WWJD ("What would Jesus Do?") is very good practice. We must evaluate our thoughts, actions, and speech and make them like those of a Buddha or Bodhisattva. What would Green Tara do? What would Kuan Yin do? What would Shakyamuni Buddha do?

My own suffering and that which I saw around me caused me to think deeply about how we create our unhappiness and how the teachings of the Buddha can help us overcome our negative thinking and habitual tendencies. Everything, and I do mean everything, is the result of my own actions. There is nothing that happens to us that we did not cause in this life or previous ones.

We spent another night south of San Francisco at Bodhi Monastery and headed east across the state to Fresno and Sanger Mission where we spent several days visiting local temples. At a presentation in Fresno, I explained again why H.H. Dorje Chang Buddha III had come to America and introduced some of the Buddha's teachings. After the presentation, those present dedicated their merit to all living beings and prayed that all would quickly become accomplished like Kuan Yin Bodhisattva. Kuan or Guan Yin Bodhisattva, also known as Avalokiteshvara in Sanskrit and Chenrezig in Tibetan, is revered by Buddhists as the personification of compassion. As I explained earlier, this Bodhisattva is already a Buddha, but continues to manifest in this realm as a Bodhisattva to help liberate living beings from all sufferings.

The Sanger Mission located near the town of Sanger on the way to Sequoia and Kings Canyon National Park is a very peaceful rural setting. Near the city of Fresno, it was a perfect place for reflection and meditation, something we had not had nearly enough time for on the trip. At the time, I had no idea that this location would be my future home and the location for what would be known as the Xuanfa Institute and later as the Holy Vajrasana Temple and Retreat Center, or that I would be moving here the following month.

We headed home to Pasadena immediately after a presentation in Santa Barbara. This phase of our Dharma Propagation Mission was over. Thousands of Westerners now knew of H.H. Dorje Chang Buddha III and why he had come to this world and specifically to America. They also knew what they had to do to enter the true Dharma.

I resumed my weekly classes at the United International World Buddhism Association Headquarters[31] in Monterey Park on the latest translations of discourses by His Holiness Dorje Chang Buddha III. After the holidays, I was given the option of moving to Sanger Mission to establish my own institute and temple. It was a perfect fit. I would miss the daily interaction with my beloved Buddha Master, but it would give me a place to develop for Western students like I had wanted. I was told I could move after the Chinese New Year, which was January 26. I filled up the big van we had used for the trip with my worldly belongings and headed north. Although the previous occupants had not quite

---

31 *Now known as the World Buddhism Association Headquarters.*

moved out, I had to move quickly as the next phase of the Dharma Propagation Mission was about to begin.

Hawaii

After a brief rest and time to move to Sanger, I was ready to start the next leg of the Dharma Propagation Tour. This time it was just the nun from Hua Zang Si and myself. We packed all our presentation gear in a golf bag carrier and another large suitcase and left San Francisco International airport on February 10 for our trip to the Hawaiian Islands.

We were very lucky to have a very enthusiastic group at the presentation I gave at the First Unitarian Church in Honolulu. I was still battling my demons and given to fits of coughing and near laryngitis. I was so unsure as to whether I could even give the presentation that I had the nun read the lecture to make sure she knew the pronunciation of all the words, just in case she would have to help. Although her English was quite good, it was still not her primary language. I know she was praying that my voice held up and I didn't start coughing again. I was, too. However, like so many times before, we were blessed, and the presentation went very well. There was so much good energy in the room and with the blessing of our Buddha Master and the Buddhas and Bodhisattvas, how could it have been otherwise? It really was amazing. For so much of this tour I had been quite ill, yet when there were Buddhist matters to be dealt with, I always was able to perform. More than once I left a hospital to make a presentation.

People are so hungry for the Dharma and do recognize just what an auspicious event these presentations are. Many wanted to hang around to learn more and help us pack for the next leg of our journey. There was one young man who came who told us he had seen the Buddha a few years before in Hawaii. I had been with the Buddha on that trip, so I could confirm that was probably correct. Another young man came because he wanted to know how to see the Buddha's artwork that had so inspired him. They were both very happy to receive copies of the treasure book, which contained many illustrations of His art. Like elsewhere, people want to know how they can meet the Buddha and learn more about the Buddha's teachings. Of course, I told them to read "What Is Cultivation?" and work to have a Dharma center on the island so that they can have a place to hear the Buddha's discourses. I told them about the most recent "Trip to the East" series that further explains much of what is in "What Is Cultivation?" and that they are being translated and I will be reading preliminary translations until they are officially recorded.

The Buddha had told the Dharma Propagation Team and repeated in a Chinese New Year discourse that the Buddha would directly teach those who would be responsible for propagating the correct Dharma to others—although the Buddha does have a few ordinary students who are not Dharma teachers, lamas, vajra masters, rinpoches, or Dharma kings, so blessed because of deep karmic connections to the Buddha and the Buddha's family from past lifetimes. Most of the Buddha's direct disciples are Dharma teachers, rinpoches and the like, but I must add, that some of the so-called "ordinary students" who do not bear honorific titles may well be holy beings who are more advanced and have higher states of realization than those who bear those titles. Titles, per se, do not tell you anything about one's level of realization or understanding of the Dharma.

I told the group that the best way to meet the Buddha is to cultivate yourself according to "What Is Cultivation?" and the related discourses and help others hear the Dharma. Of course, it is possible for those with a pure heart to meet the Buddha in their dreams and receive the Buddha's empowerments through telepathic means. I shared my own experiences and those of my students in that regard.

I had, after all, received the design for the logo that I use for the Xuanfa Institute and my original website in a very vivid dream and my Buddha Master told me that this was His way of explaining how I should propagate the Dharma (FIGURE 2 page 15). I saw a red sun riding in a yellow crescent moon floating on dharma clouds. The sun was like a mirror with seven jewels in rainbow colors around its edge. They represented good fortune, holy manifestations or miracles, the five vidyas, wisdom, compassion, sainthood, and enlightenment. The sun and the moon together are often used as symbols for the highest Buddha Dharma. They are symbols for the Dharmakaya or the Adharma Buddha. You can see them on our lineage charts and in various forms on the top of holy stupas all over the world as well as other holy places. This magical mirror of the Buddha Dharma can enable you to attain all these "jewels." You can be blessed with good fortune and happiness and avoid all disasters. You will naturally acquire the supernormal powers and extraordinary skills with which you can help others. You will perfect your wisdom and compassion to become a holy or enlightened person and ultimately achieve Buddhahood (perfection). The Buddha Dharma is marvelous and sublime! It is truly the wonderful existence of another dimension that is available for everyone. Every living being has the potential to become a Buddha!

The flight from Honolulu to the island of Maui went smoothly. There were fluffy clouds and balmy breezes and such mellowness that I understood the reason why human life on the rest of this earth was the best place to practice—better than in the heavenly realms where everything was so wonderful that you had no incentive to leave samsara or desire to practice. This was as close to heaven as one could want. There were palm trees swaying and warm sunny beaches and incredible vivid flowers of all hues and the friendliest people you could find anywhere. People really seemed glad to see you and welcome you to this little bit of paradise.

But I still had my very earthly karmas to remind me I was still part of samsara. Although my voice was great for the presentation last night, it was barely more than a squeak today. How would I do at the Maui Beach Resort Hotel presentation on Saturday? The nun took very good care of me. She definitely did not want to read my speech; although I had no doubt that she would do anything she needed to do to propagate the dharma. I had remembered a remedy our host had given me when Bodi Wentu Rinpoche and I visited her in Washington, DC last spring. Her sister was an actress in China, and we were told that she always gargled with and drank water that had been infused with tangerine peels before she went on stage. That remedy worked then, and it had worked the prior night in Honolulu, and I was counting on it again—that and our prayers and the help of our spiritual friends.

It was Valentine's Day and I wasn't certain what sort of crowd we would have, but it was a good turnout, and everyone seemed enthusiastic to hear about how and why H.H. Dorje Chang Buddha III had come to the United States. There were a few Buddhists in the crowd, but most were not affiliated with anything. All seemed to have a strong spiritual connection, especially to the island. You could sense a powerful influence of the local gods and goddesses here. Only in Crestone, Colorado, and to a somewhat lesser sense in the Appalachian Mountains had I felt this before in our travels.

We had met a delightful medicine man from the Wampanoag Tribe, an eastern woodland band that once inhabited most of New England, and his very beautiful tall and blonde Swedish wife at the airport in Maui the morning before. They were also on their way to Hilo to conduct a camp there—mostly for children. He was from a village in New Hampshire and told me he had been a Buddhist when he was young, having a statue of the Buddha and learning to meditate while he was in boarding school. It was the only organized religion that made any sense to him and he agreed that there were many parallels between the native beliefs and Buddhism. He reminded me so much of my own father who was also of the woodland tribes. I told him about taking my elderly father to his first sweat lodge and how the "Thunder Beings" had come, even though it was a very clear cloudless night, and how similar holy beings or Dharma Protectors often made their presence known at ceremonies conducted by my Buddha Master. He said he was 80 years old, but he certainly did not look it. I also told him about the Dharma Propagation Team meeting the leaders of the Taos Pueblo and how the Lt. Governor had told us about "knowing" as a child that a very great Buddha—the root Buddha—had been born in Tibet-China around fifty years ago and how happy he was to receive the treasure book.

We drove around the entire Big Island stopping on Painted Church Road near the village of Captain Cook on the Kona coast to see the Kalachakra Stupa at the Paleaku Peace Garden located there. It was a beautiful drive and the first time I had been able to see the snow-capped mountains of Mona Koa and Mona Lona. The other times I had been here they were covered with clouds. It is so desolate on the Kona side of the isle of Hawaii—just fields of cattle and old lava flows with luxury resorts dotting the coast. Highway 190-180 is further inland and up high enough that you can see everything. There are a few small villages down where the stupa is located, but the rest is pretty much uninhabited. The Hilo side of the island is quite different with lush vegetation and dazzling waterfalls and more urbanization. When we drove further south, we encountered newer lava flows, one containing the skeleton of a burned-out home that obviously did not escape the wrath of Pele, the volcano goddess. I remembered being here in the 70's and not being able to travel on this road as the mountain was still erupting and the lava flows blocked all access. Now the road had sliced through what had been molten rock and we could circle the entire island.

We were given a three lei welcome by Barbara de Franko and her friends. Although I had told her that the reason I do not notify anyone of my visits to the stupas is because it is a personal and private event, she still managed, at the last minute, to pull together seven or eight local friends to welcome us and arranged for a very nice lunch on the veranda at the Peace Center. The center was non-sectarian and had gardens devoted to many different religions including a Native American Medicine Wheel. Barbara and her friends had many questions and seemed happy with the answers I gave, based on various discourses from my Buddha Master. They asked how you know which practice is right for you and I told them that it is the one you have the karmic affinity to practice and that you DO practice. Receiving many very high and fancy tantric initiations is of no use if you do not have that affinity or do not proceed to practice them. Of course, you also need an authentic master to guide you and give you the initiation. Such a master will also be able to ascertain which is the correct dharma for you. Many of those present had followed H.E. Kalu Rinpoche and now followed Lama Tharchin Rinpoche who was coming there in a few weeks. They told us how much the first Kalu Rinpoche had loved the islands. When the reincarnation of Kalu Rinpoche visited them several years ago while still very young, he also told them of his love for the islands and that he would return when he was grown up. I ended that part of the tour with a visit to the Kalachakra stupa that Kalu Rinpoche had built (FIGURE 45).

FIGURE 45: Circumambulating the Kalachakra Stupa at the Paleaku Peace Garden on the Kona coast on the Big Island of Hawaii.

I had to ask them about my realization as to how anandamaya (the delusion of bliss) works and jokingly wondered if it was hard to practice Buddhism in Hawaii, as it was so much like living in paradise. They agreed that when you visit the islands, maybe for the first week or so of living here, you think you are in paradise. The weather and environment are so lovely and the people are kind and gentle, but pretty soon your old demons and delusions take over and you have just as many reasons to practice here as anywhere else. Also judging from the tsunami warning signs, the lava flows, and the area where we were told to drive carefully because we were in a fault zone and there were many cracks in the road, the weather and environment is not always so perfect either. A tornado touched down on a golf course and picked up and threw a 262 pound man against a building on the first day we were in Hawaii. And then there were the torrential rains with zero visibility and the 60+ mph trade winds and typhoons, but most of the time the weather is ideal.

My arms and legs were blazing red and bumpy, but I felt it was sort of a detox process whereby my body was ridding itself of many toxins. I just read in the local news that the air and water here will do that to you. The entire tour and especially to the islands had been a kind of detox for me. I had to think a lot about my practice and my cultivation and how to rid myself of harmful habits and tendencies. I firmly believe that the message of "What Is Cultivation?" contains the best medicine for all our ailments. I must continue to practice it.

Our presentation on Hilo was a bit different. We had several very serious

Buddhist disciples come and a couple who were acting very strange. It finally dawned on me, but only after I saw the young man roll what I am sure were a couple of joints, that they were stoned. Why they came, I do not know. They said they were curious and they were very polite. From my own experiences and observations, I know that many substance abusers are actually looking for some sort of spiritual path—only in the wrong places. The young man said he was a serious

Christian and asked very intelligent questions wondering if we were a lot like the Mormons whom he said believed that if you live a good moral life you will become gods. Not knowing that much about the Mormon faith, I could only answer that we did indeed believe that if you became enlightened you will become a Buddha, but that was a state that was much higher than that of the gods. They sat through most of the presentation, but toward the end, I saw the young man was getting restless and began to roll another couple of joints and then he and his lady friend quietly left. We had a very good and lengthy discussion after the presentation, mostly on how the practice of Zen fit into the lineage chart. The remaining attendees were mostly practitioners of the Zen tradition. One very dedicated young man had tried to come to the presentation in Rochester, New York, and was very happy to meet us in Hilo. He knew we were going to the stupa and had tried to meet us there, even traveling around the island twice to try to find us.

The Pacific North-West

The full team was back together for the last leg of the group effort. It was late April 2009. The rest of the visits I would pretty much be on my own. By now I had enough students in various places around the country that I could count on local support for the remaining locations. We gave three more presentations in northern California and headed to the Pacific Northwest. It was spring and the mountain roads should be good enough to come back through Idaho and Reno. I gave presentations on the treasure book *H.H. Dorje Chang Buddha III* at the Sonoma County Public Library in Santa Rosa and at the Holy Dharma Discourse Center in Sausalito, California.

The landscape was different than when we started. The intra-team fighting had ceased. Everyone was trying very hard to get along. The seeds that had been sown earlier were starting to sprout. The intensive bombardment of internet ads and reporting was paying off. We had fledgling Dharma centers established. Three of the team had been designated as Masters of Dharma Listening Sessions. They and three others had their own centers and were bringing more people to the Dharma. New students whom we had met on the way also had taken refuge and established centers where even more people could listen to the Dharma. All was as it should be.

We stopped in Mount Shasta on the way to Oregon. I gave a presentation on the treasure book at the Mount Shasta Branch of the Siskiyou County Public Library. We also presented a copy of the treasure book to the monks and nuns at Shasta Abbey. I wanted to pay my respect to the stupa of the founder of the Abbey and my first Buddhist teacher, Roshi Jiyu-Kennett (FIGURE 46). Even though it was Spring, the Mountains were still covered with a beautiful blanket of snow and it was quite chilly. You could feel and smell the awakening of the earth as a new year was beginning.

FIGURE 46: Memorial stupa for Roshi Jiyu Kennett (1924-1996) at Shasta Abbey near Mt. Shasta, California.

The team gave a presentation at the Northwest Branch of the Multnomah County Library in Portland, Oregon amidst quite dramatic circumstances. Just before I began the presentation, a violent hailstorm bombarded the library dumping several inches of hail and rain on the area. The ferocious storm with tornado-like winds only lasted a very brief time and subsided as the presentation began (FIGURE 47). Afterwards a beautiful full rainbow filled the sky. Only once before had I witnessed such a display of hail and wind and that was when I was with His Holiness Dorje Chang Buddha III in southern California. It seemed as though the heavens had opened up and diverted a river of ice over where we were. Since the dogwoods and other trees were in bloom, the ice flow was colored by many flower petals and tender green leaves and was very beauti-

124

FIGURE 47: Ice flow of hailstones outside Northwest Branch of Multnomah County Library in Portland, Oregon, just before Tour presentation.

ful. As the storm left, the lights started to flicker in the meeting room. I told the attendees how a ghost had attended one of my classes in southern California and turned the lights on and off until I thought to ask it to stop. It obeyed. The same thing happened here. I invited the ghost to stay and hear the presentation, but to please stop playing with the lights and the lights flickered one more time and remained still. I believe that this type of ghost only wants you to acknowledge their presence and means no harm. Ghost beings want to hear the Dharma, too.

We stopped in Olympia and gave a presentation in Seattle, then headed southwest across the Cascade Range toward Idaho. I gave a presentation on "H.H. Dorje Chang Buddha III Is Living in America" at the Boise Public Library and answered many questions that the attendees had about the Buddha and Buddhism and how one takes the quick path to enlightenment. I gave a presentation on the treasure book at a local yoga studio in Reno, then continued south to Carson City, Nevada. From there the team drove back to San Francisco and home, but that was not the end of the tour for me. Two more times I crossed the US in my little red Honda, and once by train and again by plane, going alone most of the way. But these trips were more oriented to setting up Dharma centers and reading the discourses of the Buddha to those I had met on earlier trips. However, there were still two new places in the Pacific Northwest left to visit—the awesome states of Alaska and Montana.

I made a solo trip to Alaska and introduced the book to a group assembled at the Z. J. Loussac Public Library in Anchorage. Many things had happened since the book was released in April 2008. Literally thousands of Dharma centers and temples had sprung up to offer people a chance to listen to the holy discourses of this great Buddha. I had just returned from Hong Kong where representatives from more than a thousand temples, associations, and other Buddhist organizations had gathered to take an exam to be able to lead Buddhists in listening to the Dharma spoken by H.H. Dorje Chang Buddha III. Fifty more were certified as Acaryas. This was the second such assembly with another being given in San Francisco in April of that year. I returned with other rinpoches and Dharma masters every year after that for several years to help administer the exam.

I also told the group that another great book of Dharma would soon be published that would further expound the highest teachings in Buddhism—*The Supreme and Unsurpassable Mahamudra of Liberation* and I urged everyone to read it, follow its guidelines, and quickly become liberated. What is available in Chinese online is part of the *SAUMOL* that relates to cultivation. Many mantras and other commentary are still missing from that as are the highest Dharmas and the first Mind-Essence. Advanced students have been transmitted some of these Dharmas like the Vajra Substitute Body Meditation Dharma or Tummo Concentration. What we have, however, provides a good basis for learning the foundational Dharma that would be required to be able to practice the higher Dharmas.

On my trip to Montana, local Buddhists and other interested residents of Helena gathered at the Law Library on Rodney Avenue to hear how Dorje Chang Buddha had come again to this earth and how this great Buddha fits in the lineage of all Buddhist sects. I also introduced the group to some of the teachings contained in the treasure book *H.H. Dorje Chang Buddha III* as well as provided examples of various Dharmas that senior disciples had received. These included the Xian Liang Great Perfection Dharma whereby the recipients were able to realize the rainbow body state in less than two hours after receiving the initiation; an advanced form of Tummo Dharma that enabled the recipient to raise his body temperature to almost 200 degrees and thus be able to destroy his negative karma and physical afflictions; the Buddhas Bestowing Nectar Dharma; and the Vajra Substitute Body Meditation Dharma where the crown of the recipient is opened so that his or her consciousness can come and go at will. This is much different from the dharma known as phowa where the crown is opened at the time of death to enable one to go to a Buddha Land or other higher realm. Some of those attending were practicing a form of phowa.

Since there were representatives from various groups within all three of the major vehicles of Buddhism (hinayana, mahayana, and vajrayana) as well as students from the local Catholic university and others, an enthusiastic and probing discussion followed the presentation. Some of those present were shocked to hear that unlike many religious leaders, H.H. Dorje Chang Buddha III does not accept offerings from His disciples. I am quite sure that was not the case with their leaders.

A most amazing thing happened soon after we crossed the border into Montana on our way to Helena. A student from Salt Lake City had come to Boise to hear the discourse I read there and help with logistics, and decided to continue as far as Helena before returning home. We had plenty of time and took our time driving through this beautiful land. It was a beautiful cool, sunny day with bright blue skies and wispy white clouds. Montana certainly deserved to be called "The Big Sky" state. The sky was immense and the seemingly uninhabited landscape went on forever. I found I was starting to fall asleep again and pulled off to catch a quick nap. We were driving in separate cars. I must have slept for 10-15 minutes and when I awoke the brilliant purple and green lights that I often see in meditation started to coalesce again. It was like it had been earlier that morning at another rest stop, when an opening appeared like a window into another dimension. That time it was not so clear, and I couldn't be sure of what I saw. It was as I imagined a portal to take you to another world would look. Once before this had appeared in my bedroom in Sanger shortly after a powerful empowerment in Pasadena. A rectangular opening appeared, and I could see inside that window. There were many Bodhisattvas or Buddhas inside looking out at me, or they appeared to be looking at me. That time the world had a ruby red glow to it—like the two giant beams of light that entered me a few days earlier during a ceremony in Pasadena. Those beams looked like what we videotaped at a stupa in Colorado. They pulsated and were alive, and a beautiful ruby red, and filled me with their power. This same phenomenon appeared many times at the Xuanfa Temple in Sanger. So, in Montana there was a bright rich purple color and an oval opening in the heavens. It was there whether I opened my eyes or shut them. I could see the opening right through the roof of the car, and I could see many ornately dressed sambhogakaya figures looking over the edge of the opening and down to where I was sitting. It was wonderful! Later I regretted that I did not ask if I could visit them.

When I returned home from this last leg of the Dharma Propagation Tour, I reported what had happened to my Buddha Master and was immediately blessed with a tummo initiation.

six

Tummo Initiation

When I returned from the final phase of the Big Blue Book tour and reported on what had happened, I was immediately blessed with a tummo empowerment and told to come back the next day for an initiation into the preliminary practices of tummo. This is one of the Dharmas that is included in *The Supreme and Unsurpassable Mahamudra of Liberation* as I mentioned earlier. My Buddha Master told me that there were five or six very high and powerful Dharmas that would be transmitted as part of *The Supreme and Unsurpassable Mahamudra of Liberation*. As the Buddha began to list them, there were even more. We have already seen students receive the Xian Liang Great Perfection Dharma where they can experience the rainbow body within two hours of receiving the Dharma. Two of the students who received this Dharma were then also able to receive the Vajra Substitute Body Meditation Dharma whereby the crowns of their heads were opened to allow their consciousness to leave and visit other realms as well as do other things here, including remaining in deep meditation.

Silver Box Discourses

These disciples were already very advanced meditators. I remember another Dharma king telling me many years ago that one of the recipients of this Dharma was spending most of his time in meditation even then. This disciple is also one who has been certified as being an enlightened being. I actually saw him tell our Buddha Master about his enlightenment experience. I will never forget it. We were on our way to the airport to catch a plane for Hawaii. I was in one car with this Dharma King's wife and Dharma King Ciren Gyatso (FIGURE 48) was driving the Buddha in another car. We passed them on the freeway and the Dharma King, normally a very reserved and solemn sort, was waving his hands in the air very excitedly. I don't know who was driving the Mercedes. It must have been on autopilot. When we returned, the Buddha asked the Dharma King to repeat his story and this time the Buddha secretly recorded it. The

Dharma King had also written an enlightenment poem that he gave. We have this recording in Chinese at some of our Dharma centers. It was so precious that it is kept in a special silver box. The Dharma King's wife felt sorry for me since I do not understand Chinese and volunteered to personally translate it for me at their home. I can't remember all of it, but one part is very clear. After explaining his experience for some time, the Buddha asked him why he had not asked the Buddha to confirm his experience. Was he really enlightened? The Dharma King responded, "I don't need to." The Buddha was delighted. That was the absolutely perfect answer. As long as you have to ask, you are not enlightened.

FIGURE 48: Dharma King Ciren Gyatso.

The Dharma of Tummo

I digress. The third Dharma that has been transmitted from *The Supreme and Unsurpassable Mahamudra of Liberation* is the Dharma of Tummo concentration I just mentioned. Tummo is the Tibetan word for "inner fire." Many who practice Tibetan Buddhism practice a form of this. I have even met people who are not Buddhist say they have experienced a sort of spontaneous inner fire like this. I believe there are Bon[32] masters who teach a form of tummo as well. There are many workshops being offered by those who promise the benefits of tummo, but they are not what we are talking about here. One of my students told me of learning Reiki Tummo from an Asian master, and while she experienced the movement of energy that made her feel good, it was not the sort of practice that is offered in *The Supreme and Unsurpassable Mahamudra of Liberation*. We have all heard of the legendary holy men of the Himalayas like

---

32 *Bon was the original indigenous shamanic religion of Tibet. Over the years, like Daoism in China, Bon has adopted many Buddhist practices, but like Daoism, it is not a branch or sect of Buddhism.*

Milarepa who can live in mountain caves for years under very cold conditions with no source of external heat and who wear very little or no clothing. There have also been televised documentaries of nuns and others drying wet shawls under subzero conditions using only their body heat. This is but a small fraction of what is possible with this kind of Dharma practice. However, today it is very difficult to see a true manifestation of tummo power.

Tummo concentration is a very high-level Buddha Dharma meditation. It is a rare holy Dharma indispensable for cultivating certain other high Dharmas and the accomplishment of the rainbow body. Regardless of what illness or disease one has, practicing tummo can eliminate it completely. One can even eliminate karmic obstructions in others with this Dharma. The perfect accomplishment in the practice of this Dharma combined with Vajra Substitute Body Meditation can lead to the accomplishment of becoming a Bodhisattva at the twelfth stage or higher. So, you can see that this is a very important Dharma for attaining liberation.

A vajra brother, Venerable Xiangge Qiongwa Rinpoche, explained the methods and stages of tummo very well in an article he wrote about making the inner-tantric Daba Buqiong and Black Jewel (Kazhuo Ande) Medicine Pills that require the practice of tummo concentration.[33] First, he explained that there are two types of practices of tummo concentration. One is Yoga Tummo from Tibetan Esoteric Buddhism. The other is the Corpse Pose Tummo regarded as "the King of Tummo" from *The Supreme and Unsurpassable Mahamudra of Liberation.* When practicing tummo, the higher the body temperature can be raised to, the higher the realization power of the practitioner. The normal body temperature of humans is between 98.6°F and 99.5°F. When the body temperature reaches a level between 104°F and 105.8°F, one is regarded as having a high fever. A temperature above 106°F can cause danger to one's life. However, practitioners of tummo concentration can attain much higher temperatures than that. My former roommate, Akou Lamo Rinpoche, practiced the Tibetan form while another vajra brother, Kaichu Rinpoche practiced the Corpse Pose form. Both were able to give demonstrations of their ability and have been videotaped using modern heat sensing technology to show their levels of accomplishment. Although a practitioner does not normally do this, they both were willing to risk losing their powers so as to help others understand the power and awesomeness of the true Buddha Dharma. Akou Lamo personally told me that her master in Tibet had warned her that she would lose her ability to practice if she told anyone what she did. I had suspected for some time that she was secretly practicing this Dharma and saw her health improve dramatically. However, as a true Bodhisat-

---

33   Ven. Xiangge Qiongwa Rinpoche, "True Stories about the Making of Daba Buqiong and Kazhuo Ande Pills and about the Iron-Clad Determiation of a Great Yogi", July 15, 2011.

tva, she was only concerned about helping living beings and did not hesitate to demonstrate her skills, if that would help others.

Ven. Xiangge Qiongwa Rinpoche went on to describe tummo practice to say that "the realization power from tummo concentration is defined by four steps. The first step is called the Initial Warmth Step. At this step, body temperature can be raised to between 115°F and 130°F but the ability of curing illnesses is not strong yet. The second step is the Joy of Heat from Meditation Step, with the body temperature raised to between 130°F and 150°F. The heat of tummo can be released at certain locations of the body to provide a relatively strong ability of curing illnesses. However, there are five illnesses that cannot be cured by this ability. Anyway, one will rarely become ill with the accomplishment at this step. The third step is the Step of Emptiness and Existence at High Temperature. The body temperature can be raised to between 150°F and 200°F. The heat of tummo can be distributed to any part of the body to heal illness by oneself, with the exception of two illnesses. The practitioner can collect the dark karma generated daily due to ignorance and burn it away with tummo. Such a practitioner can also move the heat of tummo outside of his body to cure illness and eliminate hindrance for other people or to subdue demons and evil spirits. The fourth step is the magnificent Joy at Extreme Temperature. The temperature will exceed 200°F and the heat of tummo will spread to the entire body. Master Milarepa used his realization power of this step to ignite his own body to attain the accomplishment of the Sambhogakaya and Nirmanakaya."

When I first witnessed Kaichu Rinpoche demonstrate his tummo power, I sensed that something was going wrong. The Buddha Master was quite concerned, and we were all sprinkled liberally with nectar water. What I found out later through translation was that the rinpoche had taken his body temperature very rapidly to almost 200°F, and the Buddha was concerned that he might reach this fourth stage. Something very wonderful happened after that. A very large and beautiful bright red seed character appeared mysteriously on the rinpoche's naked chest. My Dharma brother Kaichu Rinpoche is also accomplished in the Xian Liang Great Perfection and Vajra Body Substitution Meditation Dharmas.

So, we can see that the Dharmas that are being made available from *The Supreme and Unsurpassable Mahamudra of Liberation* are the very highest Dharmas in the world today and indeed have the power to liberate living beings. Needless to say, I was overjoyed to learn that I would receive the preliminary practices and begin to learn tummo.

First was the Tummo Concentration Empowerment to remove my karmic obstructions. A holy being placed the middle finger of his right hand on my throat. He held it there for a long time. We both chanted mantras. Suddenly it was like a very sharp fire shot out of his finger and entered my body. I don't know how long it lasted, but I know I screamed—the pain was very intense. This whole empowerment was videotaped and is included in several videos, including one showing how the Xuanfa Institute in Sanger, California, became empowered by H.H. Dorje Chang Buddha III as the Fourth Vajra Throne in the World. Yet it was like the Dharma Wheel empowerment I described earlier, the pain was also no-pain. I can't explain that, any better, but my Buddha Master told me this was the precursor to the Dharmakaya, to experiencing your original nature. I had experienced and seen this samadhi fire before during other forms of empowerment and initiation, but not like this. I only learned much later that the holy being performing that ceremony was Venerable Wangzha Shangzun.

Late the next day the Tummo Dharma was transmitted. I must not tell any of the details of these transmissions. I vowed that I would not, but I must say that it is a wonderful practice that I wish all living beings could learn. I am sharing this with you readers so that you can also aspire to achieving liberation with the myriad of practices available in *The Supreme and Unsurpassable Mahamudra of Liberation.*

This empowerment fire left a triangular scar that appeared to be hollow—an upside-down right triangle with the long side on the left and point at the bottom. Three other rinpoches also received this Dharma at that time. We all received it at different locations on our bodies. I am assuming that was due to our different karmic conditions. One had a huge mark on the top of his head, another on his forehead and the third on his upper lip. I have been blessed with so many of these types of initiations, but this had been the most dramatic and powerful to date.

I already described another empowerment that I had received from my Buddha Master that caused a diamond shape to form on my crown. I have never been given an explanation. When I asked about it, my Buddha Master just smiled, but I am sure it is part of His plan to help me become accomplished. Perhaps this is part of His Phoenix strategy. What I find so amazing about my Buddha Master is how he uses such different techniques to cause each of us disciples to mature in the Dharma. We all have such different karmic conditions and are so different and so our training is likewise very different. This has confused me in the past, but I am beginning to realize the magnificence and wisdom of this approach. We have become so accustomed to thinking that there is a generic solution to what is an infinitely more complex situation. I only hope that I can develop the same compassion and understanding of the different karmic needs of my students and gain the wisdom to know how to help them.

seven

Crown Opening Dharma

I once asked if I might receive the Vajra Substitute Body Meditation Dharma, but was told no, because the Buddha was afraid I would not return once I could leave this body, and I needed to be here to help propagate the Dharma for living beings. Actually, I suspect the Buddha was just being kind. I doubt if I am any way close to being able to receive such a high Dharma. In recent years I have been told I would receive that Dharma. However, I somehow manage to do something wrong and lose my merit and it does not happen.

Over the past twenty years I have been indeed fortunate to receive so many empowerments and initiations from H.H. Dorje Chang Buddha III. I have practiced the dharma of self-cultivation taught me by my Buddha Master so that I do have a modest degree of realization. My life has been dedicated to helping others learn and practice as well. I have seen many miraculous states including seeing my Buddha Master and other Buddhas and Bodhisattvas in the heavens and watching a vajra pill fly out of my hand in a dazzling red light. I was also able to awaken another vajra pill and hear and see other vajra pills sing and dance that I reported on earlier. But were these signs that I was progressing? The Buddha had said that I was, but would ordinary people be able to see the transformation? My real concern was, would I be able to help liberate other living beings? Would they believe me and follow the teachings that I had learned from my Buddha Master?

I learned of another magnificent Buddha Dharma from *The Supreme and Unsurpassable Mahamudra of Liberation* that can enable one to actually demonstrate that they have the body of a saint or holy being. It is known as the Tien Jie Mandala Ni-Wan Dao-guo Fa or Heavenly Realm Mandala Mud Pill Lamdre Dharma. Ni-wan translates literally as mud pill. Lamdre is a Tibetan term for the path and its fruit. Through this dharma, the gate to heaven on the crown of the head can truly be opened. The mud pill is also found in the meditative techniques of inner alchemy in Daoism. The mud pill crown opening was what was sought to become an immortal. Ancient emperors of China would have given their kingdoms and fortunes to be able to receive this Dharma. Ni-wan is also a Daoist term for the place where the consciousness or spirit enters and leaves the body of an immortal. It literally means a point on the top of the head that when open feels like soft mud. A newborn's skull is like this, which is the reason one has to protect the head of a baby until these openings or fontanelles can grow shut. This point is also known in acupuncture as the Bai Hui or the hundredth meeting point and is connected to the hypothalamus, pineal and pituitary glands—all parts of our anatomy that modern science does not yet fully understand or appreciate. I think this is also the Hindu Yogic equivalent of the Crown Chakra. The ni-wan also refers to the upper Cinnabar Field in Daoism or the center for intellect and spirituality. In Daoism, one refines one's essence (jing) into vital energy (qi), refines one's vital energy into spirit (shen), and refines one's spirit into emptiness. One unites one's primordial spirit to become form (an immortal) and dissipates that spirit to become formless vital energy. One is then neither empty nor substantial. That is what is called non-doing. Daoism also says one is able to receive cosmic energy through this point.

Lest there be confusion, I want to make something perfectly clear. The mud pill of Daoism is the place on the crown of the head through which one leaves the body to ascend to heaven. Buddhism also recognizes that the mud pill is the place through which one leaves the body to become a celestial being or immortal, which is one type of living being among all of the living beings in the six realms. However, what I am writing about is the Buddha Dharma and not Daoism or any other form of religion. When Buddhism came to China, the Daoists adopted many aspects of Buddhism. Still, Buddhism leads one to become a Buddha or Bodhisattva, and Daoism leads one to become an immortal. People who misunderstand what I am saying might question why I talk of a Daoist practice. This is a result of simply not understanding the teachings of Shakyamuni Buddha. Shakyamuni Buddha clearly stated in the sutras that there are six realms into which living beings can reincarnate and that the highest realm is the realm of the immortals. The ten types of immortals are described in general terms in the *Shurangama Sutra* and elsewhere, but they can generally be grouped into three classes: earth-bound immortals who continue to live amongst us, heavenly immortals who will go to the heavenly realms only after they leave this earth, and the divine immortals who can go to the heavenly realms now with their earthly bodies as well as after they leave this world. What the *Shurangama Sutra* does not say, but the Buddha explains in other texts, is the fact that those who cultivate themselves according to the teachings of the Buddha can continue their practice in these heavenly realms and go on to become Bodhisattvas. The translation that I have of the *Shurangama Sutra* is not clear on this point and appears to be discussing primarily the earth-bound immortals and not their higher forms.

However, in general, Buddhists do not seek rebirth in the heavenly realms. We know that once the good karma that enabled you to go to heaven is used up, you still have to return to the lower realms, including the hell realms, to repay your negative karma from past lives. For most people it is difficult to accumulate more good karma while in the heavens because the pleasures there are just too great. The only way to escape your karma is to become liberated. That way your negative karma cannot harm you. You are able to escape into emptiness and Yama and the hordes of Mara[34] cannot find you. However, if you have the extremely good fortune to have your crown opened, so as to be received by the highest celestial beings, and guaranteed the life of an immortal in these realms, it is most wonderful, because in that case you will be able to continue to meet and study with the highest Buddhas and Bodhisattvas and eventually be able to join them in the Buddha realms.

Although this Buddha Dharma can be transmitted to non-Buddhists as well as Buddhists and help sincere practitioners of other religions to achieve their goals of heavenly rebirth, its purpose for a Buddhist is quite different. Buddhists are also able to take rebirth in the Heavenly Realm and enjoy this paradise, but they do so in order to continue their cultivation and practice of the Dharma and eventually to be able to become Buddhas and Bodhisattvas. In the *Sutra on Loving-Kindness (Metta Sutta)*, Shakyamuni Buddha tells us that although a non-Buddhist may enjoy a lifespan in these heavens, when that lifespan ends, he must return to the lower realms to repay his karmic debts due to the law of cause and effect. However, one who follows the way of the Buddha can enjoy the pleasures of these realms and also gain liberation through the practice of Buddha Dharma while in these realms, eventually attaining the... "complete extinction of lust, hate and delusion in that same kind of heavenly existence." But there is another aspect of this Dharma that also makes it important. When one becomes accomplished in or achieves the fruit of this Dharma, one's structural body actually changes. One's bones become different than those of an ordinary being to enable one's consciousness to ascend to the heavenly realms. In this way one becomes a true holy being or saint.

Why is this important? Only holy beings or saints can liberate other living beings, and our work here as Buddhists is to help others seek liberation from the

---

34 *Yama is a great Bodhisattva who is in charge of the ghost and hell realms. He is neither a hell-being nor a ghost. Mara is also a Bodhisattva whose job is to test living beings, especially those who are on the path to Buddhahood. He and his demon followers are emanations of Buddhas and Bodhisattvas who test those engaged in self- cultivation.*

unhappiness, pain, and suffering of samsara or worldly existence. So, how do we know that someone is a holy being? There are many who claim such status and their disciples support them by calling their master a holy being, but are those who make such a claim really able to demonstrate their holiness?

There are two aspects of holy beings that distinguish them from ordinary beings. The first is that they manifest the Great Compassionate Bodhisattva State. This is a type of mind or level of accomplishment whereby everything they do is done for living beings. No matter what they do, say, or think, it is to help living beings become accomplished in the Dharma or liberated. This is the aspect of virtuous conduct. However, this alone is not enough to be designated a holy being, because, generally speaking, it cannot be seen or understood by ordinary people.

The second aspect of a holy being is that their physical body type is different from that of ordinary people and there are ways that this can be demonstrated. This is shown through miraculous events that actually change the structure of the body. The Mud Pill Holy Dharma is a Highest Form of Inner-Tantric State-Practice Initiation contained in *The Supreme and Unsurpassable Mahamudra of Liberation.* The Mud Pill Holy Dharma can accomplish this change in the structure of the body, as can accomplishment in the practice of Tummo Dharma that goes beyond the second stage. It is one way to prove that someone actually has the true Buddha Dharma and can help liberate other living beings. The process for becoming a saint in Catholicism is quite similar. A person has to have exhibited a pure, moral, and kind life and demonstrate some sort of miracle. The opening of the crown in the skull without any visible means on the surface of the skull is such a miracle! But scientific tests show that there indeed is such an opening!

As I mentioned earlier, the Mud Pill Dharma from *The Supreme and Unsurpassable Mahamudra of Liberation* is unique in that such dharma can be practiced by the practitioner of any religion. Although one needs to be a good person with deep roots of kindness, one does not need become a Buddhist to practice it. However, one must be careful in applying this dharma. It can be used to have the consciousness leave and return to the body, and it can be useful at the time of leaving this earth. But if your crown has been so opened, you must strictly abide by the Mud Pill Path Fruit Precepts. If you violate any of those precepts, you must repent that same day. If you repent a day later, your crown will close, and you will not attain liberation. But if you abide by the precepts, you will be able to go immediately to the heaven or paradise of your choice after death. You do not need to pass through the bardo. A Christian's soul would go the Christian Heaven to be with Jesus, while a Hindu would have his consciousness merge with Universal Consciousness (Supreme Cosmic Spirit) in the formless realms or go to the Brahman Heavens of the Form Realm, and so on.

In an oral discourse on the Dharma, the Buddha expounded that our crowns must be opened for us to go to any of the higher realms. What we call consciousness and others refer to as the soul or "spirit" exits the body at the time of death. The means by which it exits determines the next life. The Buddhist sutras also state that if the exit is through the soles of the feet or Yong-Quan gate, one goes to the hell realms; through the lower orifices, one becomes an animal; through the navel, one becomes a hungry ghost. The part of the body that determines where the consciousness/soul/spirit of the person goes will remain warm after the rest of the body becomes cold. If one's heart is warm and the rest of the body is cold, one is reborn to the human realm to be a human. If the throat or the throat gate is hot and the rest of the body is cold, one becomes an Asura. If one's body is cold and the Mud Pill gate, or fontanel, is hot, one becomes a deva or a heavenly being. When one is liberated and/or is reborn into a Buddha Land, the exit place will be at the Da-Le gate, i.e. the top gate right in the middle of the skull.

I remember Dr. Mitchell Levy at Zion, Illinois reporting that after the Sixteenth Karmapa departed this world, to his and the rest of the hospital staff's amazement, the area around his heart remained warm for a very long time, which would imply that he would be reborn as a human.

The Mud Pill Dharma does not enable you to become a Bodhisattva. It only enables you to become an immortal and go to the heavenly realms. It can also demonstrate that your physical body has the qualities of a holy being. However, there are many kinds of holy beings. It does not mean that as long as your crown is opened it can be said that you are a great holy being. This is true no matter what type of crown opening is received—either from the Ni-wan Dharma or the Vajra Substitute Body Meditation Dharma. These crown openings belong to the initial stage of a holy being. They are not necessarily those of great holy beings who truly attain the level of perfect liberation. His Holiness has made it very clear that even for the Dharma of Vajra Substitute Body Meditation, the opening of the crown should reveal a hole as big as an egg. Moreover, there should be a deep hole in the brain. It does not count if one just has an opening of the scalp or skull bone. His Holiness taught us that using scientific exams alone is not enough to determine the success of a crown opening. In front of the watchful eyes of many people, testing and verification of the crown opening must take place based on Buddha Dharma rules. There is 100% proof that your crown opening was successful when three peacock feathers hanging over your crown move about as a result of your consciousness leaving your body or your energy leaving your crown.

137

MRI scans of those who have received the Mud Pill empowerment show a small opening at the crown. However, the concentration powers of a small portion of those practitioners are not strong. For the sake of their safety, it is best that their openings are closed. At the time of their death, their crowns will naturally open again. There is no need to close the openings of those whose concentration powers are strong. Still, such people must strictly abide by the Mud Pill Path Fruit Precepts. I know of a devout Tibetan whose skull had many such openings from empowerments he had received from various rinpoches. His skull was retrieved from the sky burial field[35] and kept for veneration at a local temple because the lamas knew that he was a true holy being.

So, although I was encouraged to continue my Dharma practice and seek higher states of realization, my Master wanted me to have this empowerment. At the time of my Mud Pill Path Fruit Crown Opening, I wrote a vow of truth that stated the following:

"FACING WHAT IS TRUE—Becoming accomplished through the Mud Pill Path-Fruit of the *Supreme and Unsurpassable Mahamudra of Liberation* does not require the Buddha Master to touch the crown of the head or pour water onto the crown from a precious vase. The Buddha Master was on one side of the garden, and I was on the other side. The Buddha Master never came close to the crown of my head. His Holiness used His mind to accomplish this transmission. Right then and there His Holiness caused the Emperor of Heaven to descend and open the crown of my head. I clearly saw a wondrous state appear before me. It was extremely clear. Nobody would believe me. How could this be? I was worried it might have been an illusion, so I had it evaluated by a scientific instrument. That evaluation proved that what had happened was real. This fact proves that I have the qualifications of an immortal. If what I have just stated is false, I will surely descend into hell. Sincerely spoken by Zhaxi Zhuoma (See FIGURES 49, 50, and 51)."

I hope that many virtuous non-Buddhists and Buddhists alike with deep roots of kindness will also receive this empowerment.

My own experience in receiving and practicing the Mud Pill Dharma of *The Supreme and Unsurpassable Mahamudra of Liberation* was incredible. I find it difficult to describe in any way that can explain what happened in a believable way. Fortunately, I have the MRI photos that can show the success or fruit of my efforts. I truly believe that these pictures are "worth a thousand words" as far as demonstrating the results but let me try and tell as much as I

---

35 Sky burial is a funeral practice in Tibet where a corpse is left on a mountain top, exposed to the elements and consumed by a type of large carrion-eating bird. It was reserved for good people as the birds might reject someone of questionable character. The bones of holy people would be collected and used in temple rituals.

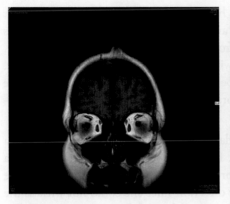

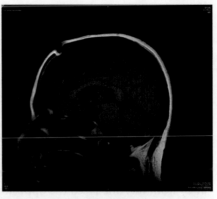

FIGURE 49: MRI frontal view photo taken as my crown was beginning to open.

FIGURE 50: My MRI Photos taken after my crown was opened

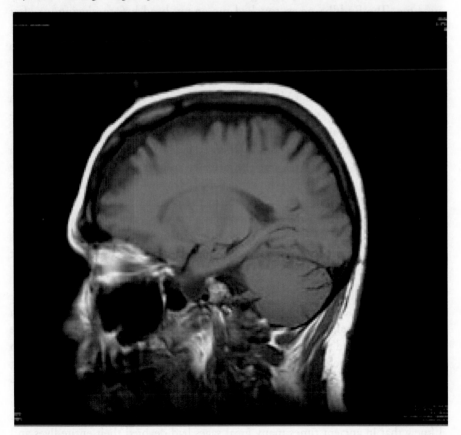

FIGURE 51: Note the very subtle consciousness leaving the opening, just after the MRI passed over the opening.

can about how they came about. As I have mentioned elsewhere, one does not usually talk about the empowerments and holy inner-tantric initiations one has received. In fact, we are prohibited from doing so according to the Dharma. This is an inviolable rule especially with respect to State Practice Initiations. However, I will describe what I am permitted to describe in order to provide non-Chinese speaking people with more specific information about the magnificence of the true Buddha Dharma.

First, it was a beautiful, balmy day. The sun was shining brightly with a slight breeze, providing ideal weather. I sat under a large orange tree next to a calm pool. My assistant and translator sat behind me and was some distance away from me. She faced the opposite direction since she could not witness the ceremony. Of course, I cannot give the particulars of the ceremony itself, but what I can tell you is that my magnificent Buddha Master was not in any way near me. The Buddha never touched me or my head before, during, or after the ceremony. In fact, my Buddha Master was on one side of the yard and I on the other during the ceremony. The Buddha used His mind to accomplish this transmission of the Buddha Dharma to me. The Buddha continued to pray for me while I practiced the Dharma. The Buddha prayed that I be a most kindhearted person, that I always benefit all living beings, that I always wish my country and its people be at peace, that I always wish all living beings be free from disasters and hardships, and that I always wish all sentient beings be eternally happy. After I received this Dharma, I sat and chanted a certain mantra silently. When I experienced a bright, distinct holy state, I began chanting the same mantra loudly to thank the Emperor of Heaven—also known as the Jade Emperor— for receiving me. My place in the celestial realms as an immortal had been ensured. Right then and there my practice of the Dharma caused the Emperor of Heaven to descend and open the crown of my head. The wondrous state that appeared before me was extremely clear. There was no doubt that something supernatural had happened!

After the ceremony my Buddha Master still did not touch my crown, including the entire time from when I received the Dharma until the year of 2010 at a medical center where I went to have an MRI image made of my head. Even if the Buddha had opened the Gate of Heaven on my crown by touching my head, such a power would have exceeded that of all of the Buddhist patriarchs throughout the generations. Even without touching my head, the Buddha enabled me to experience the supernatural state through mind transmission alone. I still wondered, "Could this just be an illusion?" It was, after all, an incredible accomplishment. I knew that in ancient times many great sages had devoted their entire lives and resources to achieving this to no avail. Why was I able to realize it?

As soon as I returned from the MRI center, I put the CD of the procedure on a computer. I knew from personally witnessing the beautiful holy state that the ceremony had been a success, but what would the MRI scans show? Would modern medical science be able to see this crown opening? Would the photos record that which is not visible to the naked eye? We were not disappointed. The results were phenomenal! The MRI image showed exactly what should appear according to a discourse given by my Buddha Master on this subject—that the Emperor of Heaven connected with me and opened my crown with a hole that was at least an inch wide. The bone around the opening even curved downward to allow for the opening. It was as if the bone had been transformed to a soft wax that could easily be shaped into a different form. Some of the images showed the opening from different angles. It was amazing! Who could believe it? Yet when I looked in the mirror, there was no sign of any change on my crown. No scars, no marks, nothing was visible to the ordinary eye. However, the sophisticated scientific instruments at the MRI center clearly showed a large opening in my crown. It went all the way through the bone into the soft tissue of my brain. It was so amazing. To the average person, this was a miracle! To a holy being, this was supernormal! I now had the body of a holy being and could prove it!

Some people have noted that I do have an indentation in my bald skull and wonder if that is the mark of the crown opening. No, it is in a different location and is a scar from a collision I had with a hard-bottomed swing as a child that had resulted in surface stiches, but certainly not the opening of the skull.

After the image was recorded, I deeply understood that my powers were not yet mature enough. Therefore, I decided to temporarily close my crown to prevent my consciousness from leaving my body and not returning or riding the clouds to heaven before my time has come. That way, I can remain in this world for a while longer. If I abide by the Mud Pill Dharma precepts, I will be received by the Emperor of Heaven and the other celestial beings and be able to continue my study and practice of the Buddha Dharma in paradise. If I become accomplished in the Buddha Dharma in this lifetime, my Da-Le gate will automatically open and I will be able to go to the Buddha Lands. Should I be able to go to the Buddha Lands, the celestial beings will come to escort me there. My Buddha Master is magnificent. I sincerely pray that all living beings have the opportunity to receive this blessed Dharma. My gratitude to my Buddha Master is without limits.

eight
The Xuanfa Institute

In January 2009, before the Big Blue Book Tour was over, I needed to re-locate to the Fresno area to what had been the Sanger Mission, the precursor to what became Hua Zang Si in San Francisco. It was a deserted ranch-style six-bed-room home on almost ten acres of land in the midst of farmland and upscale rural subdivisions and very ordinary individual homes. I thought it was perfect. When I asked the Buddha Master what I should do there, I was shocked to hear, "Start a meditation center." That is exactly what I had been trying to do for 20 years or more—long before I even met the Buddha Master. Ever since I became a Buddhist, I had used my vacations to go on retreats. I even acquired an old ho-tel-boarding house in northeast Kansas, that I converted into a retreat center with a Zen Priest friend after I left the corporate world. Now I could fulfill that dream.

Not only were there many bedrooms in this large Central California home that had been the Sanger Mission, but many of them were already equipped with double bunk beds so we could house many people. The house had been a nun-nery, while a small barn on the property had been used as the temple but was now used for storage. We needed people to help get the place in working order and create a temple and retreat center. The first retreats were mostly work retreats. People came from all over, many I had met on the tour. I tried to hold the retreats over long weekends and include a few extra days to allow side trips to nearby Yo-semite, Kings Canyon, or Sequoia National Parks just to make it more enjoyable. But things were about to get even more interesting at the temple.

In spring of 2011, I got a request to do a video about the site. I had established the Xuanfa Institute as a religious non-profit and was calling the place the Xuanfa Temple and Retreat Center. "Xuan-fa" meant to "propagate the Dharma," which I thought was an appropriate name for the end results of the Dharma Propagation Tour. I am afraid, I could not figure out what it was I was to do with this video. I understood it would be used to promote what I was doing and what was happening at our temple at our annual meeting in Hong Kong that summer, but the concepts were not getting through. We were then blessed with a brilliant and resourceful director, producer, and film crew in the form of an ex-news reporter from Chengdu named Magnolia who did understand what was wanted and who was also quite fluent in English. Under her creative eye, we assembled props, looked for sites, arranged for permits, and assembled a cast. It was a very fluid process. I was amazed at what was produced, thanks to the very talented Magnolia.

The process of doing this video enabled me to better understand and connect the many many strange things that had been happening concerning the temple property. Remember, I was already used to unexplained supernormal phenomena. Often, I only learned what something meant much later—if at all—when somehow it was translated for me. I was ok with that. Now as a result of doing this video and preparing a speech to introduce the video, I was able to make sense out of what had seemed to be unrelated events.

This story begins in 2003 when I traveled to see my Buddha Master, H.H. Dorje Chang Buddha III. Early in the morning as I left San Francisco, auspicious rainbow clouds appeared over the Oakland hills even though there was no sign of rain anywhere. Later on, I suddenly saw a colorful and large rainbow light appear in the sky. The rainbow completely circled the sun. There were also Sanskrit symbols in the sky. Just as the rainbow was fading from sight, I was able to take a picture of the bottom half of this light by focusing the camera below the sun. A dignified Buddha—H.H. Dorje Chang Buddha III—appeared in the middle of the rainbow. This Buddha became my Buddha master, who was wearing a red robe and was sitting in the middle of the rainbow. The scene was awesome and extremely wonderful. The rainbow light appeared in the sky for several hours (FIGURE 8 page 37).

This and what happened after I arrived has been reported in the treasure book *H.H. Dorje Chang Buddha III*. The Buddha Master bestowed me with two red true Holy Vajra Pills. Unexpectedly, the Vajra Pills that were in my hand started to jump. At that time the Vajra Pills jumped in my hand just as if they were alive. They not only jumped but one of them started to circle around and left my hand. It transformed into a dazzling bright red light and soared into the sky. I understood that my merit was not sufficient at that time for me to keep that pill and that it had gone to a Buddha Land or holy place for safe keeping, but that when conditions were right, it would reappear. It was also at that time, that I saw my Buddha Master, who sat far away on the dais, as the dignified bright blue Buddha Vajradhara. This was before we knew the true identity of our Buddha Master.

A thought had come to me that the arrival in this world, and particularly to America, of H.H. Dorje Chang Buddha III was one of the most important events in the history of Buddhism. We needed a stupa to mark this event and the Sanger retreat center would be perfect. However, I did not yet know why this was such a great idea.

FIGURE 52: Vajra Wheels (orbs) fill the sky as disciple unloads sandbags to stop flooding at the temple.

FIGURE 53: Rainbows and dharma wheel mandalas appeared as yurt was being constructed.

About the time I made this intention known, strange and wonderful sights began to appear at the Xuanfa Temple and Retreat Center we were establishing near Sanger. Students came to the future temple site to meditate and work on various projects. While erecting a small yurt, circular light mandalas were re-corded on many photos taken of students working there (FIGURE 52.) A rainbow even appeared together with many of these mandalas inside the yurt that we erected (FIGURE 53). Here we could see them in broad daylight.

Other mysterious rainbow light beings manifested from time to time. Sometimes they were visible to the naked eye and sometimes they could only be seen via our digital cameras. Columns of bright neon pink and sometimes vivid green light could be seen in the viewfinders of our digital cameras and students from China were even able to record this in a video. This phenomenon appeared several other times at the retreat center and several students actually saw these lights. I had also seen two of these beams of light once before at a very powerful empowerment ceremony held in the courtyard of where my Buddha Master was living.

Ghosts or spirit beings appeared and made their presence known. Lights flickered, cabinet doors opened and closed—all quite mysteriously. It seemed they meant no harm, but they only wanted to be noticed and to hear the Dharma. If their actions were a problem, I asked them to stop and they always did. I invited them to come and listen to Dharma Discourses. The ghost beings came to the Xuanfa Temple and Retreat Center to seek empowerment and learn the Dharma just as many from other realms would do.

On November 4, 2010, a magnificent Buddha Light filled the sky. It lasted all day and was very beautiful. Many people saw it in the Fresno area. It was even reported on the local news. Once a disciple looked up and saw a rainbow in the sky overhead outside the range of the Buddha Light. Other rainbows appeared in the sky as well and some disciples saw the Buddha Light repeatedly during the following week. These Buddha Lights appeared at other times as well to the delight of the students who visited the temple.

However, it was on November 8 of that year that the most amazing event occurred. We were discussing removing a pole remaining from the former chain link fence that had been part of the old dilapidated shed. I think that it had been part of a dog run. Suddenly the pole started shaking violently—like a giant tuning fork. Could it be an earthquake? When we looked around nothing else was shaking. This was very strange and scary. That plus all the unusual lights and visits from other dimensions were telling us something, but what?

I did not think it wise to remove that pole and suspected it was something quite extraordinary. So, the next day I went to see my Buddha Master, H.H. Dorje Chang Buddha III. Even though the Buddha Master was very, very busy, I was able to explain what had happened. The Buddha Master just laughed and said that I absolutely should not cut down the pole; the Dharma Protectors had come, and they were making their presence known. This was a sort of Vajra Pole that the Dharma Protectors were using to tell us how pleased they were with what was happening here. This was all most auspicious, and I should record the holy event for others. However, I found out later that this was a sign of something even more significant and wonderful that was beginning to manifest at the site. The true nature of this place as a holy place for enlightenment was being revealed. I learned that this was a sort of portal to another dimension whereby deities could communicate with living beings in this realm.

When I returned, I felt very bad that we had not filmed the mysterious shaking pole event. I was wandering around the now quiet Vajra Poles. They were not shaking at all. I muttered about how sorry I felt for not having a video that I could show to my Buddha Master and it seemed the Dharma Protectors understood as the Vajra Pole suddenly started to shake again! I was so happy to have a chance to record this unbelievable shaking Vajra Pole. This time we got the video camera and we recorded the visit. We also arranged the second building so that the second pole that had also started to shake would not need to be removed either.

On the way to see my Buddha Master, the thought had occurred to me that the new yurt we had just constructed should be used as a chapel for the Dharma Protectors. Now, this was before I knew that we had been blessed by their presence or had any understanding of what a holy place this was. For some reason, somehow, I just knew the yurt we had built was not to be used for housing disciples as was originally planned. We would build a shrine at the pole where the Dharma Protectors had communicated with us and dedicate the beautiful new yurt to them.

Why were my good students and others who visited this site experiencing such beneficial effects and life affirming experiences? Why were all these supernatural events happening here? What I found out was that the red Holy Vajra Pill that flew out of my hand during the empowerment ceremony in 2003 had flown to Sanger. All I knew then was that it had flown to a holy place for safe keeping until I was ready to receive it. This was truly a holy site and it was my destiny to develop this site into a holy retreat center where many would come and learn and practice the Buddha Dharma to transform their lives and become enlightened. In fact, one disciple who did come to stay at the temple to read the preliminary translations of the Buddha Master's sutras was able to progress very rapidly and reach a very high level of accomplishment. Others also reported making rapid progress when they did this, even being able to receive direct guidance from their yidam. I will share more on this later.

So, this would be a perfect site to establish the retreat and build a stupa marking the Buddha's coming to this world. I explained all of this at a Dharma assembly held at Hua Zang Si in San Francisco.

nine

The Fourth Vajra Throne

The pill that I had received in 2003 that then flew away manifested at the Xuanfa Institute. The vajra pill was to merge with these Vajra Poles to become one and empower the site as the first Vajra Throne in the West and the fourth one in the world. There is a video of me activating the holy pill and inviting the Holy Dharma Protectors to empower the pill, which happened. The pill danced first in my hand and then in the crystal pagoda I held. It pulsated inside the pagoda as if it were alive. It looked as though it was actually breathing. During this empowerment ceremony and a subsequent ceremony to empower certain objects, a green light flashed. Green Tara had entered the mandala to also bless the pill and the event (FIGURE 54).

FIGURE 54: Holy Vajra Pill during Empowerment Ceremony at the moment Green Tara blessed the pill.

The Holy Vajra Pill is now kept in a secured location until the auspicious time arrives to make it available to bestow its blessing on those who visit and stay at the temple and retreat center. Once in a while I will bring out the precious vajra pill itself to share its blessings with those who visit. The Vajra Poles often respond to those who come to receive their blessings. They vibrate for those with a pure heart—Buddhists and non-Buddhist alike. We will build a vajra shrine to house this precious holy object and mark how this holy object merged with the Vajra Poles to form the symbol of the Dharma of the Vajra Throne or Bodhimanda. This is how the Fourth Vajra Throne on earth was born!

And there is now a holy place in the West where students can learn and practice the correct Buddha Dharma, find true happiness, and be free from suffering. This Vajra Throne will bring blessings to all living beings, grant humankind wisdom and happiness, and enable ordinary people to become holy beings.

Now, you may ask, 'Just what is a Vajra Throne?' Vajra Thrones are sometimes referred to as Bodhimandas or Bodhimandalas and they literally can be translated as 'places of enlightenment' where both great holy beings became enlightened and sites empowered by these holy beings so that others who practice there may also become enlightened.

Before Dorje Chang Buddha returned to this world, there were only three such places in the whole world and they were all in Asia. All of the world's Bodhimandas or Vajra Thrones are very, very holy places. The first Vajra Throne is under the Bodhi tree in India where Shakyamuni Buddha was enlightened. The second Vajra Throne is at Wu-Tai Shan, a mountain in Shanxi, China. It is the Bodhimanda of a great ancient Buddha—Manjushri Bodhisattva. Many holy beings including Manjushri Bodhisattva are said to still live there and can be seen by those with great realization. The third Vajra Throne was in Tibet and it was established by Guru Padmasambhava. Guru Padmasambhava had his Vajra Throne in Tibet at Kathok Monastery where over 100,000 became enlightened and attained the rainbow body state. As I had explained while on Tour, the rainbow body is a state whereby one transforms one's body into light and at the time of death, ascends into the heavens or Buddha Lands, without leaving a body behind. Certain Christian scholars[36] have been interested in this phenomenon, as they think it may explain the resurrection of Christ and it is a practice that can be learned.

Now, what about the newly discovered Fourth Vajra Throne? The Fourth Vajra Throne in this world is the site of the Holy Vajrasana Temple and Retreat Center near Sanger, California, under the umbrella of the Xuanfa Institute, a

---

36 See page 97 for more on Father Tiso.

nonprofit religious corporation.[37] And it will be accessible to Buddhist and non-Buddhist alike.

If someone wants to learn the Buddha Dharma or listen to the Dharma Voice of H.H. Dorje Chang Buddha III and believes it, accepts it, and follows it according to the discourses of the Buddha, then that person will definitely get unlimited good fortune and be able to ascend to the heavens or Buddha Lands. Shakyamuni Buddha learned the Dharma that He expounded in this world from Dorje Chang Buddha, but He did not teach all that He learned. The world was not ready for certain more advanced teachings. Dorje Chang Buddha has come to this world again at this time as H.H. Dorje Chang Buddha III to transmit those higher teachings to those who are ready to receive them. I was told that Sanger was even more powerful than Kathok and those who come here to practice and who receive the empowerment of the Dharma Protectors here WOULD become enlightened. I was also told that this holy site was not just for Buddhists, but to provide benefit to other religions as well. All sincere cultivators of any faith who adhere to the three pure precepts of doing no harm, doing only good, and helping other living beings could practice and meditate here and become accomplished in their religion.

Anyone who comes here to sincerely practice will gain wisdom and good fortune. And, since this is a holy place, if they come here to cultivate themselves, they will gain blessings, and, if they have sufficient merit, deities may communicate with them through the Vajra Poles. Although this is a Buddhist holy site, the deities of other religions may come here as well. Buddhists, Jews, Muslims, Catholics, Protestants, Mormons, and others can come together and be blessed. Those who have visited the site have expressed a strong feeling of joy and the presence of great energetic beings. They are energized by just being here. One knows that this is a holy place. Not only has H.H. Dorje Chang Buddha III come to America, but also the Buddha Dharma has come and can be seen, learned, and practiced here.

Many of these events were discussed while we were on the Dharma Propagation Tour but it wasn't until the Holy Vajra Poles started vibrating, thus enabling us to be recognized as such a holy site, did I understand how it all fit together. The video that was made explained it even better.

The documentary video was released at the International Buddhism Sangha Association (IBSA) Conference held in Hong Kong in August 2011. The DVD also explains that Vajra Thrones, sometimes referred to as Bodhimandas, are either

---

37 *The Xuanfa Temple and Retreat Center was renamed the Holy Vajrasana Temple and Retreat Center to reflect this fact as Vajrasana means Vajra Throne in Sanskrit.*

places where a great holy being became enlightened like Bodhgaya in India or a place empowered by a great holy being where people who practice there can also become enlightened like Kathok Monastery in Tibet. The DVD shows how the Holy Vajra Pill was activated or empowered to return to Sanger and the Vajra Poles shaking in anticipation of the Holy Vajra Pill's return. The film starts with a group of weary pilgrims trekking through fields and snowy forest in search of the Truth that will relieve their suffering and finding it in the Buddha Dharma expounded by H.H. Dorje Chang Buddha III. The Pilgrims found what they were looking for and retire to prepare a celebration. They know that a special place exists near Sanger, CA where they can always find the true Buddha Dharma. This film became very popular in China causing many pilgrims to come to the temple to pay their respect to the Vajra Poles and the temple.

Pilgrimage Site

We later learned that our temple was listed on a tourism website in China as the 19th "Must See" place to visit in the U.S., ahead of the Metropolitan Museum in New York. A group of students visiting the temple from Sichuan confirmed the fact that we are a very popular site and that they had a photo of our temple in their temple. I think this is largely due to the popularity of the video we filmed about being recognized as the Fourth Vajra Throne or Vajrasana in the world today. There is a student in China who told me she watches that video every day. The students were thrilled when the Vajra Poles responded to them and quivered as they often do (but not always). One group of students said they had chanted mantras while driving from Los Angeles and again after they arrived. Maybe the Dharma Protectors had heard and were greeting them.

Non-human Residents and Visitors

The Buddha Master had emphasized the Buddha Dharma is not just for humans, but for all living beings. We have had our share of non-humans show up and their manifestations are told throughout this book. I know I must do more to help living beings of all sorts, and I learn from the non-human residents and visitors as well as the human ones. Dharma Duck (actually a very large goose with a Mohawk and an attitude) who came and guarded the Institute for a summer has left, but before he left, he gave me a painful bite to register his complaints. When we listened to Dharma discourses, he would try his best to join us either by flying at the window or pecking at the door. We finally opened the door so he could listen, and he seemed content. We gave him a blue vajra-bodhi pill to help develop his affinity to learn the Dharma (FIGURE 55). He must have felt abandoned when I left Sanger to take care of Dharma business, because when I returned, he let me know that I need to pay more attention to the needs of others, or at least that is how I interpreted his actions. We must all continue our cultivation.

FIGURE 55: Dharma Duck receives a vajra-bodhi pill at Holy Vajrasana Temple

We see many spirit forms, especially around the Holy Vajra Poles. If you take photos at night with a flash, you may catch them. We often make food offerings to the hungry ghosts outside the kitchen door. The spirit forms we photographed there were very round and appeared to be quite fat. I do not know if there is a connection, but I thought it was quite amusing. We want them to be fed and happy and to come and listen to the Dharma talks (FIGURE 56). The *Supreme and Unsurpassable Mahamudra of Liberation* has a section devoted to how we should pay our respects and make offerings to the local gods or devas.

FIGURE 56: These "fat" ghosts or light beings appeared where we left food offerings for them. We often capture photos of wispy transparent beings elsewhere at the Temple, but only these appeared to be quite plump.

ten

Remodeling of the Temple

After the temple was designated a Vajra Throne, things changed. We had to remodel the temple to make it a suitable place for such an honor. First, the temple was renamed as the Holy Vajrasana Temple and Retreat Center. Then I began work on the plans. All my training in city planning, landscape architecture, and civil engineering, and experience in project management was finally of use—maybe. I survived the Fresno County Planning Commission hearings, revised the plans to make the closest neighbor happy and it looked good. Actually, the neighbor's ideas were very helpful and resulted in a much better design. She did not want any two-story buildings with monks being able to see her nude sun-bathing. She has actually been a great neighbor. I doubt if I could have survived without her as she has taken responsibility for the flood irrigation of the fields around the temple and our jointly shared irrigation ditch. She once arranged to have a tractor and trailer come to move my car after another neighbor let the primitive irrigation system run too long and flooded my driveway.

We would have a short-term retreat center and individual cabins for long-term solitary retreats. The geologist did not give us many options for septic tanks, but we figured out a way to do it. The process was maddening. The project had to be reviewed by an endless number of governmental agencies, but we finally answered their concerns. However, the very same day the county finally gave their approval to proceed, I was summoned to Pasadena and told I would need to open a second location in the Mohave desert in Southern California. I quickly had our architect change the building plans, so we could start remodeling the existing house and bring it up to code and meet handicap accessibility and other requirements to be used as a temple, but the infrastructure and site work we just finessed. Maybe the desert move would not happen. Maybe I would not be able to move there. I did not want to install driveways and parking until I knew what I would be doing.

In any event, the temple design for the Sanger site would need to be changed and less ambitious. We would not be able to build the covered walkway to the Holy Vajra Poles with the 21 prayer wheels and ornate Tibetan carved columns. The stupa and individual cabins would be at the desert site. We would continue to remodel the temple, but it would be a smaller structure that we would keep as a local temple. We still needed to add ADA handicap accessible bathrooms and change the entrance way.

Gift of Three Buddhas

We already had the main statutes for the Buddha Hall. In January 2012 Reba Jinbo Rinpoche and I had flown to Las Vegas to bring back three magnificent golden statues of Ancient Buddhas–Shakyamuni Buddha, Manjushri Bodhisattva, and Kuan Yin Bodhisattva. Both of the Bodhisattvas are really Ancient Buddhas who have come back to this world as Bodhisattvas to help living beings develop their wisdom and compassion so that we, too, can become Buddhas. They were gifts from another rinpoche and his wife who were not able to use them due to zoning problems. The main statue of Shakyamuni Buddha was an exact replica of the giant statue at Hua Zang Si and was based on a painting done by the Buddha Master. The statues were lovingly and carefully wrapped, first in silk, and then in many layers of bubble wrap. Then they were taken out of their existing home and loaded on a rental truck. Reba Jinbo Rinpoche carefully constructed a frame to hold the precious cargo in place and drove the truck and me back to Sanger. It was a long day, especially for Reba, but well worth it to have these statues in place in Sanger. We literally redesigned the temple to hold them. We would tear out the fireplace and chimney in the old recreation room, remove the wall between that room and the living room, fill in the sunken living room, and close off the kitchen area with a soundproof fire wall. The three statues were the foundation for our main altar (FIGURE 57).

Flaming Jewel Tibetan Columns, Prayer Wheels, and more

After learning that our focus should be more on the new Buddhist Village and the Ancient Buddha Temple complex to be built in southern California, I had to re-evaluate my plans. I had already commissioned the beautiful flaming jewel Tibetan columns for the walkway to the Holy Vajra Poles that would hold the copper prayer wheels we had purchased from Nepal. That part of the project would need to be redesigned and probably completed at the Ancient Buddha site in the desert. The stupa would also need to be built there. We would remodel and create a small temple in Sanger that was code compliant. We had to install a new septic system no matter what. A rainy season had proven that the old one was rusted out and the leaching field was non-existent. The prayer wheels and most of the Tibetan columns were placed in storage. A major flooding of the living and dining room area had rendered what we had been using for the retreats as non-functional.

FIGURE 57: The Three Buddhas in place as the main altar at the Holy Vajrasana Temple.

FIGURE 58: Flaming Jewel Tibetan columns inside of the Holy Vajrasana Temple at Dorje Chang Buddha Lineage Tree Altar.

We redesigned the entryway to use two of the Tibetan columns and give us a grander entranceway. Jiangba Luosang Rinpoche donated a lovely crystal chandelier for the entryway that had been in his home in Germany. Three more of the Tibetan columns could be used to enhance the interior and create another altar (FIGURE 58). Construction started in earnest with the new septic system being installed in December 2014. The main remodeling started early in 2015 and continued until a new wing was added to house the American Disability Act compliant bathrooms.

Bodhighara

Early, before the sun was too high, a dedication ceremony was held to establish a Bodhighara (Bodhi Tree Shrine) at the Holy Vajrasana Temple (FIGURE 59). Over 100 people including Holy Virtuous Ones, rinpoches, acaryas, Dharma masters, lay followers, and others attended the May 2014 ceremony which was held near the Holy Vajra Poles. I even brought the Holy Vajra Pill to the Dharma Assembly to bless the young Bodhi Tree and those present (FIGURE 60). I then read an original gatha paying homage to the Vajra Poles that were located next to the assembly.

FIGURE 59: Bodhi Tree at the Holy Vajrasana Temple, Sanger, California.

155

FIGURE 60: Zhaxi Zhuoma with Holy Vajra Pill at Bodhighara Dedication Ceremony at the Holy Vajrasana Temple and Retreat Center

The Sri Maha Bodhi Tree (Ficus religiosa) in Anuradhapura, Sri Lanka, is the oldest living human-planted tree in the world with a known planting date. The sacred tree, a descendent of the historical tree under which Shakyamuni Buddha sat to become enlightened in Bodhgaya, India, was brought to Sri Lanka in 288 BCE by the Ven. Sangamitta, the sister of Ven. Arahath Mahinda. The two venerables were the daughter and son of the Emperor Asoka who sent them as missionaries to the island. It has been tended by an uninterrupted succession of guardians for 2,300 years, even during the periods of foreign occupation and the many civil wars.

Sri Lankan Heads of State have sought the blessings of the Sri Maha Bodhi before commencing any important work. It is a very important site of pilgrimage for the devout. I visited this holy living symbol of the Buddha's Enlightenment in Sri Lanka in 2012 with friends. Our guide told us after we left the site that a few years earlier the Tamil Tigers had machine gunned the pilgrims visiting the tree, but that story was not publicized. Anuradhapura is near the northern part of the island and close to the Tiger's territory. We also noted very discreet military installations near the site, but when we were there, the soldiers were just mowing grass.

156

This descendent of the Sri Maha Bodhi Tree was installed as a Bodhighara near the Holy Vajra Poles at the site of our Holy Vajrasana Temple in Sanger. It is a precious reminder of how Shakyamuni Buddha sat under its ancestor over 2,500 years ago and obtained Anuttara-Samyak-Sambodhi. We express our gratitude to Shakyamuni Buddha and to His teacher, Dorje Chang Buddha for bringing us the most complete Buddha Dharma that can enable us to likewise become enlightened. We give our most humble thanks and offer our devotion to the magnificent Manifestation, H.H. Dorje Chang Buddha III who empowered this site as the Fourth Vajra Throne (Vajrasana) in the world today.

New Wing Installed—Vajra Poles Respond to Contractors

Early in 2015, the main remodeling of the building began and continued until a new wing was added to house the ADA compliant bathrooms. While working on the remodeling of the Holy Vajrasana Temple, Sean and Adam of Pacific Construction reported that they and Reuben, the electrician, had experienced the Vajra Poles shaking and could not believe what they saw. First one pole would shake, then stop while another started to vibrate until all five had exhibited their powers. When they told their supervisor, Charlie, he refused to believe them as did others they told. Understandably, it is hard to imagine that such a portal to other realms exists in this world. They were most fortunate to witness this, as many travel to this site from all over the world and may not see anything or only a slight tremble. The construction crew said a slight wind did come up, but in no way could that breeze cause the poles to behave like they did. Sometimes there is a certain type of wind that seems to accompany the poles, but at other times the poles do not move at all even in strong gales. It appears as if the poles cause this special wind to arrive and not the reverse. The poles are known to shake quite violently, but sometimes they only tremble or pulsate as if sending a coded message and sometimes they just stand there and do nothing. Visitors have also reported seeing light and waves of energy surround the poles. Those who come and meditate with the poles report being able to quickly enter a deep and profound state of concentration. These poles are amazing and seem to respond so differently to the different people who come to see them.

Bravachakra (Wheel of Life) Installed

In 2017 a large representation of the Wheel of Life (Bravachakra) was painted and installed in our Holy Vajrasana Temple and Retreat Center (FIGURE 61). This image is a symbolic representation of samsara or cyclic existence, dating to the time of Shakyamuni Buddha and holds the keys to ending suffering as taught by the Buddha. This original image was given by the Buddha to his friend, King Bimbisara of Magadha to explain samsara to King Rudrayana (Udayana). The other king had given King Bimbisara a very expensive gift of a jeweled robe and King Bimbisara did not know how to return the favor with something of equivalent value. The Buddha painted this image (or had it painted) and told the King that there was no greater gift he could give his friend. It is said that the other king became enlightened upon receiving and studying the gift. It is also said that Shakyamuni Buddha instructed His monks to have this image painted on the walls of every monastery so that ordinary and illiterate people could learn the true nature of samsara and how to escape it.

This is now one of many wonderful sites to see when you visit the temple. When the artist and his friend arrived with the painting and prepared to install it, they, of course, paid their respects to the Holy Vajra Poles. All five of the Holy Vajra Poles responded by immediately shaking to greet them.

FIGURE 61: Bravachakra (Wheel of Life) painting installed at Holy Vajrasana Temple.

158

eleven

Meditation Retreats & Classes

The Early Retreats—2009-2014

Over the years we developed different types of retreats at the temple. They started out to be primarily work and Dharma listening retreats as we prepared to modestly develop the temple facilities. I had preliminary translations of many of the Buddha Master's discourses and was allowed to read them to the students. At first, I could also make recordings of them that the students could take back to their Dharma centers, but some students violated their agreement and made copies and we had to recall all the recordings. Students continued to visit the temple to hear the Dharma discourses, meditate, take refuge, receive Dharma, and to work on many projects.

Rinpoches affiliated with the Xuanfa Institute visited the Institute and helped with various projects to develop and maintain the site. One morning, while posing for a group photo, a very bright golden orb of light appeared, pulsated and vibrated over their heads and disappeared. It was visible to those taking the photos and was captured on their digital cameras, and very briefly on a video camera (FIGURE 62). This golden light had also appeared on other photos and once outside the library window. A similar orb was captured in a video moving through a wooded area near the river that ran past the retreat center in Thailand where our meditation retreat was held in 2015.

The rinpoches shown in FIGURE 62 were on their way to attend a meeting with their Buddha Master in Pasadena, California. They were also able to attend an empowerment ceremony where they participated in a Dark Dharma Assembly on that trip. I am often able to arrange for my students to attend either private group meetings or Dharma transmissions with H.H. Dorje Chang Buddha III. In March of 2013 there was a special Dharma assembly originally intended for Western students to receive instructions on how to practice Zen meditation. However, once the Chinese students heard about this, there were many more Chinese students there as well. This Dharma transmission resulted in *The Great Dharma of Zen* that is included as Appendix A. Recently, whenever it is possible, I try to take those who attend retreats at the temple to see the Buddha Master at the end of the retreats.

FIGURE 62: Pulsating golden orb appears at Holy Vajrasana Temple over the heads of rinpoches who were on their way to meeting with H.H. Dorje Chang Buddha III.

Detail of golden orb as it enlarges.

Sometimes Benxin Chiren Rinpoche (Jason Wu) was able to come to the temple and do simultaneous English translation of many of the Buddha Master's discourses for us. His translation and comprehension skills are such that he can listen to the discourse in Chinese and at the same time give us a translation in English. In 2012 we started the Xuanfa Five Vidyas University (XFVU) to provide more options for students to

160

gain background in Buddhist studies online and to study the Dharma we had available from the Buddha Master; major sutras and commentaries; and the lives of patriarchs, matriarchs, great Bodhisattvas, and Buddhas. As a result of Benx-in Chiren's translation work I learned how the Buddha taught us to study His discourses using the Seven-Dharma System. Our retreats and classes were then oriented to use that method, but more on that later. During this time disciples would come and meditate with the Holy Vajra Poles (FIGURE 63).

FIGURE 63: Meditating with the Vajra Poles at the Holy Vajrasana Temple

On-the-Road Phase—2014-2015

Because we needed to remodel the old ranch house, install a new septic system, and make other improvements, the major retreats were planned to be held at other locations during the remodeling phase. When the contractors began in earnest in 2015, we started doing retreats in China, New York, Thailand, and Hong Kong. Most of these were week-long retreats. His Holiness has said that it takes at least seven days for it to be a real retreat. It takes that long to settle into the silence and schedule and quiet yourself to be able to truly concentrate.

Our retreats in both mainland China and Thailand were longer retreats. The retreat in China was held on a lake in a bamboo forest at a yoga studio. Esoteric Buddhism is considered a form of yoga and many who attended were both yogis and Buddhists.

FIGURE 64: Naga guarding the Thai Retreat Center.

Our first Thai retreat was held at a private retreat center on the banks of the Chao Phraya River, just north of Bangkok. Statues of nagas (FIGURE 64) guarded the center while golden globes of light like what we had seen at our temple in Sanger could be seen moving through the adjacent jungle-forest. The last day of this retreat included a trip to the Buddhamonthon (Buddhist Mandala), a park devoted to Buddhism and a gift of the Thai king to his subjects. It was dedicated in 1957 to commemorate the birthday of Shakyamuni Buddha who was born approximately 2,500 years earlier. The entrance is graced with a beautiful 57-foot statue believed to be the tallest free-standing statue of Shakyamuni Buddha in the world. It is a popular place for "Liberating the Animals (fish release)" ceremonies as the fish and other animals are very well protected. Many other disciples from nearby Dharma Centers joined the group and brought even more fish to be liberated (FIGURE 65).

This was also the site where H.H. Dorje Chang Buddha III had given a discourse that was attended by many beings from other realms. Many types of birds and fish came to the area. These animals, along with dogs and insects, became totally still as they respectfully listened to the Dharma. The nearby lake started to surge up in waves. A large, dark gold-colored fish used its tail to stand up by itself on the surface of the water along with a small black fish and a silver-white fish. All three fish paid homage to the Buddha Master. His Holiness said that the large fish was really a dragon who had transformed itself into a fish (FIGURE 66).

I saw something like this happen when the Buddha Master once visited our temple at Sanger. The very large and brightly colored Koi who inhabited the pond on the property all aligned themselves, stood on their heads and did a little dance for the Buddha. I am told that they continued to dance like that even af-

162

FIGURE 65: Buddhamonthon Fish Release, Thailand, 2015.

FIGURE 66: Dragon and other beings attend discourse given by H.H. Dorje Chang Buddha III at Buddhamonthon, Thailand in 1999.

ter the Buddha Master left, but I did not see it. I also saw a school of fish follow the Buddha Master like little puppies as the Buddha walked next to a lake in a

Japanese Garden in the San Francisco Bay Area (FIGURE 67). Other students reported similar experiences of the Buddha Master's interaction with animals. There is a beautiful video taken in Mexico when a flock of birds come after the Buddha Master prophesied that they would and did a sort of aerial ballet in a rainstorm. Copies of that video are available at many of our temples. Most of the many dogs that live with the Buddha Master do prostrations to Him. The cats, not so much, but there is one who I think is the father of one of our temple cats who sleeps like a guardian outside the door of His bedroom.

FIGURE 67: School of Koi following the Buddha Master at a Japanese Garden south of San Francisco.

After holding a short meditation retreat and meeting with students, we held a Blessing of the Animals Ceremony in Hong Kong after the Thailand retreat in 2015. Pet owners brought their animal companions to take refuge in the Three Treasures and receive blessings. Twenty dogs, eight cats, two birds, and four turtles received the refuge vows and came forward with their owners and handlers to receive a sprinkling of holy water and a Vajra-Bodhi Pill to help develop their affinity for the Dharma and be able to continue to listen to the Dharma in their next life (FIGURE 68). Several had been listening to the Dharma discourses with their masters before they took refuge. All were very well behaved. One cat even cried after taking the Vajra Bodhi Pill.

FIGURE 68: Blessing of the Animals, Hong Kong. A miniature collie just received a sprinkling of holy water and a Vajra-Bodhi Pill.

Seven-Dharma System Seminars & the Xuanfa Five Vidyas University —2016-2018

Students from China, Canada, and various parts of the USA attended a retreat and seminar on how to listen to Dharma discourses at the Holy Vajrasana Temple over a Fourth of July weekend. Benxin Chiren Rinpoche gave a simultaneous translation of several discourses by H.H. Dorje Chang Buddha III that were recorded in 2000. These Dharma discourses warned us that it will be fruitless if we do not abide by the Seven Dharma approach to listening to discourses presented in these discourses. The non-Chinese speakers were given a dispensation to be able to immediately start taking notes since it was so hard for them to even hear the discourses. We would have two-day retreats over a weekend or longer and Benxin Chiren Rinpoche could translate for us. I also read from a transcript of a recording done in China of a Grand Debate that served as an example as to how the Dharma should be debated or discussed by disciples and explained certain important and profound Buddhist principles. With this background the students prepared written summaries of the discourses and formed questions that were then debated by those present.

This was all part of the courses sponsored by the Xuanfa Five Vidyas University. Those who were enrolled in the class for credit agreed that the Seven Dharma process mandated by the Buddha Master was extremely helpful in gaining an understanding of some of the very profound principles contained in the discourses. This was the first time that XFVU had attempted to make a course available in both Chinese and English although the earlier attempts at bilingual retreats had gone very well. We are attempting to adapt this process to studying translations we have of written texts by the Buddha Master on our online Zoom classes with the Lemonade Sangha, which I will describe later.

In 2018 I received preliminary English translations of both the *Supreme and Unsurpassable Mahamudra of Liberation* and *Imparting the Absolute Truth through the Heart Sutra*. Realizing the importance of both of these amazing sutras, I focused our efforts on making them available to other English-speaking disciples. I realized that these were what we should be focusing our Buddhist education on as well. These were the sutras we should study and follow. All I could do was read from these translations at the temple or sometimes at other locations. Nothing could be released in print until we had an official translation. I then dissolved the Xuanfa Five Vidyas University (XFVU) until such time as they were available to be used as texts.

The Seven Dharma System of Listening to Dharma Disourses

1. Listen to get basic concepts—do not take notes.

2. Listen again to see what you missed and again to questions raised by other students.

3. Listen again, but take notes and record what you hear (Non-Chinese speakers may start with this step) asking questions of translator, observe who asks what questions.

4. Listen again and correct your notes.

5. If possible, listen again; discuss with other students; prepare questions to be used in "debates", forming questions for which you have answers and those you do not.

6. Debate questions with other students; moderator makes sure every student asks at least one question and every student has an opportunity to answer at least one.

7. Reflect on what you have learned and prepare a written talk to propagate these teachings to others.

H.H. Dorje Chang Buddha III Discourses

twelve
Changing Form

Early in 2014 the Buddha Master showed me two photos of Himself, one as a beautiful young man and the other as a gnarled, wrinkled, very old man (FIGURE 69). I had heard about him doing a major transformation but had not seen any evidence of this feat.

FIGURE 69: Photos of H.H. Dorje Chang Buddha III taken on October 18, 2012 (left) and October 19, 2012 (right) above an altar at Chua Thai Son, a temple in DaNang, Vietnam.

They were remarkable photos and can be seen with a statement by the Buddha Master denying he had done anything special in the book *Learning from Buddha.* See FIGURE 96 on page 244 for the image in this book and the words that always accompany the photographs.

When He showed me the photos I remember laughing and saying, "But I saw you do this ten years ago". He asked me to explain and I told him the story described below. He then asked me to tell that story at the Grand Dharma Assembly in Hong Kong that would be held in March to release His sutra *Imparting the Absolute Truth through the Heart Sutra,* A poster printed with the two contrasting photos and how they came into being was also going to be revealed to the thousands of disciples who would attend.

The following is from my Hong Kong speech:

"I thought for some time, just which great Bodhisattva is my Buddha Master? Then I had a shocking experience that I have not shared publicly. I actually saw my Dharma King Master drastically change His appearance in a very short period of time. Even though my Buddha Master had predicted that He would on such and such a day take on the negative karma of others and would not be available to meet the public, I was not prepared for what I saw. He appeared on the predicted day looking very ugly and old—His face was bloodied as if He had just been severely beaten. His eyes were swollen and half closed! There were many people standing around, but they seemed to be accepting of this condition. I had been thinking that, because of His accomplishments in both exoteric Buddhism and esoteric Buddhism and the Five Vidyas, my Master must be a Buddha, but how could this be true when He looks so old and decrepit? I could barely stand looking at my beloved Dharma King Master when He was like this. Remember, at that time we did not know that our Dharma King Master was a Buddha. In less than an hour, I looked again, and my Buddha Master had changed to a beautiful young man. I was shocked. Oh, my God. How could this be? My Master is a Buddha! What I was thinking is true! He is not just a Bodhisattva, but a Buddha. I looked around, but no one else was shocked or showing any reaction at all to what had just happened. I looked again at my Master and He just smiled. He put His finger to His mouth and quietly said "**shhh**" and I realized that no one else had seen this transformation, but I knew this fact about the Buddha. I was not to tell anyone. I had seen my Buddha Master totally transform His appearance before everyone knew about this ability. Now because of the fact that the Buddha Master's ability to change His appearance from old to young is known internationally, I can tell you all what I experienced, and you will be able to see photos similar to what I saw. Amitabha!"

Return-to-Youth Pill

I had the good fortune to be at the Buddha Master's hermitage when He came out of an extended retreat. He met with a few of us and blessed each of us with a small blue "Return-to-Youth Pill." After taking that pill my hair changed from white and grey to the original light brown or dark blonde of my youth and I felt quite young. I even let my hair grow, just to see for sure. The transformation did not last, but it was quite amazing. My change was nothing like what the Buddha Master did and as I remember it, we were told that these pills were not related to the change described above. I merely wanted to share this experience to give others an idea of the sort of things that happen when you are around the Buddha.

thirteen

H.H. Dorje Chang Buddha III's Paintings Sell for Tens of Millions

In case any proof was needed of H.H. Dorje Chang Buddha III's accomplishments in the Craftsmanship Vidya, you could look at the art market's response to His work. The paintings of the Buddha Master have been selling for millions of dollars for decades. In May 2000 a very large painting of a lion and two cubs titled "Majesty" sold for $2,125,327 at an international auction followed by the sale of another large painting of an Arhat "Venerable Da Li Wang (Sadapralapa)" in October of that same year for $2,207,912. I know of four museums built to display his paintings to the public: near where He was born in Sichuan Province China, in Hong Kong, and in San Francisco and Covina, California in the US.[38] More recently in 2015, two smaller paintings sold for much more at Gianguan Auctions in New York City. The small mounted ink-on-paper painting titled "Ink Lotus" sold for $16,500,000 to an anonymous American buyer (FIGURE 70) while "Loquat," a composition of colored ink washes, calligraphy, poetry, and prose sold for $10,200,000. The Buddha Master's wife, Dr. Yuhua Shouzhi Wang, is also an internationally acclaimed artist with a grand exhibition of her paintings at the Louvre in Paris, France in 2019. She also sold the ink painting titled "Pomegranates in a Bamboo Basket" for $1.27 million that year.

One of my favorites and the first painting by H.H. Dorje Chang Buddha III that I ever saw was a copy of a stunning painting of Kuan (Guan) Yin Bodhisattva that my acupuncturist had in Asheville, North Carolina. In fact, it was Doctor Kuai who introduced me to the works of Master Wan Ko Yee, as He was then known. I am sure that seeing that painting helped convince me to learn

---

38 Contact https://www.hhdcb3cam.org/ for more information on the H.H. Dorje Chang Buddha III Cultural and Art Museum in Covina, CA and https://www.iamasf.org/ to read about the International Art Museum of America (IAMA) in San Francisco, CA.

FIGURE 70: "Ink Lotus" a painting by H.H. Dorje Chang Buddha III

more about and eventually follow H.H. Dorje Chang Buddha III. Years later I was able to see an original of that painting when I was with the Buddha Master in California. I am not sure it was the exact same image, because I believe He painted several versions. It was amazing. You could see every hair on the Bodhisattva's head, or it appeared that way. I remember how impressed I was with the detailed brushwork. We have another copy of that painting hanging in our main Buddha Hall at our temple in Sanger. I also remember seeing a large and very detailed embroidery of that image that someone had done in China as a tribute to the Buddha Master. This painting of Kuan Yin Bodhisattva (FIGURE 71) and both of the two paintings mentioned above that sold for millions in China are all featured in the Big Blue Treasure book *H.H. Dorje Chang Buddha III* as examples of His "Fine Brushwork" style, but the Buddha Master painted in many quite different styles including another of my favorites of the Indian Patriarch Bodhidharma done in His "Freehand Brushwork" style shown in FIGURE 73 on page 182.

FIGURE 71: "Kuan Yin Bodhisattva " by H.H. Dorje Chang Buddha III

Much has already been written about the Buddha Master's paintings, sculpture, calligraphy, etc., in various art books, so I will not repeat more about that here. The above was just to provide context for the following story I really want to share and to authenticate the value of the Buddha Master's artwork for the next chapter. I want to tell you about my personal favorite painting that He drew for me in a few minutes on plain typing paper using a black Sharpie. It's of a pensive panda on a cliff and it hangs in my Buddha Room (FIGURE 72). I mention it to not only tell of my Buddha Master's talents, which are amazing, but to tell of His ability to empower others. After he finished the Panda sketch and another one of plum blossoms, He threw the magic marker to me and told me to copy them... and I did. Now mine were not perfect reproductions of what He had painted, but they were pretty close and infinitely better than anything I have ever drawn before or since. I know of other students who have become professional artists after receiving His empowerment to do so. I learned much later in Asanga's *Bodhisattvabhumi* that one of the reasons a Bodhisattva seeks to perfect the Craftsmanship Vidya is to teach the craft to others so as to attract them to the Dharma. It certainly worked on me.

FIGURE 72: Sharpie sketch of "Panda on Cliff." by H.H. Dorje Chang Buddha III.

fourteen

Persecution of H.H. Dorje Chang Buddha III in China

You may have seen that H.H. Dorje Chang Buddha III was in trouble with the law in China and had fled to America to escape prosecution. It is true that at one point, INTERPOL had issued a warrant for His arrest. What you may not have heard was the true story behind those accusations and what happened to resolve those issues and you may not know how the Buddha Master responded to these charges. I want to share what I know about those events.

The Buddha Master was persecuted in China by corrupt officials who were in powerful positions at the time in two provinces where he had lived and who did so to cover up for their own crimes. It took over a decade for the truth to be revealed as to how the then Party Secretary of Sichuan Province Zhou Yongkang and the then Secretary of the Politics and Law Committee and Chief of the Public Security Department of Guangdong Province Chen Shaoji had false-ly fabricated cases to persecute Wan Ko Yee[39] to cover up their own extensive corruption. An arrest warrant was issued, and the case elevated to the national level with China requesting involvement of the International Criminal Police Organization (INTERPOL) after Wan Ko Yee left China. In 2010 Chen Shaoji, who also later served as the chairman of the Political Consultative Conference of his province, was tried and sentenced to death (with stay) for embezzlement and corruption. I believe the other official and others were also jailed. The case is well documented and quite fascinating, but what I wanted to report on was how the Buddha Master handled the whole mess.

I remember that when we were working on the Big Blue Treasure Book, the Buddha Master showed me a huge binder that His attorney had compiled for INTERPOL to counter the charges. Some charges were so ridiculous, they were funny. As I recall, the Chinese officials were trying to pin extortion charges or

---

39 *Wan Ko Yee was the Buddha Master's name before he was recognized as H.H. Dorje Chang Buddha III*

something like that on the Buddha Master. They had one person testify that not only would Master Wan Ko Yee not accept a large donation, Mr. Yee wanted to give the student money or maybe only accept one dollar. I forget the details but how could that be extortion? The so-called victims in the case would not testify against their Buddha Master, but instead praised Him.

There were serious charges, but they were simply not true. Several corrupt government officials had stolen valuable artwork and tens of millions from the Buddha Master and from His students and were trying to cover their tracks. They were eventually found out and received their just rewards. The Chinese do not fool around on these matters.

There was another part of the scandal that I even played a very small role in and went to Hong Kong to give testimony as to the good character of my Master at a very large press conference held in December 2014. One of the so-called "victims" who also testified at that press conference was Mr. Lau Pak Hun, a very wealthy Hong Kong developer and vajra brother, who the corrupt officials claimed had been defrauded of $60 million Hong Kong dollars. The truth of the situation was that, yes, this gentleman had been defrauded of that amount of money, but the Buddha Master had nothing to do with that deception. The developer had tried to give that amount of money to his Master, that was also true, but the Buddha Master would not accept it. The Buddha Master finally agreed he could use the money to establish a museum to house some of the Buddha Master's paintings and other artwork. The woman who was put in charge of the museum did establish the museum (I have friends who attended the Grand Opening), however, she took the bulk of the money, including a loan on the museum, and gave it to her brother to invest in his factory. An audit of her accounts revealed what had happened and even though she had highly placed political connections, she was sent to prison. All of the other charges against the Buddha Master were similarly debunked, the charges dropped, and the Buddha Master cleared of any wrongdoing.

There are still false articles on the internet concerning this matter. It was a juicy salacious affair. However, the Buddha Master never appealed or complained about the framing, persecution or slandering against him. When asked why He had not even published INTERPOL's conclusion from the investigation to refute the rumors, H.H. Dorje Chang Buddha III said, "The thing that I want to do is: I will bear all negative karmas and sins of living beings, I will give all my good karmas and merit to you. If I show that to exonerate me, the people who slandered me would not get exonerated. Then, who will bear their sins and negative karmas?"

fifteen

Dharma of Selection: Jin Gang Fa Man Ze Jue Dharma Assembly

I know I have written about many extraordinary things that happened about or around the Buddha Master, and many incredible Dharmas have been transmitted or exhibited, but I think the Jin Gang Fa Man Ze Jue Dharma Assembly held in September 2015 is still the most amazing practice of Dharma I have witnessed. It is a Dharma in Tibetan Esoteric Buddhism for determining the result sought through selection; in this case to determine the status of two Buddhas and a Bodhisattva. Around twenty venerable ones, Dharma kings, and rinpoches including myself, participated in this Dharma led by Great Rinpoche Wangzha Shangzun. The decisions by the Dharma of Jin Gang Fa Man Ze Jue[40] determined that Sakyamuni Buddha is a true Buddha, H.H. Dorje Chang Buddha III is a true Buddha, and Master Hui Neng, the sixth patriarch of the Chan (Zen) School, was not a Buddha but was the incarnation of a great Bodhisattva.

There are many different Dharmas of selection, but this one is one of the highest. It can be used to determine the true or false status of any holy being. In this world, this Dharma and the Dharma of Forecasting the Future are the highest among the Dharmas of decision by selection. The Dharma ranked next is the holy inner-tantric Dharma of "Bai Fa Ming Men Hei Guan Ze Jue (a Dharma specifically used to determine the correct or wrong result)." The next lower Dharma is the Dharma of dropping divine pieces to receive divine instruction, which is at the inner-tantric level. Then, there are lower, outer-tantric Dharmas of lot-drawing from a golden vase, rotating a tsampa[41] ball, watching a sacred lake to see the result, and others. This Dharma can only be possessed and commanded by holy

---

40 *Also referred to as "The Vajra Fa-Man Determination by Holy Selection Dharma." It is used to determine the authenticity of the reincarnation of a Buddha, Bodhisattva, Arhat, or rinpoche.*

41 *Tsampa is a staple in the traditional Tibetan diet consisting of ground roasted barley and yak butter.*

ones at the level of great Mahasattvas or higher. Only a holy one who has the realization of performing holy inner-tantric initiations that are close to the level of state practice can perform the Dharma of Jin Gang Fa Man Ze Jue.

The Buddha Master's most senior students were present to witness Wangzha Shangzun perform this most solemn Dharma. First, the Dharma was performed to verify the status of Sakyamuni Buddha. The beseeching document stated, "We respectfully beseech a verification from the decision by selection. If Sakyamuni Buddha is truly a Buddha, a crown made by strands of hair will be put on the head. If not, there will be no crown." A portrait of Sakyamuni Buddha was laid on an ordinary four-legged dark-brown flat table. Then, a pinch of sand from the Ganges River with the color of light camel wool was picked up and put on the portrait at a spot of hair at the top of the Buddha's head. Wangzha Shangzun began to practice the Dharma at a Dharma dais, which was about 13 feet away from the table. After a ritual of knocking a wooden fish, ringing a bell, waving a Vajra, performing mudras, and chanting mantras, twelve documents written on yellow papers were burned. We all saw with our own eyes that the sand placed at the spot of hair at the top of the Buddha's head began to disperse with inconceivable changes. Every grain of sand seemed to be alive. All sand grains moved individually with miraculous transformations. Sand grains connected with each other to form strands of hair standing in the air. The strands of hair then automatically formed a crown of hair, which very naturally and wonderfully stood up above the top of Sakyamuni Buddha's head. A scene of adding a crown of strands of hair to the Buddha's top-knot was manifested, proving that Sakyamuni Buddha is a true Buddha.

Immediately after that and on the same table, the Dharma was conducted again for H.H. Dorje Chang Buddha III. The beseeching Dharma document stated, "We respectfully beseech a verification from the decision by selection. If H.H. Dorje Chang Buddha III is the incarnation of the primordial Sambhoga-kaya-Buddha Dorje Chang Buddha, a crown made by strands of hair will be put on the head. If not, there will be no crown." Wangzha Shangzun practiced the Dharma following exactly the same ritual as before. After the twelve documents were burned, the sand of the Ganges River with the color of light camel wool that had been flatly put on the spot of hair at the top of a photo of H.H. Dorje Chang Buddha III's head suddenly had the miraculous transformation of being elevated upward. Sand grains connected with each other to form strands of hair standing in the air. The strands of hair then automatically formed a crown of hair. A 3-dimensional crown was put on the head of H.H. Dorje Chang Buddha III in the portrait, proving that H.H. Dorje Chang Buddha III is a true Buddha coming to the world!

The last decision by selection was to verify whether the Sixth Patriarch Master Hui Neng had been a Nirmanakaya Buddha. The beseeching Dharma document wrote, "We respectfully beseech a verification from the decision by selection. If the Sixth Patriarch Master Hui Neng is a Buddha's Nirmanakaya, a crown made by strands of hair will be put on the head. If not, there will be no crown." As before, Wangzha Shangzun practiced the Dharma following the same ritual and the twelve documents were burned. Everyone saw that the sand of the Ganges River with the color of light camel wool placed at the top of Patriarch Master Hui Neng's head had no movement or change at all. Therefore, the conclusion was that Patriarch Master Hui Neng was not a Buddha's Nirmanakaya. So, a lower-level status had to be verified, i.e. to determine whether Patriarch Master Hui Neng was an incarnation of a great Bodhisattva or not. The second beseeching Dharma document wrote, "We respectfully beseech a verification from the decision by selection. If the Sixth Patriarch Master Hui Neng is an incarnation of a great Bodhisattva, a crown made by strands of hair will be put on the head. If he was not at the level of a Bodhisattva, there will be no crown." After Wangzha Shangzun practiced the Dharma, a Dharma crown was put on Master Hui Neng's head. Sand grains formed a crown of hair. However, because Patriarch Master Hui Neng was not a Buddha or a Bodhisattva with Universal or Wonderful Enlightenment, as stipulated by the Dharma, the crown of hair did not stand up into the air and become a 3-dimensional crown but was formed on a flat plane. However, it was very naturally structured and absolutely not something that can be made by humans. It was also amazing, but not as spectacular as the three-dimensional models for the Buddhas.

It took over five hours for Wangzha Shangzun to perform these three Dharma ceremonies. To show the magnificence and extremely truthful nature of the crowning process through determination by the Jin Gang Fa Man Ze Jue Dharma, each of us attending the Dharma assembly took a test to crown the visage using the sand from the Ganges River. As it turned out, none of the holy and virtuous ones present who are at the levels of Golden Button Grade 2, Golden Button Grade 1, and Blue Button Grade 3 were able to crown the Buddha's portrait with sand from the Ganges River. There was no manifestation of power of Buddha Dharma to cause miraculous changes. This proved that the great Dharma of Jin Gang Fa Man Ze Jue could only be practiced by extremely great holy and virtuous ones at the level of Golden Button Grade 3 or higher. No one else possessed the realization to practice the Dharma successfully.

Wangzha Shangzun was very dissatisfied with himself for the first session. He said that his cultivation was shallow and lacked merit and virtue and that his own karmic forces caused him not to practice this Dharma of decision by selection perfectly. However, the truth was that a few of us who were witnessing this Dharma became so excited that we caused a disturbance and that was what caused the outcome to not be completely perfect. Seeing such a holy state was simply too much and those students could not control their emotions and shouted loudly and pushed others so they could barely see what was happening. I remember being pushed aside so that others could get a closer look.

For this reason, Wangzha Shangzun decided to hold a second session of the Dharma assembly. Before the second Dharma assembly started, Dharma King Gar Tongstan (Ciren Gyatso) made the rules on behalf of Wangzha Shangzun. He announced that onlookers could get closer to watch but no one was allowed to speak loudly or push others. All must have the mind focusing on being respectful before moving closer. Then Wangzha Shangzun practiced the Dharma. The second Dharma assembly had a perfect success with extremely magnificent manifestations, proving again that Sakyamuni Buddha is a true Buddha and H.H. Dorje Chang Buddha III is the incarnation of the primordial Sambhogakaya-Buddha Dorje Chang Buddha. In the process, the sand of the Ganges River of the light camel wool color placed at the top of the head exhibited unimaginably miraculous transformation. A loose-hair crown changed into a head-covering crown and a thick-hair crown changed into a thin-hair crown. The strands of hair gathered or separated as required at different places to knit into a naturally perfect crown. Every sand grain had its own independent life. Some walked extremely fast; some wandered around casually; some followed twisted paths; some traveled past the boundary and then came back; and some climbed from the bottom to the top. The sand grains followed each other one by one to form strands of hair that stood into the air without falling. Eventually, a knot was formed to create a perfect crown for the Sambhogakaya-Buddha. Then, Wangzha Shangzun snapped his fingers to perform a mudra and the strands of hair fell into a pile of sand with no trace left of the crown. Wangzha Shangzun issued a Dharma decree to distribute the sand of the Ganges River (which became Vajra Sand after the Dharma was performed) to all who were present. Every attendee received a share of the Vajra Sand that manifested the holy crown worn by the genuine incarnation of the Buddha. I used mine to make a kind of holy pill that was used in a specific tantric initiation so that I could share them with my students.

The situation at the time was that the Dharma was practiced with the same table, at the same position, following the same ritual, and using the same sand of the Ganges River. However, the three hair crowns created were completely different. There was one Bodhisattva two-dimensional crown and there were two Buddha hair crowns that were three-dimensional and stood into the air. The latter two were also different from each other in terms of shape and structure.

All of us attendees on the Dharma assembly that day took an oath to testify for the above reported true facts, "We all attended the Dharma assembly for determining the status of the Buddha by the Dharma of Jin Gang Fa Man Ze Jue as practiced by Wangzha Shangzun. We clearly understand and believe in the law of cause and effect. What was stated above is true and without any false statement. If we lied to deceive people, we not only will not become accomplished but also will descend into the three lower realms to undergo extremely miserable suffering. If what was stated above is all true, we wish and pray that all living beings be able to learn the true Dharma of the Tathagata from H.H. Dorje Chang Buddha III and Sakyamuni Buddha, attain perfect good fortune and wisdom, and become accomplished and liberated to benefit countless living beings."

sixteen

Tea with Great Holy Wangzha Shangzun

I have been often asked what the most excellent and great holy Wangzha Shangzun is like. I have had the good fortune to meet him several times in different forms and situations. In one case I did not know who he was until much later. In addition to successfully conducting the amazing and very high level Jin Gang Fa Man Ze Jue Dharma Assembly to determine who was and who was not an authentic incarnation of a Buddha described in the last chapter, he is a most impressive and powerful elder man who is worthy of our respect. I have met many Dharma kings of different sects, but no one is like Wangzha Shangzun. His power and virtue surpass all of them.

After the ceremony, I had the extreme good fortune to meet an attendant of his who speaks English and requested to prostrate to the Shangzun, which to my surprise, was granted. It is very difficult to meet him. The attendant told me that, to date, probably less than 100 persons in the U.S. have had the good fortune to meet him privately. The attendant took me to the place where this great Mahasattva was staying. I was very excited to be able to see him again.

I understood that Wangzha Shangzun mostly speaks Tibetan, but I was told he can also speak Mandarin Chinese. I found out since that meeting that he also speaks English and can appear as a tall Caucasian.[42] His voice was as I had remembered from the ceremony. Seeing him up close, I realize that he is probably over six feet tall and in excellent health. I had guessed that he must be at least sixty as I knew he had spent 45 years in seclusion in Tibet, but from his appearance guessed he could be even younger. His attendant told me that the Shangzun had already turned 93. He is very spirited and looked like and had the energy and bearing of a much younger man. As for his appearance, he has a

---

42 *The World Buddhism Association Headquarters also confirmed this in Answer #13 "...*
Wangzha Shangzun had a completely different appearance every time when He received eminent monastics and great virtuous ones," February 28, 2018. I also experienced his presence
very differently on another occasion.

most remarkable full beard, large kind eyes, bushy eyebrows, a rectangular face, and is bald, or was at that time.

I was reminded of images of Bodhidharma, the "barbarian" with such a beard and eyebrows who went to China from India, only Wangzha Shangzun is considerably more handsome than the great patriarch of Zen is usually portrayed to have been. (FIGURE 73) However, what is most impressive is his incredible modesty and humility. This is what it is like to be in the presence of a great holy being!

FIGURE 73: "Bodhidharma" painting by H.H. Dorje Chang Buddha III

I had wanted to meet him to express my gratitude for the empowerment I received at the Jin Gang Fa Man Ze Jue Dharma Assembly, but also just to show my respect because I knew that only someone of very high attainment could have performed that Dharma. When I offered him prostrations, he would always tell me to prostrate instead to H.H. Dorje Chang Buddha III. His attendant told me that this holder of three gold buttons at a Shangzun level always carried an image of the Buddha Master with him and did this. When he went back to his living space, the first thing he would do was to put H.H. Dorje Chang Buddha III's image and Shakyamuni Buddha's image in a high place and make offerings to them. I again prostrated, but it was just as before. Wangzha said, "The Buddha Master is here. You should prostrate to the Buddha Master. How can I accept your prostrations?" The other Dharma kings I have met always accepted and even arrogantly awaited my prostrations while silently seated on their thrones. Wangzha Shangzun is certainly the top chief great Dharma King among all Dharma kings, but he is still so humble. I was very touched. Again, I realized how very, very fortunate I am.

Wangzha Shangzun is very easy to communicate with and very amiable. Every sentence he says with a smile. He also provided me with hot tea having his assistant serve me using traditional china teacups. I accepted the teacup and put it aside on the table. Wangzha then told me that "the quality of this tea is not very good. It comes from Tibet and is called Old Eagle Tea". However, the fragrance of the tea, was so wonderful that it betrayed his humble portrayal. I requested from Wangzha Shangzun how to practice the Green Tara Mirror Altar Dharma (Jing Tan Fa). The Shangzun said, "First you have to have a good mirror. Then you get the Dharma transmitted through holy inner-tantric initiation. The most important thing is that you should practice according to the Buddha Master's teachings, and let all people know that they should do good and cease evil. It is then very easy to succeed with this Dharma. But you should decide by yourself if you want to practice this Dharma. The Buddha Master proposed that we should cultivate ourselves and opposed the miraculous. I am not telling you to practice this Green Tara Mirror Altar Dharma."

The time flew by so quickly. My mouth was dry, and I realized I needed to drink the tea, but when I lifted the cup, the cup was so heavy it was as if it were glued to the table. I couldn't move it even when I exerted a lot of force. I was so surprised. I put that cup on the table. How can I now not lift it? This time Wangzha Shangzun saw what was happening and told me, "It is no use to use force. Force cannot lift it. You have to use your mind to lift it. When your mind is not attached to anything, everything will follow your mind." Then Wangzha Shangzun asked me to lift it again. Very strange. It was as if it was weightless. I easily lifted it and also when I opened the cover of the cup, there was a moving image like a video in the cover. I clearly saw a picture of one of my fellow brothers from the past and a moment when I was in Japan. It was very clear, but it quickly started to disappear. I was really surprised. I used my eyes to follow the cover. After a while it completely disappeared. Then the Shangzun said. "Any object can be used as a mirror." So, I suddenly understood why my mind and my cultivation are so important and cannot be replaced by anything else.

I pray that each of you take advantage of this most fortunate fact that the H.H. Dorje Chang Buddha is living in this world now and practice the Dharma that you learn. I also pray that you all quickly become accomplished.

Namo H.H. Dorje Chang Buddha III! Namo Shakyamuni Buddha!

I then humbly prostrated and offered special thanks to Wangzha Shangzun for teaching me this important lesson.

seventeen

Testing in the Holy Realm

In 2014, the World Buddhist Association Headquarters (WBAH) first began a program to test the qualification of venerable ones, Dharma kings, rinpoches, monastics, masters of Dharma listening, Dharma masters, laypeople, and others. This was to help Buddhist cultivators choose masters who possess virtue, cultivation, accomplishment, and Buddha Dharma. There were 3,273 people who officially took the written test of 100 problems on sutras, vinayas, and shastras (commentaries). However, in the end, only 1,085 of them were qualified to take the examination in the holy realm. It was a complicated process. Even after reaching a high enough score on the written test, there were other tests and finally the examination in the holy realm, which was executed in the Eight Winds in Samsara Battle Position and the Vajra Battle Position. Manjushri Bodhisattva and Mahamayuri Vidyarajni Tathagata are the yidams of the Holy Test. Each session of the exam was witnessed by seven holy ones and ten additional witnesses. I was one such proctor and as such was able to witness the tests in both the large and small battle position.

After practicing Dharma, divining pieces are given to the candidate taking the examination to drop privately to receive the divine forecast by Manjushri Bodhisattva. Then, the candidate enters the Eight Winds Battle Position to demonstrate his/her cultivated abilities and accomplishment from practice. One has to break through the destination zone to walk into the land of safety to pass a certain grade level which will be indicated by the corresponding buttons on one's Dharma attire. You may keep taking the exam as often as you can advance. You reach a level where you can progress no farther. At that point you are able to check what Manjushri Bodhisattva predicted in His divination and it is always the same as the level you just reached. There has been not even one disagreement in a candidate's grade level between that determined from breaking the battle position and the prediction by the divination. This general description is true whether you perform in the small or large battle position.

The grades ranged from three levels of blue buttons to three levels of gold buttons. The highest, a three gold-button Shangzun level, is considered a non-receding Bodhisattva who is not required to take the examination. However, the presiding proctor overseeing the battle positions, Venerable Wangzha Shangzun, even though he did not need to do so, wanted to set an example and requested on His own initiative to take the examination. All those with gold buttons belong to the category of holy virtuous ones. Another level was added that fell between gold buttons 2 and 3, called a lotus level.

Originally, the highest level below a gold button level was a Blue Button Grade Three Plus 2 Black Buttons called Da De or Great Virtuous One and below that was a Blue Button Grade Three Plus 1 called a Xuan De or Propagating Virtuous One, which is what I achieved when I first took the test in the holy realm. When my work was reviewed later, I became a Da De, the status I hold at the time this book was written. That of course can change either up or down. Any of us below the highest three gold-button category can recede and fall to a lower level if we violate the precepts and do not continue our cultivation and practice.

A student asked the gurus at the World Buddhism Association Headquarters (WBAH) about the use of sutra debate as practiced in certain Tibetan schools as a requirement in receiving a geshe[43] degree to test one's level of accomplishment. They were told that obtaining a geshe degree "...does not mean that they possess true Buddha Dharma because a geshe is merely a scholar of empty theories. The degree absolutely cannot represent the holder's accomplishment in true realization power. Only the written exam of 100 questions based on sutras, vinayas, and shastras and the most sacred and solemn holy exam can be ironclad proof of one's true knowledge and realization power.[44]

A very wise student observed after taking this exam in the holy realm that there was no doubt that you were being observed and the Dharma protectors were there keeping an eye on you—you could not fool them or lie to them. This may be one of the most important aspects of this effort. It gives us faith and evidence that there are higher beings out there who know what we are doing and not doing.

---

43 *A geshe is a Tibetan Buddhist academic degree considered to be equivalent to a PhD. It is emphasized primarily in the Gelug lineage, but also awarded in other traditions. The geshe curriculum is thought to be similar to what was taught at the great Indian Buddhist monastic universities like Nalanda.*

44 *World Buddhism Association Headquarters (WBAH) Inquiry # 20190101, December 1, 2019.*

eighteen

Kuan Yin Bodhisattva's Great Compassion Dharma Assemblies

I want to give a little background on the Dharma of Empowerment by Kuan Yin's Great Compassion. There are two stages to this great Dharma—the generation stage and the perfection stage. The generation stage only has about a 3% manifestation and can be learned successfully immediately, regardless of whether the learner is a good person or a bad person. This person receiving that empowerment can then empower living beings to enter the state of the Dharma right away. On the other hand, the perfection stage which requires the cultivation of Bodhi Holy Water includes a 97% realization of accomplishment and is very difficult to achieve. It has been said that "to perfectly cultivate the holy water that penetrates the Dharma bowl (as you do to generate Bodhi Holy Water) is more difficult than climbing to the sky."[45]

"The precepts and disciplines of the Dharma of Empowerment by Kuan Yin's Great Compassion are very rigorous. The precepts stipulate that the master practicing the Dharma must spend the entirety (minus expenses of conducting the ceremony) of the offerings collected within 15 days on releasing living beings in captivity and carrying out good deeds such as the relief of poverty or disasters. If not acting according to this precept-stipulation, one would violate the precepts of this Dharma and break the essence of abiding by the precepts. One would lose the lineage right away. Once the lineage is lost, the Dharma will be directly taken over right there by the Mara King's demonic descendants and becomes a demonic dharma. The master will then become a demonic master. In this type of situation, this Holy Dharma would become a demonic dharma doing poisonous harm to living beings. H.H. Dorje Chang Buddha III mentioned such possibility long ago in the book *Learning from Buddha*."[46]

---

45 *World Buddhism Association Headquarters Public Announcement #20170112, November 15, 2017.*

46 *World Buddhism Association Headquarters Public Announcement #20170111, November 2, 2017.*

His Holiness Dorje Chang Buddha III did transmit the generation stage level of this great Dharma to several of His senior students. I do not believe He does this anymore. I was fortunate to receive that transmission. We can hold Dharma assemblies using this Dharma but we absolutely cannot receive any personal benefit from them. Disciples are most generous in their offerings after they receive the beneficial effects of the Dharma, but the offerings must go to help other living beings. It cannot be used as a temple fund raiser or to enrich the master performing the ceremony.

H.H. Dorje Chang Buddha III told another rinpoche before that rinpoche held such a Dharma assembly in Hong Kong, "**Holding the Dharma assembly to benefit the great masses is a good thing. However, you must clearly understand the Dharma I expounded in the recorded Dharma discourses. You must remember to practice the ending (concluding) practice of releasing living beings from captivity to truly benefit the great masses with great compassion. Otherwise, you will be a heretic using the name of Buddhism.**"[47]

In *Learning from Buddha,* the Buddha Master tells us that this Dharma is the easiest to practice. He said that "as long as one has the power of lineage, that is sufficient. You can succeed in practicing it the very same day you take up the practice of it. The next day, you can convene people, empower all of them, and lead them into a supernormal state. However, there must be Dharma-protecting people on the scene to protect the safety of the attendees who are empowered. This is to prevent attendees, who may jump or move about uncontrollably after they enter a supernormal state, from hurting others who are on the floor or beside them."[48]

The Buddha Master also said that the concluding practice of dedicating the offerings received from such an empowerment is the most essential and the best part of the Dharma. He told us that "**were it not for its concluding practice, I would not advocate practicing this Dharma. I all the more would not transmit this Dharma in the world. Why should we release captured living beings? All living beings have been our family members since beginning-less time. They are the same as humans. It is just that their degree of intelligence and their appearance are different from those of humans. Still, their consciousness is the same as that of a human. That is why in real life we see that some animals can even rescue people, some can do math, some can sing, and some can dance. I even saw a dog that was able to play a highly difficult piano melody. Moreover, the dog played it very precisely. We must help them and rescue them. Furthermore, we**

---

47 *The Office of H.H. Dorje Chang Buddha III Public Announcement #50, September 13, 2016.*

48 *P. 26, Preliminary translation of Learning from Buddha.*

must not hurt any living being even in the slightest. We can only rescue them."[49]

I conducted my first Kuan Yin Bodhisattva Great Compassion Dharma Assembly in downtown Clovis, California in January 2017. This was the first time this ceremony had been conducted in English. Buddhist and non-Buddhists from the Fresno, Sacramento, San Francisco, Los Angeles areas as well as from New York City, Salt Lake City, Sri Lanka, Germany, Cambodia, Taiwan, Thailand, and Shanghai and various parts of China attended. I told those present that the Great Bodhisattva Kuan Yin would come and empower all present, help remove obstacles from their lives, and enable those who could keep the three pure precepts (avoiding evil, doing good, and rescuing living beings) to have good fortune and much happiness. After the ceremony there were many emotional and moving accounts of what happened. Illusory states and movement were manifested and people were empowered.

FIGURE 74: Heartwood Kuan Yin Bodhisattva's Great Compassion Dharma Assembly held in 2017 in Hendersonville, North Carolina.

The Great Compassion Empowerment was also held in April at the Xuanfa South Dharma Center, located at the Heartwood Refuge and Retreat Center in Hendersonville, North Carolina (FIGURE 74). Many of those participating experienced profound encounters from the Great Compassionate One and found old illnesses and pains disappear and emotional blockages released. Some had

49 *Ibid.*

188

immediate relief, and others only noticed that long-standing aches and pains were gone after the ceremony. People came from all over the United States as well as from Canada, China, and Sri Lanka to participate. The ceremony was part of a Dharma assembly held to invite Kuan Yin to appear and bless all who were attending. Some felt a cool breeze and others saw various lights while they swayed and danced involuntarily. Several shared their experiences with the group after the ceremony.

The ceremony was part of an extended weekend seminar and retreat that focused on *Learning from Buddha* and translations of other discourses by H.H. Dorje Chang Buddha that I read. Benxin Chiren Rinpoche, from Pasadena, California, provided simultaneous translations of recordings of the discourses. The next month I held another similar Kuan Yin Dharma Assembly in Salt Lake City with the help of the Xuanfa Utah Dharma Center.

FIGURE 75: Kuan Yin Bodhisattva's Great Compassion Dharma Assembly held in 2017 in Thailand.

Later that year I went with Gesang Suolang Rinpoche and other students to conduct two more Kuan Yin Bodhisattva's Great Compassion Empowerment Dharma Assemblies at a beautiful private retreat center located in the parklike suburban Nongjok District of Bangkok, Thailand (FIGURE 75). After all of the Dharma assemblies, the participants would come forward and explain what they had experienced as shown in FIGURE 76. The Dharma Assembly was followed by a fish release ceremony performed as part of the Kuan Yin Bodhisattva Empowerment. The first of these Dharma assemblies was for volunteers who received the empowerment of Kuan Yin Bodhisattva so that they could serve as Dharma protectors and help others the following day.

FIGURE 76: Testimonials given after Kuan Yin Bodhisattva's Great Compassionate Dharma Assembly, Thailand.

FIGURE 77: Class on *Learning from Buddha* after Dharma Assembly, Thailand.

I also read in English (and had translated into Thai by Kunlanat Makboon) preliminary translations of Dharma Discourses given by H.H. Dorje Chang Buddha III and transmitted Dharma in a charming and unique concrete "tree house" (FIGURE 77.) Gesang Suolang Rinpoche from Salt Lake City, Utah, and Gongjue Tuji Rinpoche from Cologne, Germany joined in leading chants early every morning from the Holy Vajrasana Temple Hymnal. Gongjue was able to stay in the tree house in a most unusual suite above the meeting room. He has the Xuanfa Dharmazentrum (Dharma Center) in Cologne.

FIGURE 78: Disciples from the United States, China, and Taiwan who served as dharma protectors, in the Founder's Room at the Chua Thai Son (temple) in Da Nang, Vietnam just before the Dharma Assembly.

Gesang and I left Thailand for Vietnam to conduct three more Kuan Yin Bodhisattva's Great Compassion Empowerment Dharma Assemblies at the precious Thai Son Pagoda (temple), in Da Nang. Khatas were offered, along with chanting and prostrations to the Holy ones. We paid our respect to our Buddha Master whose photo not only graced the main altar, but also the private altar next to the monastic quarters (FIGURE 78).

Many received healings and various forms of empowerments. Some even saw the magnificent Great Bodhisattva. Some spontaneously started singing, dancing and doing graceful mudras that they had never done before (FIGURE 79). Everyone was very happy. Even the fish, frogs, and critters that were released into a nearby creek were jumping for joy and eager to return to their homes, receiving the refuge vows in the process (FIGURE 80). Two weeks later more turtles, crabs, and other living beings were released into the Han River within sight of the Golden Dragon Bridge and according to the requirements for concluding Kuan Yin Bodhisattva's Great Compassion Empowerment Dharma. In fact, the most important aspect of the Kuan Yin Great Compassion

191

Empowerment Dharma, as the Buddha Master said, is selflessly benefiting and helping living beings.

FIGURE 79: Kuan Yin Great Compassion Dharma Assembly held in warm rain at Chua Thai Son (temple), Da Nang, Vietnam.

FIGURE 80: Captive animal release after the Kuan Yin Bodhisattva's Great Compassion Dharma Assembly, Da Nang, Vietnam.

I did not hold animal releases to fulfill that requirement for the Dharma Assemblies we held in the States. Instead, I got a special dispensation to use the money collected to help bring the Dharma to captive human beings in prison. I needed an extension of the requirement to use all the offerings within 15 days of the event as it takes much longer to accomplish anything in our state prisons. I will write more about that later.

The warm rain that fell on the last Dharma assembly seemed to add to the mystery of Kuan Yin Bodhisattva's presence as warm breezes wafted across the beautiful white sand beach to the temple. Da Nang, Vietnam is deserving of the title, the Riviera of Asia. It is not surprising that Kuan Yin Bodhisattva should make such a pronounced presence in Da Nang during the ceremony. Her images are everywhere. The small temple where we performed these Dharma assemblies was located on one of the five famous marble mountains in Da Nang. The marble is harvested to make many beautiful statues which are seen everywhere and many of those statues are of Kuan Yin Bodhisattva.

Later, with Gesang's help, I also conducted an all-day class in Da Nang to discuss the book based on discourses given by H.H. Dorje Chang Buddha III entitled, *Learning from Buddha* (FIGURE 81). The tiny temple was packed as was the patio outside the temple with disciples who were eager to hear the Dharma. An English translation of that precious sutra is now available on-line and discussed more later on.

FIGURE 81: Disciples crowd into Chua Thai Son (temple) to eagerly hear a reading of *Learning from Buddha.*

However, I must confess that once again I was quite sick for most of this trip. It seemed I always overestimated my strength and underestimated the difficulty of travel as I had earlier in Hong Kong and on the Dharma Propagation Mission. It started in Thailand and by the time we got to Vietnam I knew I needed help. I cannot say enough good things about the care I got in a local hospital and the kindness of our hosts and the students. I would manage to rally for the classes and ceremonies and gave refuge vows and Dharma to many students, but the rest of the time I was in bed. Gesang was wonderful, as usual, and kept me on a complex, but strict schedule of meds. It had been almost that bad in Thailand. We stayed at a private retreat in Thailand that had floating restaurants on a beautiful lake and a spa with all sorts of treatments and wonderful hosts, but I was mostly too sick to enjoy it. Gesang and others had to conduct the fish release while I suffered. I am so grateful to have such talented and generous students.

nineteen
Personal Retreat

We had been offering up to 30-day private retreats at the temple and in March 2018 I decided I needed to take one myself. It had taken me over a month to recover from my last Asian trip and I wanted to reflect on what I was doing wrong. I had just received preliminary translations of both the *Supreme and Unsurpassable Mahamudra of Liberation* and *Imparting the Absolute Truth Through the Heart Sutra*. I had perfect and trustworthy students who came to the temple to feed me and take care of anything that would come up. I had three goals: strengthen my personal practice, which I never seemed to find enough time for, contemplate how I could better promote the correct Buddha Dharma to non-Chinese speakers, and to study those two preliminary translations. My intention was to cut all internet-phone contact and personal contact with the outside world.

I can only report, I was only partially successful. I was very grateful to all who worked to give me this time. I know how difficult that can be for most of us to have thirty-days to just focus on practice and learning the correct Buddha Dharma and to not worry about worldly matters. I was very grateful. I was also very grateful to my two vajra brothers who enabled me to have the preliminary translations to study and all the other translators who helped make that possible. I hope that they will be available soon, but you can read them, too, if you do a retreat at the temple.

There are a few recommendations I made to myself and anyone else wanting to do a private retreat:

1. Have a plan before you start your retreat. I wasn't ready even though I deferred starting for a week. There were still things I needed (or thought I needed) to do that carried into the retreat and caused me to keep my computer and phone. And, I did not have a plan of what to do on the retreat itself.

2. Don't allow yourself access to the outside world. Even though I greatly reduced my phone-internet contacts, I still kept some channels open. Everyone else cooperated beautifully and tried to support me, but I still persisted. DON'T DO IT! I came out a couple of times and had a hard time regaining the practice. Absolutely no phones, internet, or computers should be allowed. There is a reason you do these retreats with no possible outside contacts and not in your usual living space with all its comforts and distractions. We do have a Dharma Protector chapel and a special Dharma that the Buddha Master gave me to practice there (FIGURE 82). You cannot have any forms of electricity there—not even a match, candle or flashlight! Sonya, a nun who stays here at the temple, did a retreat and stayed there last month during the Covid-19 quarantine. The other nuns took her food. But I thought I could do it in my quarters. My support crew did leave food for me. I was wrong. DON'T DO IT. Find a way to be and stay isolated from distractions. The next time I try this I will use the chapel.

3. I reviewed and read (and posted) the translations that Benxin Chiren quickly provided on answers to critical questions from the virtuous ones at the World Buddhism Association Headquarters. There is a lot to be learned from these, especially on inner-tantric initiations. I wanted the other English-speaking disciples to have these teachings. Although I rationalized that I was doing "Dharma Work", I should have completed that work before I started my retreat.

4. I also reread Jamgon Kongtrul's *Retreat Manual*, written in the mid-nineteenth century on the Tibetan approach to their traditional three-year, three-month retreat with guidelines on how to prepare, life within, and life afterwards.

5. With all of the above, I was able to establish a daily schedule based on an increased understanding of what my practice should be and how all the pieces fit together. I have been most fortunate to receive many Dharma practices and initiations over the 18 years I have followed His Holiness, but I was not sure how to practice them in an integrated manner. Now, I feel I can.

6. Thirty-days is not enough time. I only really got started the last week.

I learned more how not to do a retreat, but it was still constructive. The integrated practice plan was helpful. I did come up with ideas on how to better propagate the Dharma. The most important outcome was my resolve to be more aggressive in taking the Dharma to the English-speaking world. I already had a mailing list of over 2,000, but many were primarily Chinese-speakers. I would continue sending a monthly newsletter to them, with mostly photos of what was happening at the temple and some Chinese translation, but I would create a database of non-Chinese speakers, focusing on the people who only understood English and post a weekly blog. It would be more informal than the newsletter and I would try to tell my stories. I called this blog "Thus Have I Seen (or Heard)". It was actually the precursor to this book. I took the "128 Evil and Erroneous Views" from the *Supreme and Unsurpassable Mahamudra of Liberation* and talked about them and whatever else was current.

FIGURE 82: Dharma Protector Chapel at the Holy Vajrasana Temple.

I think the blog was successful. I could tell how many were at least opening the blog and also clicking links to other articles. I do not know how many read any of it, but some did and were quite supportive. I wish I could say the retreat got me back to where I wanted to be in doing my daily practice. I became progressively more discouraged and frustrated that we could not get the discourses and writings by the Buddha Master released in English. I was allowed to read them at the temple, but that did not reach many people. My health was deteriorating so that it was very difficult for me to travel. I did not think I was long for this world, and I was not making good use of my remaining time. My world seemed to be falling apart and I seemed unable or unwilling to help myself or to seek help.

I did go to my Buddha Master and received the *"Phoenix and Chicken"* discourse I mentioned in the Preface. What was I to do?

twenty
Holy Fire Ceremony

There were several extraordinary Dharma assemblies held in Pasadena that I did attend after my retreat, even though it was becoming increasingly difficult for me to even drive to southern California. I was able to continue holding some English classes at the Amitabha Buddha's Temple of Compassion and Wisdom in Rosemead, California and even started a series of classes in San Diego with the much appreciated and bountiful support of Helen Pan. I would not have been able to do any of this without her help.

One very rare Dharma assembly was held in Pasadena, California on September 19, 2018 and I was able to attend it—a Holy Fire Ceremony. It is believed that this Dharma has not been performed anywhere in the world for over 80 years. Pabongka Dechen Nyingpo Rinpoche (1878-1941), a Gelug lama in Tibet, was one of the last known masters who could perform this Dharma. Common fire offerings are frequently performed in Tibet, India, and elsewhere to halt disasters, remove hardships and difficulties, eliminate hindrances, and increase good fortune. I had attended such a ceremony in North Carolina many years ago, long before I had even heard of my present guru. It was one of the first Tibetan ceremonies that I experienced. However, in terms of the empowerment generated, it bore little resemblance to the Holy Fire Mandala Homa[50] Dharma that was practiced here. Those who had the good fortune to attend not only received the initiation to be able to practice this Dharma, which is considered the "king" or greatest of all Dharmas to eliminate living beings' sins, hindrances, and dark karmas, but also were able to witness the subduing of evil, malicious demons and the successful subtle presentation of "Secretly Sending a Petition to a Bodhisattva."

I had such good fortune to attend and personally saw the Vajra Female Mahasattva ignite the fire in the specially prepared mandala stove using a flashing

---

50 *Homas is a Sanskrit word that refers to a ritual in which an offering is made in fire.*

ray of light that burst into flames. We all kneeled to kowtow to pay respect and followed the ritual to start praying and burning our homas. I was not personally in a place to see the Vajra Female Mahasattva arrive, but I certainly saw the blaze of light that caused the fire to ignite.

A disciple took the initiative to put the Vajra demon-subduing bowl used in the holy fire offering on a small flat-surface table upside down. Prior to this, other disciples had very carefully cleaned the table and the bowl in front of all of us. According to the Dharma, the bowl would gather and capture the demonic, opposing, and malicious karmas of everyone present at the fire offering site. The demonic beings would be suppressed inside the bowl. The demons tried to escape from the bowl. At this absolutely critical moment, a sound of "hong" or "hum" was heard. A lightning bolt launched by Vajra Female Mahasattva turned the malicious demons and dark karmas inside the bowl into foul-smelling crushed powders. The demonic souls were then brought to the Buddha Land by Buddhas and Bodhisattvas, to be taught and reformed under rigorous control there.

Then the great Dharma of "Secretly Sending a Petition to a Bodhisattva" was practiced. All attendees at the site saw that with a tremendously loud "hong" or "hum" from the Vajra demon-subduing bowl, the edge of which was air-tight, being closed by the surface of the table, lightning-like fire instantly rose from the edge of the bowl and immediately went out. Someone then turned the bowl over. There was nothing inside or under the bowl. The "one petition" to be secretly sent to the Bodhisattva had already been taken away. It simply disappeared without a trace while we watched with our eyes wide open.

As an aside, all the smoke generated from the burning demon bodies and the fire did not cause the smoke detectors in the ceiling of the Buddha Hall to go off or cause water to sprinkle down. That was a more worldly sort of miracle.

It was at this ceremony that we learned Dharma King Gar Tongstan (FIGURE 48, page 129) would leave this world that night as he had predicted. He said that he would pass after this last Dharma assembly. This ceremony was what he had been waiting for. I knew this great Dharma King. He had been very kind to me. He was the enlightened one I wrote about earlier who had his enlightenment experiences recorded in the "Silver Box Discourses." I was not able to attend his passing although others with whom I was staying did. The ceremony was exhausting, and I had to rest. He is greatly missed. He was able to "pass away in a state of perfect accomplishment before the ink dries" as he predicted in his farewell letter to the Buddha Master. He was truly an enlightened being just as he had said he was when he told our Buddha Master of his awakening. He left behind shariras; unprecedented relic-flowers in green, blue, yellow, white, and black; and a tooth-relic signifying his holy status (FIGURE 83).

FIGURE 83: H.E. Venerable Gar Tsongstan IV Dharma King Ciren Gyatso's sharira.

twenty-one

True Compassion

I do want to try to express what I have learned about compassion from my Master, as I consider it the most important Dharma I have received. Like karma, it is complicated and not always what you might think it is. It is helping someone in such a way that they may become liberated, and not giving them what they want or what you think they want or should have. Only an enlightened one has such wisdom to know what that is. Only an advanced Bodhisattva or Buddha can see the past and future karmic conditions of that person. That is why it is so important for us to first become enlightened ourselves only then can we truly help others. Do we not do anything when we sense an injustice or see someone in pain? I said it is complicated.

> ### Great Compassion for My Mother Bodhichitta Dharma
>
> 1. *Understanding who my mother is*
> 2. *Bearing in mind kindness*
> 3. *Repaying kindness*
> 4. *Loving kindness*
> 5. *Compassion*
> 6. *Renouncing greed*
> 7. *Eliminating attachment*
>
> **H.H. Dorje Chang Buddha III**
> **What Is Cultivation?**

Interventions without knowing the facts of the matter might not be a good thing, but we need to apply the two sets of seven principles for developing bodhichitta as best we can and always look deeply at our motivation, and weed out any selfish attachments that may adversely affect our decisions. Too often we intercede to make ourselves feel or look good and not to help anyone else. Always introspect and keep checking your true motivation, and pray for guidance.

I will give an example. My Buddha Master told a story about one of my vajra brothers. Everyone else was laughing, but I was horrified. I said, but what he did was despicable! "Yes, what he did was despicable," my Buddha Master agreed and continued on with the story. I could not put that down. I fumed and I fussed and went home and fumed and fussed some more. I couldn't sleep that night. That was not right! How could the Buddha let such behavior continue? How could my other vajra brothers and sisters just laugh about such outlandish and selfish behavior? I was so angry over all this, that I was prepared to go the next day and ask that my name and pictures not be included in the treasure book *H.H. Dorje Chang Buddha III* if this person was also going to be in it. That is how upset I was and how absurd my behavior was.

But first, I had to read a translation of one of the Buddha's discourses to a group of students. I managed to calm down enough to do that, but it was still my intent to go to my Buddha Master and make my request as soon as I was finished with the class. I came to one sentence in the discourse and it hit me like a bolt of lightning. I was so ashamed. The Buddha said something about the fact that the Buddha had all sorts of disciples. Some were very great Bodhisattvas and some were bums and scoundrels. Only then did I get it. This vajra brother may have done something quite despicable, but he was a living being and the Buddha was still going to teach him. Also, there were very many virtuous things that this

> ### *Bodhisattva Correspondence Bodhichitta Dharma*
>
> *1. Self and others are equal*
>
> *2. Exchange between self and others*
>
> *3. Benefit others before self*
>
> *4. Dedicating merit*
>
> *5. Fearlessly protect the dharma*
>
> *6. Effectively lead others to correct practice*
>
> *7. Renouncing myself to help others build good karma*
>
> **H.H. Dorje Chang Buddha III**
> **What Is Cultivation?**

person also did. I was like that too. I made many mistakes, but still my Buddha Master continued to teach me. The Buddha never gave up on me, although I have been ready to give up many times. And just maybe there were more reasons as to why the vajra brother behaved the way he did than I understood. Instead of asking to be taken out of the treasure book, I went to my Buddha Master and repented for my ignorant, arrogant, erroneous, and evil views.

In the sutra *A Monk Expounds the Absolute Truth to a Layperson*, written by the Buddha when he was quite young, the Buddha expounded that the conduct of Bodhisattvas is much different from the conduct of ordinary people. In the mind of Bodhisattvas, there is no differentiation between good and evil. At every moment, they are examining their own faults. They immediately correct their slightest faults. They never see the faults of other people. They also do not see their own good fruits. They constantly hope that living beings will soon escape from the cycle of reincarnation. This is true compassion and profound.

We have added a new chant to our morning service that the Buddha Master transmitted while on a road trip with His senior students entitled "The Wrongs of Others Are My Wrongs" along with the two branches of seven principles on developing bodhichitta listed above from the "What Is Cultivation" as part of our daily reflection. This reflection is part of our daily homework.

The Wrongs of Others Are My Wrongs

The wongs of others are my wrongs.

To regard others and yourself as one is great compassion.

A true cultivator regards the mistakes of others as his own mistakes.

Do not talk about the wrongs of others.

Do not make known your meritorious deeds.

Speaking of your meritorious deeds shows you dark karma.

Dharma Discourse given on the "Trip to the East Coast"
H.H. Dorje Chang Buddha III

I have one more personal experience on how Holy Beings are different from ordinary beings, not only in how they exhibit compassion, but in other matters as well. At one time I was with the Buddha Master's wife almost every day. I was helping her learn English and she was helping me learn Chinese. I even had lunch with her and the Buddha Master often during this period and I was able to observe the Buddha Mother in many situations. One thing I remember was that it was very difficult for me to explain sarcasm to her in an English article we were studying. It was not a concept she seemed to have had previous experience with. However, the most remarkable thing happened when her mother died. I know she loved her mother and had not seen her for many years, but I had no awareness that her mother had passed on. It was only when her mother's beautiful and elaborate shariras arrived that I realized what had happened (FIGURE 84). Holy Beings and ordinary beings are different.

FIGURE 84: Elder laywoman Wang Cheng E-Fen's sharira

twenty-two

The Five Vidyas

I have finally come to realize that you must have an understanding of the Five Vidyas to begin to understand what the Buddha Master is teaching us. However, as of yet, very few of the discourses given by the Buddha Master on the Five Vidyas have been recorded or released for publication in English. I will try my best to offer what I have seen, heard, and understand about the Five Vidyas. Please understand that this has not been reviewed or approved by the Buddha.

The five major vidyas are classified as 1) Craftsmanship and sometimes also arts and/or technology (silpakarmasthanavidya), 2) Healing (cikitsvidya), 3) Sound (sabdavidya), 4) Causality or Buddhist logic (hetuvidya), and 5) Inner Realization (adhyatmavidya). A classic Buddhist education in India and later in Tibet would include training in all of these along with five minor vidyas. The minor vidyas are rhetoric, lexicology or ornate diction, phonology or prosody[51], dramatics or dramaturgy, and astronomy. Sometimes vidyas is translated as sciences, or knowledges, or branches of learning, but that is not quite the right concept.

H.H. Dorje Chang Buddha III has explained that these five major categories are much more complex and subtle than the normally translated headings would suggest. To think of them as just five items or categories of knowledge would be incorrect. We would be wrong in our understanding of the Five Vidyas. Vidyas is an ancient word from India that is used in many different contexts to mean different things. Taken literally, it represents the opposite of ignorance or misconception about the nature of reality, which is avidya[52] or darkness. You might say

---

51 Prosody is the musical or metric structure of language. It can relate to versification and rhythm, but it is also the patterns of stress and intonation in a language, your manner of speaking or expressing yourself.

52 In Sanskrit a word can be negated by adding "a" to it, thus "vidya" or brightness becomes "avidya" or ignorance or absence of light.

that vidya then represents the essential truth of everything or all that is bright and good. Actually, it is as Venerable Akou Lamo Rinpoche clearly stated in the book *H.H. Dorje Chang Buddha III*, "...the Five Vidyas are not that narrow. Everything in the universe can be classified into five aspects of brightness and darkness. To develop everything that is good in the universe and that benefits living beings is classified as 'bright.' That which confuses and is bad is classified as 'dark.' This is the real meaning of the Five Vidyas of which the Buddha spoke."

The Buddha Master explained that the Five Vidyas in the Buddhist context represent the underlying principles of the universe. They are comprehensive and profound and totally encompass everything in the universe with life or without life, the spiritual and the material. Everything—all dharmas—are contained in the Five Vidyas. All animate and inanimate, conditioned and unconditioned phenomena in the entire universe are expressed in the Five Vidyas. It is essential that they be understood and mastered, if one is to obtain the full power of the Buddha Dharma. You could even say that they are the Buddha Dharma. That is because the Buddha Dharma includes all truth, including the truths of modern-day science. However, strictly speaking, these truths are not Buddhist truths or truths that belong to Buddhism. They are the underlying principles of truth and the original nature of all phenomena. They represent the entire interrelated Truth of the Universe. There cannot be a sixth vidya. There are only five and those five contain everything. That is why His Holiness has told us that it is heresy to refer to the Five Vidyas as merely five sciences or areas of knowledge or learning.

The Five Vidyas are the manifestation of the powers and wisdoms of holy beings—they represent the realization of Buddhas and Bodhisattvas. Perhaps the current Wikipedia definition of "transcendental knowledge leading toward Brahman" is closer to what the Buddha Master is teaching us than the concepts about them currently held in modern Buddhism. They are the results of what holy beings do and they include everything in the universe that helps living beings. The Chinese translated the Sanskrit Five Vidyas into "wu ming (五明)", which literally means the five brightnesses. This is really closer to their true meaning than the usual more prosaic English translation of sciences or knowledge and learning. The Chinese character for "ming" is composed of the ancient characters for the sun and the moon representing the source of all illumination. The principles expressed by these five categories contain the clarity of the true science of enlightenment. H.H. Dorje Chang Buddha III often talks about this brightness. Once He expressed concern that the improper transmission of the Buddha Dharma would cause the world to lose this light. That is why we must be so careful in transmitting this Dharma. When one can understand these five principles, one understands everything and can do anything! I think it is best that we just use the Sanskrit term and do not try to translate it.

You must know that the true Five Vidyas are neither hollow theories from books nor the so-called five major vidyas or five minor vidyas as defined by most Tibetans. The Five Vidyas refer to the mastering of the rules of change that govern all spiritual and physical existence of myriad phenomena in the universe. Buddhas and Bodhisattvas have acquired this mastery. What is not good, these holy beings turn into good. What is useless, They transform into usefulness. They are unimpeded in their power of debate. They know the correlation between science and logic, and which concepts are mutually constructive or mutually destructive. They turn afflictions into bodhi. They have attained liberation from death and rebirth and are at the pinnacle of transcending the mundane to become holy. They are greatly enlightened and capable beings who have attained accomplishments at the levels of Equal Enlightenment Bodhisattvas, Wondrous Enlightenment Bodhisattvas, or Buddha.[53]

There is no one on this earth who has mastered these Five Vidyas like our Buddha Master. Others talk about it or may say they have, but where is the evidence of their mastery? It is not enough to express an abstract understanding or hollow theories about helping living beings. A true master must be able to demonstrate concrete results and skills in these areas. I think it took many of us a long time to understand why our Buddha Master talked so much about the Five Vidyas. We only had a superficial understanding of what was meant. I know I did. In fact, I had never even heard of the term before the Buddha Master started teaching us about them. The treasure book, the Big Blue Book, *H.H. Dorje Chang Buddha III,* documents His mastery of the Five Vidyas.

The Buddha gave a number of discourses, both private and recorded for public distribution on the subject and still we were confused. I could find very little written about them in English, but bit by bit I began to understand their significance. I did find one reference on how an ancient ruler had wanted to convene a council of the most advanced followers of the Buddha to develop a common ground for understanding the Dharma. He kept raising the bar as to who could attend to have only the finest practitioners present, but there were always too many. Finally, the criteria he used was to only admit those who had mastered the Five Vidyas. That was a small group and they were the most advanced minds in his kingdom.

I did finally find an English translation of Master Asanga's *Bodhisattvabhumi (The Bodhisattva Path to Unsurpassed Enlightenment)* that at least mentioned the five branches of learning, but it was obviously with a greatly diminished definition from how H.H. Dorje Chang Buddha III explained them. This is one

---

53 *World Buddhism Association Headquarters (WBAH) Reply to Inquiry #20190101, op.sit.*

of the volumes of the *Yogācārabhūmi Shastra,* the classic commentaries of the Yogachara tradition. The Dalai Lama in his forward noted that this book not only outlines the practice of meditation and cultivation of the Six Paramitas, "... but encourages the acquisition of broad knowledge and general education in the pursuit of enlightenment. The focus of that education is the five sciences (vidyas), which include the study of Buddhist and non-Buddhist philosophical views, grammar, logic, medicine, and crafts." The translator of that book did offer a more detailed definition stating that "Learning the Dharma includes all five of the major branches of learning: (1) the inner sciences, (2) the science of logic, (3) the science of grammar (sound), (4) the science of treating disease, and (5) the science of the categories of crafts and occupations." He also provided more detailed descriptions of what each of these five categories contained and how they contributed to the training of a Bodhisattva.[54] Mastery of all five categories is required for one to become a Great Bodhisattva just as much as accomplishment in the Six Paramitas. However, the understanding of these categories is nowhere near that provided by the Buddha Master.

Even given the narrower definitions of the Five Vidyas offered by Asanga, the *Bodhisattvabhumi* offers interesting motives on why a Bodhisattva seeks to master the Five Vidyas or branches of learning:

For the arts and technology (crafts and occupations) there are three: amassing wealth to be able to easily benefit sentient beings; to enable oneself to be held in high regard by sentient beings so that they will listen to you expound the dharma; and to be able to benefit sentient beings and attract them to the Dharma by providing them with knowledge of a craft.

For healing (medicine) it is to be able to cure many varieties of illnesses contracted by sentient beings and to promote the welfare of the greater populace.

For sound (grammar) it is to generate trust in one's speech or presentations, and so that one can engage in orderly discourse.

For logic it is to gain an accurate and complete knowledge of what is incorrectly or poorly taught or described in the body of teachings; to be able to refute objections that are raised by others; and to instill greater faith toward the teachings of the Buddha.

For the inner science it is to learn and put into practice the Buddha's speech and be able to fully reveal these teachings to others.

---

54 *Pp. 171-191, Asanga,* The Bodhisattva Path to Unsurpassed Enlightenment, *as translated by Artemus B. Engle, 2016.*

I do believe that it is partially the unavailability of the Yogachara literature in English and the lack of emphasis on the Third Turning of the Wheel of Dharma that has made it so difficult for Western students to grasp the significance of the Five Vidyas and even perhaps to having the karmic affinity for learning the Dharma of H.H. Dorje Chang Buddha III. I know that reading Engle's translation, which I did not do until I started writing this book, helped me to understand why my Buddha Master had stressed both cultivation and the development of the Five Vidyas —even with Engle's limited definition of what the Five Vidyas were. We learn and propagate Dharma in what we do—in everything we do: mundane and holy acts alike. Daily life off the cushion or meditation seat is just as important as our mind training on the cushion.

In 2019 The World Buddhism Association Headquarters (WBAH) responded to an inquiry from a disciple who asked about some other Chinese students who were claiming to have received geshe degrees from a Buddhist academy in Tibet, and that they had achieved the Five Vidyas upon passing a sutra debate. I already discussed the geshe degree in "Chapter 17—Testing in the Holy Realm," but this response also helps explain how diminished modern Buddhism is concerning what the Five Vidyas are and that they are not something that can be attained through sutra debates or scholarly discussions. "The Five Vidyas are the results of true realization power, not a sliver of the true essence of the Five Vidyas can be obtained through empty debates. One has to truly present results that can be seen. These results must be superior to the highest standards that experts can achieve."[55] The WBAH also comments on how misinterpreted the Five Vidyas are in Buddhism today in that they represent one single discipline and are limited to such pathetically simple matters like medicine, music, religious knowledge, crafts, etc.

The Craftsmanship Vidya, for example, "...is not just about being able to carve butter flowers, draw face masks, make Tangkas, create oil paintings, ink paintings, water-color paintings, pastel paintings, graphite sketches, wax crayon paintings, chalk paintings, or spray paintings, or make sculptures. Having accomplishment in all these aspects and surpassing experts of national standing still cannot be considered as having true Craftsmanship Vidya. There are infinite aspects to true Craftsmanship Vidya, which does not only include painting, but also construction, architecture, sand sculpting, sculpture, decoration, landscaping, scenic creation, lighting design, styling of clothes including shoes and hats, hair styling and ornamentation, wall hangings, curtain design and patterned decorative windows, interior furniture and interior design, color decorations of pavilions, colorful gift wrappings, knotting and ribboning, and even one's man-

---

55 *Op.cit. WBAH #20190101.*

nerism including how one carries oneself when one walks and sits, and in one's dignified presence, etc. One must attain the level of an international expert in every single aspect. Simply speaking, only when one attains the highest level of enjoyment in all things of beauty in the universe can one be considered to have attained the Craftsmanship Vidya."[56]

This vidya is usually referred to as craftsmanship or art and technology, but the Buddha Master told us it is also much more. It not only includes the ability to create works of art, like sculpture or painting, or technological innovations, but also anything where you express yourself— from making facial grimaces where you turn a frown into a smile, to applying makeup, to the clothes you wear. The Buddha Master warned us that to foolishly say that this only includes painting is wrong. "The Craftsmanship Vidya is much more than merely painting. If it were merely a craft like painting, then shouldn't Yun Sculpture not be part of the craftsmanship vidya? Shouldn't artistic sculptured landscape scenes also not be part of the Craftsmanship Vidya? Shouldn't the alteration and tailoring of clothing likewise not be part of the craftsmanship vidya? All of these are in fact part of the craftsmanship vidya. As I said a moment ago, haircutting or hairdressing is also part of the Craftsmanship Vidya. How a model walks on stage is part of the Craftsmanship Vidya. This is a type of artistic expression. Everything that is beautiful and artistic is included within the Craftsmanship Vidya. Whatever brings enjoyment and happiness to people is part of the Craftsmanship Vidya. Sitting in a dignified manner, as straight as a bell, totally conforming to the appearance of a member of the sangha, is also part of the Craftsmanship Vidya. The Craftsmanship Vidya contains the manifold changes. In short, things that embody that which is good and things of art are all part of the Craftsmanship Vidya. You must understand these things!"

H.H. Dorje Chang Buddha III also told us that the Craftsmanship Vidya represents the two aspects of our outward expression and our spirit. Our spirit is included in the Craftsmanship Vidya. Take, for example, the case where someone's spirit is full. How is it full? Such a person is very self-confident. He feels that the expression of his spirit is very beautiful. This is also part of the Craftsmanship Vidya. Some actors in plays have stage fright. Although on the surface they very much appear to have craftsmanship, their spirit lacks craftsmanship. When some people take the stage, not only do they appear well, they are full of spirit. They think that they will certainly be the best. Their spirit is very full. This spirit is part of the Craftsmanship Vidya. This is extremely profound.

Another example is the Healing Vidya, which is not just about curing hu-

---

56 *Ibid.*

man beings, animals and birds of their illnesses. "It also means having the ability to optimize conditions of and resolve the problems of living beings as well as inanimate objects. Only that can be considered the Healing Vidya."[57] It is fixing anything that is broken and/or improving anything. It also includes anything where you take something coarse or rough and then refine or correct it. It includes everything where something goes from a bad state to a better state. The Healing Vidya includes all activities that improve a situation or thing. For example, revising a draft manuscript, repairing a clock, or any other revision, repair, alteration, or activity that raises the quality of something is part of this vidya. Anything that is refined or changed to be good is considered part of the Healing Vidya in this ancient way of understanding universal principles.

This Vidya of Sound or speech does not simply involve spoken or written words or singing. H.H. Dorje Chang Buddha III once explained that singing is only part of the Sound Vidya. The Sound Vidya includes all types of sounds, such as the sound of breathing, the sound of an earthquake, the sound of an erupting volcano, the sound of a firearm, the sound of a gentle breeze in the forest, the sound of a roaring tsunami, the sound of an air whistle on a boat, the sound of buzzing insects, all of the intermingling sounds of nature within the universe such as the sound of flowing water; the sound of us debating, speaking, reciting literature; and so on and so forth. All sounds, produced by everything that can produce sound, that are pleasurable to living beings are included within the Sound Vidya. It can also involve hand gestures or other forms of communication. Broadly speaking, it also includes the ability to communicate with other species and types of living beings both on earth and beyond. His Holiness asked us, how could you say that the Sound Vidya is simply spoken words? Such an interpretation is terrible! The sound of rain is part of the Sound Vidya. All delightful sounds and any sound that is beneficial to living beings emitted from animate beings or inanimate things comprise the Sound Vidya.

I once asked His Holiness if a certain jazz musician who was so enthusiastic about His Holiness's calligraphy—who was attracted to the rhythms of the writing even though he knew no Chinese, maybe "heard" them? I was told, "Yes." There is an energy that can be felt and heard as well as seen and that is expressed in the Sound Vidya.

On another occasion the Buddha Master explained the Vidya of Causality or Buddhist logic. For example, this vidya is often translated as "logic" but it is not the logic of Western philosophy. It is the logic of the Law of Cause and Effect. Understanding this principle can enable you to see both past (causes) and

---

57 *Ibid.*

future (effects). His Holiness pointed to a lamp and explained that the darkness and lightness of this lamp creates different karmic reactions. There is one effect if the lamp is lit and another if it is turned off. When the lamp is in different positions it also creates different effects. He also picked up a teacup and explained the cause and effect of drinking the tea. Taking the lid off a teacup is the cause. Vapor or steam arising from the tea is the effect. Taking the cup in your hand and bringing it to your mouth is the cause. Slaking your thirst is the effect. He has given many, many examples of how this principle works— from the causes that result in a single hair falling to the collective karma of nations or groups of people that results in either prosperity or disaster. H.H. Dorje Chang Buddha III told us that the Causality Vidya relates to all matters and all Dharmas, all levels of conditional and unconditional phenomena, the entire logical relationship among them, the relationship of cause and effect, and so on. What the Causality Vidya covers is countless.

Inner Realization, is the hardest to understand and is unique to Buddhism. "...Inner Realization Vidya is the summation of the other four vidyas. This vidya refers to the high-level manifestation of inner realization power such as inner realization power of physical body that is exuded from one's appearance and that can be applied to external objects. One who has Inner Realization Vidya has transcended the ordinary and entered the holy realm, and They can communicate directly with Buddhas and Bodhisattvas. They are extraordinary, wondrous and majestic to the utmost."[58] It is often defined as inner science. For example, H.H. Dorje Chang Buddha III can use his inner skills or realization to understand all things in the universe like the palm of his hand. This includes everything about all sentient beings and all things without consciousness (non-sentient). He was able to answer the question raised by me concerning the Five Vidyas by means of this inner science. His inner science skills are transformed into wisdom. He then used speech skills to deliver the answer. His Holiness has told us that the internal vidya refers to inner realization powers. The Buddha Master said that these inner realization powers are very deep. There are the inner-tantric initiations. At the highest level, this includes the magnificent, limitless, complete, and perfect enlightenment powers of the Buddha. It includes the ability to hide Mount Sumeru in a tiny mustard seed. All of this is part of the inner realization of the inner vidya. Some people say, "This inner vidya is actually supernormal powers!" It includes the accomplishment state of the Buddhas and Bodhisattvas. Such enlightenment and realization states are included within the Inner Realization Vidya. Understanding one's mind and seeing one's original nature is a state of realization that is part of the Inner Realization Vidya. Although it is certainly

---

58 Ibid.

putting "...into practice the Buddha's speech..." and revealing "...these teachings to others," as Asanga said, it is certainly also a lot more.

H.H. Dorje Chang Buddha III explained that some acts are connected with more than one vidya. Take, for example, a barber or hairdresser. The act of cutting hair belongs to the Craftsmanship Vidya. However, taking a bad head of hair and fixing it up belongs to the Healing Vidya. For another example, a car breaks down. When a car repairman takes that broken car and fixes it, that is called the Healing Vidya. Yet another example is when there is a weather imbalance and it does not rain. A few projectiles are shot into the air that stir up [seed] the clouds and cause rain. This method of handling the problem is a type of healing of the earth. It is also part of the Healing Vidya. Another example would be when problems arise during your meditation. You request the Master to point out where you are making mistakes and how to get on the right path. The Master's instruction will cause you to visualize correctly and show you how not to be attached to phenomena. That is also part of the Healing Vidya. In short, the Healing Vidya includes that which is huge in the universe as well as that which is as minuscule as dust.

Thus, H.H. Dorje Chang Buddha III told us that the Five Vidyas are not just five items of science or knowledge. Casually select a tiny part of any of the Five Vidyas, and you will see that it contains thousands of scientific items. Isn't labeling the Five Vidyas as the five sciences a form of trampling upon the Buddha Dharma? We should expose anyone in the present or past who spoke of the Five Vidyas in such a way, whether he be a Dharma king, great rinpoche, or great Dharma master, for such a person cannot represent the mind-seal teachings of the Buddha. Mastery of the Five Vidyas is the perfect realization of the magnificent Buddha. It is a brilliant achievement that can be manifested. This is the Five Vidyas.

Only a very great Dharma king or Buddha could understand and expound on these principles in their entirety. When H.H. Dorje Chang Buddha III gave the impromptu discourse on which much of this chapter is based, the dozen or so disciples in the room were radiant and extremely appreciative. It was a very auspicious and wonderful occasion. I must humbly offer my apologies and beg forgiveness for what I captured from the translation of that magical moment, but I felt it was so wonderful that I wanted to share it with others, even though I am sure this account inadequately expresses what was said.

The Buddha Master demonstrated accomplishment in all of the activities identified by Asanga, and so much more. It is not so much that what other religions offer and what we have now in Buddhism are wrong, but rather, so incomplete. It shows how much we have lost of the power of the true Buddha

Dharma and why H.H. Dorje Chang Buddha III came back to this world to show us that power. Different Buddhist sects and also certain non-Buddhist groups understand some aspects of these vidyas, but only a Buddha can understand these universal truths in their entirety. This knowledge was the Buddha's awakening—His "Enlightenment." These five principles existed before the coming of the Buddha and were not changed or altered by the arrival of the Buddha. However, the Buddha was able to comprehend the inner-most truth of these principles and thus gain their power. That is part of what is meant by the term Buddha Dharma. Dharma is a Sanskrit term that can have different meanings in different contexts. It is usually thought of as the holy teachings of the Buddha (capitalized as Dharma), but it is also used to mean all phenomena or the universal principles underlying all phenomena. When you understand the meaning of Buddha Dharma, you can see that these meanings are not different. You can also understand just how marvelous the true Buddha-dharma is and the power it has to transform.

Achievements in the Five Vidyas represent the highest accomplishments in the Buddha Dharma, and the highest comprehension of both the conditional and unconditional worlds. They are what holy beings do, pure and simple—they represent the realization of holy beings. How could anyone be called a holy being who could not show mastery in at least some of the Five Vidyas? Buddhist books tell us about the accomplishments that a true vajra master must possess. They mention that an accomplished one should excel in all Five Vidyas, yet most who claim to be masters cannot demonstrate proficiency in all of these areas. Even the famous historic Dharma kings have not reached the levels manifested by H.H. Dorje Chang Buddha III. In the current world there are certainly no others who can reach this level! He is able to obtain the help of the devas and the Dharma protectors, at any time, to help him with his work. These devas and Dharma protectors can accomplish things at thousands of times the speed of ordinary human beings. Some of H.H. Dorje Chang Buddha III's works of art would have taken decades to be completed by conventional means, yet His Holiness can turn out masterpieces in only a few hours or sometimes even a few minutes. I know. I have seen His Holiness start a work of art and I have come back a few hours later and seen a completed masterpiece. Some of H.H. Dorje Chang Buddha III's art-work resembles withered vines or petrified wood or ancient coral that takes thousands of years for nature to produce, yet when His Holiness called the deities to help, they aged in a matter of minutes.

When I first introduced H.H. Dorje Chang Buddha III's achievements at an exhibition in Southern California in 2006, I started by saying that everything that was seen—all 200 examples of 18 different categories of work—were from the Buddha Dharma. H.H. Dorje Chang Buddha III is an extremely accomplished artist, poet, writer, inventor, etc., because He has complete realization of the Buddha Dharma. His manifestation of prajna wisdom or the various vidyas as seen in His art and innovations exceeds that of any other Dharma king in history. And these exhibits were only a very small sampling of the creative genius of this great being! They did not include His Holiness's work as a healer, nor His accomplishments in the martial arts, nor His musical achievements, nor His holy writings and discourses, etc.—all of which are considerable. Although I used those words to introduce my Buddha Master, I did not yet know He was a Buddha, nor did I really understand the truth of what I had said or anything about the Five Vidyas.

Remember what Penor Rinpoche said in 2008. He told me that my Master was much higher than he was and that it was a good thing that such a high being should incarnate in these Dharma-ending days. He also said that such a being should demonstrate many miracles and supernatural powers.

In a recent class given on the Five Vidyas during which I shared an early draft of this chapter, I asked the students how they felt the Five Vidyas impacted their lives and practice. The results were quite insightful. One student, a very talented craftsman, said he now realized that what he had always done for any-one needing something fixed was a kind of healing—making the world better, a Bodhisattva act. Of course, it was also part of the Craftsmanship Vidya. I told another story of a friend, a gifted pianist who would go to nursing homes to play, only to find the pianos there to be woefully in need of tuning. He then taught himself how to tune pianos and proceeded to "heal" the nursing home pianos as well as perform the Sound Vidya of bringing joy to others. Another student, a professional dancer from Mexico, told how she and her partner, who are also disciples of H.H. Dorje Chang Buddha III, started dancing for those in shelters, prisons, nursing homes, and the like. They had to hold benefits to raise money to do this, but they found that they were not only spiritually rewarded, but were able to perform in places they never thought possible, and started receiving anonymous donations. They even danced for H.H. Dorje Chang Bud-dha III. The Five Vidyas are just what Bodhisattvas do.

It is important to realize that this mastery and very high level of accom-plishment is available to all who learn and practice the correct Buddha Dharma. We, too, can acquire this marvelous transformative power.

twenty-three

Your Yidam

In His book *Learning from Buddha,* H.H. Dorje Chang Buddha III provides the definitive definition of "Buddha-Dharma." He gives a one-sentence summary stating that "In Buddhism, the perfect practice of the preliminary practice, main practice, and concluding practice is called Buddha Dharma." This practice relates to "Yidam" practice. I am not going to discuss how you do these practices. You can read about them in *Learning from Buddha,* which is now available online in English. I do want to share my observations and experiences about an important aspect of this Buddha Dharma—your relationship with your Yidam.

The Buddha Master tells us that "**your Yidam is the holy being presiding over the particular Dharma you decide to practice in order to attain accomplishment.**" The Buddha Master also tells us we have to face our Yidam and the Dharma protectors of our Yidam. And you cannot hide from either your Yidam or the Dharma Protectors. You may wonder how you know who your Yidam is. As you advance in your practice, you may receive a particular Dharma of Selection and be told who your Yidam is. As I understand it, this is probably a being that you have already achieved some accomplishments with in past lives and you are already familiar with the Dharma associated with that Yidam. Many of us start this practice with Kuan Yin Bodhisattva as our Yidam and follow the "Vajra Yoga Perfection Dharma" that you can find in *True Stories about a Holy Monk.* Many different other Bodhisattvas or Buddhas can serve as yidams including Shakyamudi Buddha, Amitabha Buddha, Green Tara, Manjurshri Bodhisattva, or Sarvanivarana-Vishkambhin. You may be fortunate to receive other Yidam practices from authentic Dharma masters and rinpoches. However, you only do one Yidam practice at a time, but you may also follow different Yidams through the course of your spiritual career as you evolve in your spiritual practices. (FIGURE 85)

FIGURE 85: My painting of the Female Buddha, Green Tara.

I was told that if you cannot receive a Dharma of Selection, you may select the Yidam for whom you have the greatest affinity. In fact, you do not pick the Yidam, the Yidam actually picks you. However, you must continue your cultivation, keep your precepts, and not hold any of the "128 Evil and Erroneous Views" denoted in the *Supreme and Unsurpassable Mahamudra of Liberation* for this to happen

Do not be frustrated if something is not clear. If you are not progressing in your Yidam practice, go back and reflect on your cultivation. You should be doing this three times per day anyhow. If you are not keeping the precepts or developing your bodhichitta, you cannot progress. If your cultivation is good, your Yidam may come and teach you what you need to know. I have had that happen as have several of my students.

Once I was not clear on how to visualize a particular mantra and my Yidam showed me how to do it. I have a student who does not live near California and who is unable to visit either the Buddha Master or me very often. He is a serious, sincere, and compassionate cultivator and does have a very good relationship with his Yidam. She has helped him on many matters. I recently received an email from him telling me how much he had gained from his last trip to the Holy Vajrasana Temple and being able to study *Imparting the Absolute Truth through the Heart Sutra*. Even though he was only able to study this Dharma a short time this trip, he gained realizations which he didn't get in all the previous years he had studied here. He said, "It made a deep impact on my life and I am very grateful that I was able to read even this little bit of it. Since then I was reflecting even more on how our daily lives relate to achieving accomplishment in the Dharma, how cultivation and Dharma practice need to go together. I often compared it with breathing, like inhaling and exhaling following one another and both are necessary to keep [your] life working. This morning I received an instruction from [my Yidam] on this topic while I was doing my Dharma practice which I would like to share with you."

He went on to explain that his Yidam told him that he should see that cultivation is like collecting firewood. Doing a Dharma practice is like igniting a fire. If we have not collected enough wood (or any at all) the fire of wisdom cannot burn. So even a kind thought is like a dry twig that will fuel the fire. Cultivating ourselves seriously and not slipping in any moment is like piling up a huge amount of firewood which will cause the fire to burn strongly and result in accomplishments.

I was delighted. He said I could share the teaching as an example of how our Yidams do teach us, but we must do the practice and cultivate our behavior. The Buddha Master tells us in *Learning from Buddha* that if you learn one of the Mind Essences from *The Supreme and Unsurpassable Mahamudra of Liberation* ..."to the point of proficiency and put it into practice, you need not worry about not being able to learn Buddha Dharma. Even if I, your Master, do not teach you, the Yidam will teach you."

twenty-four
What I Did

In October 2019 a Chinese documentary was made about Buddhism in general and the role of H.H. Dorje Chang Buddha III and His teachings in society, and the impact they are having and will continue to have on society. The China International Education TV from Beijing interviewed me and other senior students of the Buddha Master at our temples. They filmed the Holy Vajrasana Temple and the Holy Vajra Poles. Senior students and the abbots of other temples were asked other questions, but I was asked, "For Buddhism as a universal religion, besides promoting and inheriting the traditions, in which areas can we explore to adapt it to the modern world, to satisfy the religious needs of the mundane world, and to connect it with the values of the civil society, so that the development of Buddhism can sustain itself forever?" We were given several options on questions to answer and I picked this one. It was a subject that I had thought most about. It was one of the factors that prompted me to write this book. How can the correct teachings of Buddhism become an integrated part of our modern world and be sustained in that world? I had been drawn to the Buddha Master because I felt in my heart—long before I even suspected that He was a Buddha—that His teachings of Buddhism were like what I imagined the original teachings of Shakyamuni Buddha were like when He walked on this earth. That was what I had been looking for. Only, the Buddha Master was presenting them in ways that were adapted to the modern world in which we lived. My passion, my wish was to be able to help bring what He so marvelously taught us to the English-speaking world.

Given that, my answer to the question posed by The China International Education TV was, "H.H. Dorje Chang Buddha III has told us that we must work to uphold the laws and aspirations of our nations and live together in harmony with others. The other unique and powerful influence of Buddhism is that it is inclusive of all, thus enabling it to have influence over other religions and belief systems. It does not promote dogma or teach that other belief systems are intrinsically evil. It does not require loyalty to any worldly leader. We have no pope or worldly hierarchy. One can remain Christian or Jewish or Daoist or what have you and still practice the Buddhist path and become an enlightened or holy being—a Bodhisattva.

"I remember H.H. Dorje Chang Buddha III advising me before I spoke to a group of young Catholic men that not all Bodhisattvas are Buddhist. That is how Buddhism spread to other countries, it absorbed much of the local customs, including the local deities, while teaching the methods of enlightenment taught by Shakyamuni Buddha. H.H. Dorje Chang Buddha III has given those of us living in the modern world the *Supreme and Unsurpassable Mahamudra of Liberation* that is available at many levels to enable us to become enlightened and be free of all suffering. One does not need to become a Buddhist to learn and practice this Dharma.

"We are building a Buddhist village around Holy Heavenly Lake in Hesperia, California that will serve as a model and center for Buddhist and non-Buddhist alike to come and learn and practice the Dharma; enjoy Buddhist art and architecture; and experience the spirit of Buddhism from a variety of different cultures. I plan on building a small temple and center there to help serve local English and Spanish speaking followers using indigenous adobe structures and "hermit caves" for those wishing to do long-term intensive retreats. I am also hoping to introduce some local Native Bodhisattvas to help make the teachings of the Buddha more 'real' for local people."

They only used the first paragraph of my answer in the documentary, but I thought the rest of the answer captures my intent for the work I am doing or want to do in this world, and how I want to apply what I have both "seen" and "heard" from my Buddha Master. It sparked something in me that caused me to have hope again—to face my demons and stop being so chicken-like, and to reevaluate what I was doing. What was working and what was not? Why was this so? What could I do?

In order to realize that dream of reaching out to make the Dharma more real for local people, I had started several initiatives in addition to what I had been doing at the Holy Vajrasana Temple in Sanger to bring the true Dharma brought to this world by my beloved Buddha Master and that reestablished the original teachings held by Shakyamuni Buddha for our modern times. I would add this book as another initiative as well. I was particularly interested in sharing the teaching of the Buddha with non-Buddhists. Although you do not need to become a Buddhist to benefit from the teachings of the Buddha, if you continue to study Buddhism, I do believe your relationship to your original beliefs will evolve.

The initiative that I felt was most personally rewarding was work I had started with the prison community of women at the Central California Women's Facility at Chowchilla, California. I had dropped it when I was not able to go there because of my health and other restraints. The second initiative was the community of Spanish-speaking Buddhists, started in Northern California, but also on hold. The third was the start-up Dharma center in the Mojave Desert at the Holy Heavenly Lake site of the future Ancient Buddha Temple and Buddhist Village that we started in January 2020. These all had potential, but then the pandemic hit, and everything came to a stop. Let's see what the pandemic did, but first let us look at each of these communities.

I still had faith in the Buddha and the Dharma, but in myself—not so much. Long before the virus, I had scheduled the month of June 2020 to be free of all events—no retreats, no trips, nothing. I would devote myself to the Dharma and beseech the Buddhas and Bodhisattvas to help. They always did when I asked, but I had been too depressed or maybe embarrassed to ask. I knew that was wrong, but I lacked the will to change. It did not work out that way. I did not go on retreat. Instead, I wrote this book and devoted my time to the work of establishing and supporting an International Lemonade Sangha. I will explain how that happened, but first, let me tell what happened to the other three initiatives.

2018—Chowchilla Sangha

Part of the vow I took after conducting the Kuan Yin Bodhisattva's Great Compassion Dharma Assemblies that were discussed earlier, was the vow to contribute any offerings made during those assemblies to freeing captive living beings. In most cases this involved releasing captive wild animals, insects, birds, or marine life, but I wanted to do something for captive human beings who were held in our local prisons, too. Normally this action must be done within a few days after the event, but I got a dispensation because of the red tape involved in doing anything in the California state prison system. I could send them Buddhist books and buy Dharma instruments for their chapels (after extensive and time-consuming vetting), but what else could I do? Most of our books were still in Chinese.

I developed a strong desire to do prison work after returning from the Standing Rock Sioux reservation in September 2016. I had traveled there with Gesang Suolang Rinpoche and met Bhikshunni Pannavati and other Buddhists to join the Dakota Access Pipeline protests and to see first-hand what was happening, to show support for their cause, and to join the Oceti Sakowin[59] camp (FIGURE 86). Gesang and I had also gone on to the small Mandan, North Da-

---

59 *The proper name for the people commonly known as the Sioux is Oceti Sakowin, meaning Seven Council Fires. Each of the Seven Council Fires was made up of individual bands, which were based on kinship, location and dialect — Lakota, Dakota or Nakota.*

FIGURE 86: Standing Rock Encampment—our camp was under the tree with the maroon and saffron Eternal Knot Tibetan door hanging from the tree.

kota, jail for a separate protest concerning a native woman who was incarcerated there. All of this caused me to remember a vivid vision I had had many years ago where I was told I should help those in prisons. I was also told to construct a tipi and paint it with certain symbols, which I did, but that is another story. I had tried to do work with prisoners when working with the Kickapoo Nation while I was in Kansas and often asked for guidance of tribal leaders on what I could do. Finally, a wise Pottawatomie Medicine Man told me, "Know that not all prisons have walls." With that I proceeded along other paths, but that mandate was always there to work with those who did have physical walls confining them. When I came back to the temple from the Standing Rock reservation, I was determined to do something to bring the correct Dharma to inmates. After I explained what I wanted to do to my Buddha Master, He was delighted and encouraged me to do so.

I started by contacting a Buddhist Chaplain group I had trained with earlier in the San Francisco Bay Area. I remembered that some of the group were working in prisons. I had not been able to join the class field trip to San Quentin[60], but I serendipitously received an invitation to a seminar on prison

60 *San Quentin, is a notorious maximum security state prison for men in Marin County, just north of San Francisco. It has California's only death row for male inmates and the largest in the United States, holding 700 condemned men in 2015 with a capacity for 715. Chowchilla has the only death row for*

chaplain work being sponsored by the group, I believe the same weekend after I arrived home from Standing Rock. I signed up and went to the Bay Area for the seminar and a reunion of my fellow students. I was able to find out from the other students where the closest prison to our temple might be. It turned out that perhaps the largest female prison in the world was less than 45 minutes away from the temple, north of Fresno, near Chowchilla. There had been two women's correctional institutions there, but as they reduced the population of female prisoners, one had been converted to male use. I stopped to check them out on my way home from the Bay Area Chaplain seminar. That only gave me a glimpse of their bleak exterior and the name of the person to contact about visiting the facilities. I contacted the most delightful rabbi who was not only in charge of the Jewish prisoners, but also had those who were or considered themselves to be Buddhists. As it turned out, he was interested in doing more to seek out those of Buddhist persuasion or interested in Buddhist practice and was very eager to have some help. The California State system does not have any Buddhist Chaplains, even though they have every other conceivable group represented. In recent years there had been a lot of emphasis on religious freedom and meeting the inmates' spiritual needs. So, after personal TB tests and much red tape, I was given permission to enter the prison and meet with the twenty to thirty women there who were interested in Buddhism.

I tried to meet at least once a month with this group of inmates. Seven women took refuge. Since the women hold jobs at the prison and cannot always arrange their schedules to attend our classes and services and are both released and transferred to other facilities, it was often a different group that attended each session. It was challenging, but very rewarding. The women are amazing, eager to learn the Dharma, and very insightful. Not all of the group I met with are "releasable" but are "lifers" —some with no hope of parole. They understand impermanence and karma—in spades. It is something they face head-on every day. I do not think that is true for all of the women in the prison, but for the ones who find their way to Buddhism, it is true. One of the most serious students is like this. She is not only working on herself; she works to bring others to the Dharma as well. I am very impressed with these women and their spiritual capacity and affinity with the Dharma.

Guard towers located around the octagon-shaped site are occupied by armed guards keeping a watchful eye on the inmates. I was not allowed to wear

female prisoners, but they would be transported to San Quentin for execution should that happen, as San Quentin has the State's only execution chamber. There has not been an execution there since 2006. San Quentin was also the site of a major scandal during the Covid-19 outbreak when infected prisoners from another prison were carelessly shipped there, infecting and killing many of the San Quentin prisoners.

maroon or any other colors worn by the inmates–they even confiscated a chartreuse handkerchief I once had with me. They are very careful about anything that can be used for gang communication. And, yes, the women have gangs that control their behavior both inside and outside the prison walls. I also found they have alcohol (known as pruno, hooch, or toilet wine)— being very resourceful in what they use to ferment what I understand is a deadly brew. I found this out because one prospect told me she could not take refuge when she found out what our five precepts entail. I had not anticipated that.

The chapel is a sort of oasis where the women can go to participate in spiritual programs of just about anything you can imagine. I witnessed a very touching scene where one of the inmates came to see the chapel staff to give a teary-eyed goodbye after she just found she had been released. It seemed she didn't really want to go. It is scary on the outside, too. The chaplains and religious volunteers were special.

Things are very severe and whatever you are doing can be interrupted at any time by blaring loudspeakers announcing where you need to be or what you need to do. It is hard to find time to concentrate, but the women here seem to be able to do it. All the inmates are counted several times during the day. Once there was some sort of disturbance when I was leaving, and all the women had to instantly drop and remain on the ground until control was reinstated. With armed marksmen watching every move and having authorization to shoot. You do not deviate from protocols. They installed video cameras everywhere in the Chapel after I started going there, so we were constantly under surveillance as well. And the rules concerning what you can and cannot do are maddening—no hardbound books or notebook binders are permitted. It is amazing what can be weaponized. They warned us at orientation that the system does not negotiate to release hostages. Once I had my own "brown-card," I could at least bring a suitcase in with my books and lunch, but before, I could not even carry a purse. Once, all of the chaplains were away from the chapel for a short time and I was given the alarm to carry on me. I am not sure what would have happened if I had pushed the alarm bell, but I was warned that I would not want to find out and I believe the person who warned me.

I finally did get a glimpse of what the rest of the prison, aside from the Chapel, was like and how some women lived when I was taken to the "Condemned Housing" where the inmates with death sentences and those considered more dangerous were housed. It was not what I expected. The good rabbi warned me that there was no way he could describe the experience and he was right. This is the only facility in the state having a death row for females. There were 23 or 24 women, of which five had indicated they are or want to be Buddhists. I believe all those on death row have been convicted of murdering at least one person. Some have been there for over 20 years. Several have exhausted all hope of parole or appeal. At present the State is not executing anyone, but that could change at any moment. California has not abolished the death penalty. I was only able to meet three of the Buddhist women there and spend time with two, but I still hope to return. There is no place to sit, and you have to put on an armored vest to enter, but they are so eager to learn Dharma that it is worth the effort. They do have access to some books and just discovered a correspondence course from I think the Amitabha Buddhist Society, a Pure Land Group. I am not allowed to offer any correspondence-like program since I have physical access to the prisoners. You cannot do both. I did donate as many books as I could along with certain Dharma instruments. I have acquired several supplies of malas (Buddhist rosaries) that some of the women wanted and could have if they met the strict prison standards. So far, I have not been able to give them malas. One set was too big, another had tiny metal beads, and so on. Everything is heavily vetted.

I had to stop visiting the prison because of restrictions on visitors and my failing health issues. I miss the classes and the inmates very much. I suspect I learned as much as anyone. I am not sure if I will ever be able to return and that saddens me. The chapel is a long walk deep within the prison and I am not at present physically able to make the trek. Perhaps when the Covid pandemic is over and it is safer to go out, I will be able to meet them at the prison again, but for now it may be best that I develop another means to communicate with them.

2019—Spanish Sangha and Bilingual Classes

Last year, I met a young Hispanic man from Ecuador who wanted very much to learn more about the Dharma and was quite interested in the Buddha Master. He had studied and practiced Buddhism for years and it shows. I think he found me via our temple website. He has a young and quite spiritual wife from El Salvador and young children. She still has limited English skills, so he would try to translate any of the English readings that I gave. They lived near an Amtrak line in Stockton, California that also runs to Fresno as well as the Bay area. The train schedule was such that I could arrive and leave the same day and still have enough time for a class, enjoy lunch with them, and return before nighttime. I could handle that. Other Spanish students were able to join us from the bay area and several local non-Spanish speakers came as well. Another excellent translator joined the group and the two translators worked very well together to translate whatever I would read from the Buddha Master. They were wonderful classes. Those of us who did not understand Spanish also benefited from the process and the discussions (FIGURE 87). Our hosts had to relocate to

San Jose to be closer to work and we started holding the Spanish Sangha classes at Hua Zang Si (FIGURE 88) until the novel corona virus of 2019 hit.

FIGURE 87: Reba Jinbo Rinpoche with Blanca and Edwin Miranda at their home in Stockton, California during a dharma class for the Spanish Sangha in Stockton, California.

FIGURE 88: Class for Spanish Sangha at Hua Zang Si in San Francisco, California. Zhengzhi Shi helped with the drum and bells

Perhaps we will be able to start online classes with Spanish translation when we recover from the pandemic. We could reach more students that way, as there are Hispanic students in southern California who would benefit from these classes as well. Hesperia, where we now have a new Dharma center and hope to build another temple has a sizable Hispanic population, too.

2020—Xuanfa Holy Heavenly Lake Dharma Center at Hesperia

Remember in 2014 when I was told that I should move my long-term retreat center and start another temple for Western students in the desert in southern California? Well, that site is located in the small modest town of Hesperia in the Mojave Desert. Our site has 130 or so acres next to the usually dry Mojave River and contains a beautiful lake. It had been a sort of horse ranch and equestrian center with facilities for weddings and the like around the lake. I learned that the lake was a very special place, located on underground aquifers and the location of powerful crystals (FIGURE 89). It was a holy site and was going to become an even holier site as my Buddha Master was planning on building His residence there along with His Ancient Buddha Temple. It was to be developed as a Buddhist village with a series of canals connected to this magical lake. Different Buddhist groups would build their temples there. Others would develop shops and businesses related to the activities of the temple—a sort of Buddhist Vatican City. My plans are to start another temple or Dharma center for non-Chinese speakers and have facilities for long-term retreats.

FIGURE 89: Zhizang Shi (Sonya) at Heavenly Lake, Hesperia, California.

On the first Sunday in January, 2020, we held our first class in temporary quarters. We now have 27 members of our Meetup group and several continued attending the online classes after we could no longer go to Hesperia because of the quarantine. One regular drives from Scottsdale, another from Salt Lake City, and several more come from San Diego and the Los Angeles area. I am very enthusiastic about this group, too. True, we are sort of in the middle of nowhere in the Mojave Desert, but we are also where H.H. Dorje Chang Buddha III will be moving and have his main temple, and I still hope to start another Holy Vajrasana Temple there with Long-term Meditation Caves (FIGURE 90). For now, I will continue meeting with them via the virtual Lemonade Sangha.

FIGURE 90: Model of Proposed Long-term Adobe Meditation Cave/Hermitage.

So, what is the Lemonade Sangha? In early Spring of 2020, the Covid-19 pandemic outbreak caused us to close the temple to visitors and retreatants and stopped any travel or holding of classes anywhere. I had wanted to do distant learning for some time. We had started the Xuanfa Five Vidyas University in 2012 and did reach a few students. My intent was to enable us to have a program that allowed for long-term retreats by students from China who needed student visas to be here that long. Of course, it would serve other purposes as well, but there were few Western students who were any way close to being able to do a three-year plus retreat and the Chinese students who were, needed student visas. I did hold a number of Seven-Dharma System Seminars on various topics that were also helpful. I wanted it to be part of the XFVU program, but that never really worked out. I finally stopped XFVU, at least until we could get approved English translations of the major texts by the Buddha Master and hopefully of several of His discourses. That may still happen and with the use of Zoom meetings we may be able to offer those programs again.

When the virus was just beginning to have an impact on us, the rabbi chaplain at the women's prison called me, to see if I was ok. The Chowchilla Sangha was concerned about my well-being. That was a wake-up call. I was so ashamed. I should have been calling about them. I immediately wrote them a long letter advising them on what they could do during the lock down and promised to keep them up-to-date with what was happening with me and our temple by sending them edited Blog articles. I was too late. The rabbi's email sent back an automated message that he was not able to be at the prison either. That initiative was on hold, but it fired me up to start the Lemonade Sangha.

I talked with several of my students and we all agreed our lives were not that different. In fact, this sheltered-in-place order was not all bad. It gave us more time to devote to our practice and an opportunity to reassess our lives and recharge and reflect on our Dharma and cultivation practice. So out of this lemon called Covid-19 or the Corona Virus, we made lemonade. I wanted to start this effort as an invitation-only event. We were warned about zoom-bombers who were crashing many Zoom projects. That might create bad karma for anyone tempted to profane the Dharma.

I started with a mailing list of over 160 selected from the people who had been frequently opening my blog. The first Zoom based class on "What Is Cultivation?" was quite successful. There were over 75 who registered from eight different countries for either the Sunday afternoon classes or the related open mike discussion groups held every Saturday morning during the first four-week period. Over 35 persons participated in at least half of the class sessions. We will continue these events as long as there is interest. I suspected that when we were no longer under house arrest, the attendance would diminish as people became "busy" again. That happened, but not so much. There was a core group that remained interested.

We also started virtual morning services Monday through Friday at 6:00 am and at 7:00 am on Sundays. I pledged to continue the Saturday morning discussion forums or open mike sessions and the Sunday afternoon classes. These hours enable students from both Europe and Asia as well as all of North America to participate.

This virtual temple may be our primary temple and it was certainly the fire I needed to both do what I needed to do with my practice and to sit down and write this book. I want to reaffirm that the Dharma does work—that the Buddhas and Bodhisattvas and Dharma Protectors will support you, if you let them. You still have to be open to that help and have faith in yourself. You do need to be that phoenix and rise up again and again. I am reminded of a Christian saying that the only difference between a saint and a sinner is that the saint never gave up. That applies to becoming a holy person in the Buddhist sense as well. The Dharma is wonderful and powerful and the empowerments may help clean out hindrances and obstacles, but the key is what you do. This practice is driven by you and the fact that you do have a Buddha Nature that is the same as that of all who have become holy beings— as do all living beings. The Buddhas can show us the path. We have to follow it ourselves.

twenty-five

What Can You Do?

In this book, I tried to convey my personal experiences on tour, at the temple and beyond, and to describe my own awakening through the various teachings, empowerments, and initiations I was most fortunate to receive. That was intended to show what is possible. But how does that help you, the reader? As of the time this book was written, there are still very few Dharma discourses or Dharma texts available in English for you to study and follow and you may not be able to learn directly from the Buddha Master or receive His empowerments and initiations. What can you do? I've given a lot of thought to this matter and usually end up feeling very sad. I must confess to shedding many tears over this matter and the fact that more do not yet have the karmic affinity to learn the true Buddha Dharma. What I want to share here is my best take on what you can do if you cannot read or understand Chinese, because we do have the foundational teachings in English. And I am going to assume a few more critical texts will be published by the time this book is published, or soon thereafter. All of this is to help those who cannot understand Chinese learn the true Buddha Dharma. This simple book is intended to help augment all these efforts.

I already told you the Buddha Master told me in a dream how I should propagate the Dharma when He helped me develop the logo for the Xuanfa Institute. He said I should use the following seven jewels to propagate the Dharma.

1. Good Fortune: Following the teachings of the Buddha can enable you to have good health, wealth, to avoid disasters, and enable you to have the resources you need to be able to both practice the Dharma and bring others to the Dharma.

2. Holy Manifestations or Miracles: I have shared some of my experiences with the supernatural abilities of holy beings who do follow the teachings of the Buddha.

3. Five Vidyas: Following the Buddha's words you, too, can obtain super-normal powers and extraordinary skills and learn how to behave like a Buddha or Great Bodhisattva. These are explained in Chapter Twenty-Three.

4. Wisdom: You need to study and practice *Imparting the Absolute Truth Through the Heart Sutra* and other texts as per the following strategy to learn the correct Buddha Dharma.

5. Compassion: See Chapter Twenty-Two and the following strategy.

6. Sainthood: See Appendix B on the paths to develop your wisdom and compassion to become a Holy Person or Saint.

7. Enlightenment: You are able to escape the suffering of samsara and will ultimately become a Buddha.

This strategy for learning the correct Buddha Dharma has not been approved by the Buddha Master, so it can only be offered as background research. It is only what I have observed, heard, and experienced. Please quickly develop your wisdom to be able to know what is true and take what works for you.

I believe with all my heart that H.H. Dorje Chang Buddha III offers us a system of practice that can enable us to have good fortune and happiness in this life and the ability to become holy persons so that we can also become accomplished in our compassion and wisdom to end the cycle of birth and death in samsara and to be able to truly help other living beings—all our relations. His teachings represent the original Buddha Dharma taught by Shakyamuni Buddha over 2,500 years ago that has enabled many to become enlightened and be liberated from the painful cycle of birth and death. He has corrected errors in understanding and translation that have crept into what we think of as Buddhism today and presented the truths known and revealed by Shakyamuni Buddha. And He does so in succinct, understandable, and direct ways that are appropriate for this time and place.

I will continue to share what I have in preliminary translations at our temple and any other way I can for as long as I can. And I will continue to practice the Dharma I have and cultivate myself. We must all pray that official and correct translations be quickly made available in English and available to everyone.

twenty-six

Published Works in English by or about H.H. Dorje Chang Buddha III

The Big Blue Treasure Book, *H.H. Dorje Chang Buddha III*

This amazing book contains the documentation of who H.H. Dorje Chang Buddha III is, how we know that to be true, and evidence of His mastery of the Five Vidyas. It also includes many important teachings, but only one "What Is Cultivation?" is translated into English. This is a book that gives some context to who the Buddha Master is and His teachings. This is the book we distributed and discussed in the Dharma Propagation Tour we did in 2008-2009 (FIGURE 21 page 68). The main sections of the book were published both in English and Chinese. The best source of this or any of the books mentioned below is Dharma Voice Publishing, LLC: at 656 East San Bernardino Road, Covina, CA 91723, U.S.A.

Cultivation of Character and Cultivation of the Mind

I start with the understanding that we need to develop both our character and our minds, in other words, our compassion and wisdom (prajna). And we need different strategies for each. The first we do through cultivation in the world using concrete actions and the second through cultivation of our mind with concentration (zen) and the practice of certain dharmas. There are many methods. The following teachings will usually focus on one or the other or sometimes on both. You can find all of the online references below at the temple website (https://holyvajrasana.org) unless another reference is provided. I try to offer classes either at the temple or online on these sutras. You can find a current temple schedule again on the temple website or find links to the online features on my weekly blog at https://zhaxizhuoma.org. You may also find some of these references at https://www.wbahq.org, the website for the World Buddhism Association Headquarters.

The Dharma of Cultivation

The good news is we have translations of this most fundamental Dharma in English: *The Dharma of Cultivation Transmitted by H.H. Dorje Chang Buddha III* also known as the Dharma discourse *"What Is Cultivation?"* This is what you need to get started and to guide you throughout your journey on the path to enlightenment. I talked about it at the many presentations given on the Big Blue Book while touring the fifty states as it is the main introduction to the Buddha's Dharma in that book—at least in English. I have included several quotes from that book in this book.

The Dharma of Cultivation is based on a discourse given by H.H. Dorje Chang Buddha III in response to a question raised by a rinpoche (me) concerning how to best propagate the Dharma to Western students. It was such a special transmission that it was included in the treasure book *H.H. Dorje Chang Buddha III* in both Chinese and English. When the discourse was given, beings came from the holy realms and illuminated the room.[61] It is the foundation that everyone needs to understand how to manage your karma and ultimately become a Buddha. Without this Dharma and the actual practice of this Dharma, it is doubtful that any of the other Dharmas will be effective. This text is included online in English and other languages.

The Great Dharma of Zen Practice

This teaching is to help you develop your mind—to acquire wisdom, transcendental wisdom or prajna. You can find the *Great Dharma of Zen* in Appendix A of this book and online. This translation of a discourse originally intended for Western students provides background on the origin of zen practice, as well as instruction on how to do the meditation practice and instructions on how to remove obstacles to practice. Unlike other zen practice manuals, this Dharma also introduces three mantras that will help you be able to meditate. The mantras are not included online or in this book. Holy Dharma like this cannot be transmitted electronically. You need to be transmitted those by a vajra master who has the authority to transmit them.

I pleaded with the Buddha Master for years to provide meditation instructions but was always told I needed to practice cultivation first. I needed to understand impermanence, then I needed to have firm belief. With such a foundation, I needed a mind determined to leave the cycle of reincarnation. Then I would be ready to make true vows and be able to develop a mind of diligence. After that I would be ready to receive precepts, and only then would I finally be a suitable

---

61 *This encounter with the holy beings is described on page 52"*

235

vessel to learn meditation. The eighth right view of proper cultivation was bodhichitta. All eight if these right views need to be acquired in the proper sequence.

Supreme and Unsurpassable Mahamudra of Liberation —128 Views

The next text I would add is the *Supreme and Unsurpassable Mahamudra of Liberation (SAUMOL)*. I am adding that even though it was not yet available in English when I finished this book, partly because I believe it will be available by the time this book is published or shortly thereafter, and partly because, like the first two texts, you do not need to become a Buddhist to practice it, and also because the *SAUMOL* explains the different techniques needed to practice cultivation and zen (meditation). I would then add the "128 Evil and Erroneous Views" that are part of the *SAUMOL*. They are already available online in a preliminary English translation. With an understanding of these views, you can evaluate other Buddhist teachings and Buddhist teachers. The *SAUMOL* has been translated and hopefully should soon be available online. In fact, it was partly in anticipation of the *SAUMOL* finally being available in English that prompted me to write this book.

Parts of this book by H.H. Dorje Chang Buddha III are already available online in Chinese. Included are the "Xiamen Most Excellent Oceanic Mind Essence;" the "The Ultimate Bodhicitta for Attaining Dharma-Nature True-Suchness Oceanic Mind Essence," which includes "Verses Explaining Phenomena," a "Vajrasattva Practice," and a "Concluding Practice;" and the "128 Evil and Erroneous Views." Most of the mantras and the dharmas are not included. A preliminary translation in English of brief discourses on each of the "128 Evil and Erroneous Views" by H.H. Dorje Chang Buddha III is available online and has been highlighted on my blog and included in the Lemonade Sangha classes. These dharmas offer a more advanced form of cultivation practice. They enable you to develop bodhichitta. You are training yourself to think, speak, and act like a Bodhisattva.

One of the dharmas included in the *SAUMOL* explains how to practice a dharma to make offerings to local ghosts and gods or devas (FIGURE 91). First, you need to explain to them that you know you have disturbed them by invading their space, but that you will bring them benefits. You ask that they protect and assist you in accomplishing all your endeavors so that you can perfect your practice and realization of the Buddha Dharma. You also assure them that you will share and let them enjoy the merit you gain. I didn't know this, but it was what I did when I asked the Huichol deity about leaving shamanism to follow my Buddha Master. I also wrote about how another student had serious problems when she did not negotiate or seek the approval of local deities before she built on their land.

Why do we do this? You may think this silly or crazy. When a group of us met with the Buddha Master after a March 2019 retreat, we asked why the local and land gods or devas were important. We were told that local gods are living beings, but they are beings from another dimension, not humans. They can help you with worldly things or secular things because they still have feelings. The holy Dharma protectors and Bodhisattvas will not, because they no longer have feelings and only care about cause and effect and you becoming liberated. They do not care about mundane things nor have any emotional attachments. We can still request and receive help from the ordinary samsaric beings. They can still help us with our worldly life—family matters, businesses, financial matters. We need to respect and help all living beings, even some we cannot usually see or communicate with.

FIGURE 91: Spirit House at the Holy Vajrasana Temple

A third mind-essence, "**Root Master Oceanic Mind Essence**" has not yet been transmitted. I already discussed several State practices from the *SAUMOL* earlier including the Vajra Substitute Body Dharma, the Xian Liang Great Perfection Dharma, Tummo Concentration Dharma, and others. These are very high State practices that require inner-tantric initiations and empowerments. There are also enhancement dharmas that I can transmit that are very helpful for your practice and help prepare you for more advanced transmissions.

The titles given above are from an early translation of this text and may change in the final printed version. I do not know how or when the *SAUMOL* will be distributed, but I will publish that information on my BLOG at https://www.zhaxizhuoma.org. You can also check at https://www.wbahq. Currently, I am reading a preliminary translation of "The Xiaman Most Excellent Oceanic Mind Essence" for our Sunday Service that starts at 6:00 am on Zoom every week.

Dharma Discourses

You should also listen to or read the Dharma discourses by the Buddha Master, if you can find a Dharma center or temple that has them in English or has someone who will translate them for you. There are a few that are now recorded in both English and Chinese. These (and hopefully others) will also be available online at the "Dharma Voice" through the World Buddhism Association Headquarters. Keep checking there at https://www.wbahq.org. You should use the Seven-Dharma system discussed earlier as a guide on how to listen to and/or read them. The four bilingual Dharma discourses that currently exist are:

"The Intrinsically Existing Truth of No Arising and No Ceasing in the Universe and in Human Lives Realized by the Buddha Was Not Created by the Buddha."

"Taking Refuge to Become a Buddhist Disciple and Practicing According to the Teachings of the Buddha Will Eradicate All Sins, Including the Retributions of Descending to Hell. You Can Naturally Become a Great Holy Person with Enormous Supernormal Power, Boundless Good Fortune, and Be Free from Birth, Aging, Sickness, and Death."

"Living Beings Are Lost in Their Deluded Self, Not Seeing Their True Self."

"Many People Have Deceived Themselves Yet They Do Not Even Know."

There are many discourses you should try to read or hear. There are two that provide teachings that we include as chants in our daily service taken from a series of discourses given by the Buddha Master to a group of His senior students on a trip to the East Coast in 2009. They traveled in a caravan in RVs and at night when they stopped, the Buddha Master would give a Dharma discourse. I did not go on this trip but had on other occasions had the good fortune to be part of the entourage who traveled with the Buddha Master when this happened. All of the discourses on this particular trip were especially wonderful. Six nights were spent on transmitting the Dharma as commentary on the *The Sutra on Understanding and Realizing Definitive Truth* listed below. Another favorite on considering other people's mistakes that the Buddha Master had His disciples chant before He gave the second part of an exceptionally profound discourse on determining who is a true master is included earlier in this book[62]. And it is part of our daily reflections on what we have learned from the Buddha. The Buddha stressed that no one should be considered a master and attempt to teach others without holding and practicing this view.

Eight Winds

Gain & Loss
Honor & Disgrace
Praise & Ridicule
Pleasure & Suffering

---

62 *Page 204*

However, it is lesson eight in that series, "Cutting Off the Twenty Dharmas Relating to Ordinary Feelings" that I include on any "must read or hear" list as well as in our daily chants. These are key in our quest to become a holy person. The Buddha Master said, "If we are to reach the holy state, we must thoroughly discard the delusion-based deeds of ordinary people that hinder us and bind us to samsara and must thoroughly discard those things that cause us to be unable to end cause and effect." They are *Fame, Gain, Prosperity, Decline, Good Fortune, Gladness, Increase, Decrease, Antipathy, Resentment, Anger, Hatred, Scheming, Defamation, Seizing, Harming, Illness, Suffering, Parting, and Death.* They are a more detailed rendering of the Eight Winds or worldly dharmas that Shakyamuni Buddha said must be abandoned in order to lose attachment to self and become a holy being. You may have encountered them in other Buddhist literature. In this discourse the Buddha Master gives a brief description of each of these twenty dharmas of ordinary feelings and explains how they cause us to be unable to end cause and effect and thus remain in samsara. The Buddha Master tells us that if we can cut off these twenty dharmas relating to ordinary feelings, we will no longer be entangled by attachment to self, which is the root of samsara.

True Stories about a Holy Monk

True Stories about a Holy Monk is a Dharma book about Dorje Losang, a senior disciple of H.H. Dorje Chang Buddha III, that contains a complete yidam Dharma practice of the Four-Armed Kuan Yin Bodhisattva with a preliminary, formal, and closing practice. It also explains holy nectar and shows examples of different types of nectar. It has been translated and published in English. Dorje Losang left this world in 2004 leaving many shariras as proof of his accomplishment (FIGURE 92). There are other articles about Dorje Losang on our temple website (www.holyvajrasana.org).

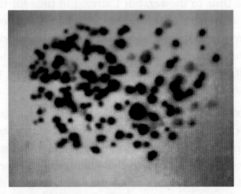

FIGURE 92: Elder Dharma King Dorje Losang's sharira.

Imparting the Absolute Truth through the Heart Sutra

Next, you should try to find a way to at least read or hear the introduction to the content of this sutra on prajna in *Imparting the Absolute Truth through the Heart Sutra* and the discourse given at the end of that book on how to realize prajna. This discourse covers "Not ignoring Cause & Effects;" "Take Refuge and Arouse Bodhichitta;" "Contemplation of Impermanence;" "Three Pure Precepts;" "Ten Good Characteristics;" "Four Immeasurable States;" "Dharma of Preliminary Practices;" "Dharma to Pass Through Barriers;" "The Six Paramitas;" "Correspondence with the Buddhas and Bodhisattvas;" and other topics. These are not the heart of the sutra, but they will give you an idea of what this profound text offers and what you need to do to obtain the fruits of the sutra.

I don't expect to see the entire text of *Imparting the Absolute Truth through the Heart Sutra* to be available to the public in English for some time, but I am hopeful we can at least be able to study the introductory and implementation parts sooner. I also hope I am wrong and an English translation will be available soon. The last draft translation that I have is almost 800 pages, so this is a monumental work of translation. The main translator has submitted it for review, but this will take time. The main text of *Imparting the Absolute Truth through the Heart Sutra* uses every word or phrase of the *Prajna Paramita Heart Sutra* to transmit us the Dharma relating to prajna. Since it is transmitted by a Buddha, it then also becomes a sutra. The entire text is essential to studying, understanding, and finally realizing emptiness.

This text is so important that a very spectacular Buddhas Bestow Nectar Dharma Assembly was held in March 2014 in Pasadena to honor the publication of *Imparting the Absolute Truth through the Heart Sutra*. I remember receiving an urgent phone call one morning telling me to come immediately to what later became the Holy Miracles Temple—over 200 miles from our temple. I didn't even have time to shower, but I arrived in time for the very memorable ceremony. There is a video of this ceremony where three-colored nectar spontaneously appeared in a special bowl with no one conducting the ceremony (FIGURES 93 and 94). The nectar was then used to make the ink that stamped the memorial edition of the book that was released later that year in Hong Kong (FIGURE 95).

This book by H.H. Dorje Chang Buddha III was released in Chinese in 2014 but it is not yet available in English. It is based on a series of very famous discourses given in China in the 1990s, using the text, meaning, and principles of the *Heart Sutra*. It clearly explains the relationships between mind, Buddha, and living beings. It tells everyone what the absolute truth of Buddha Dharma and liberation is. Several years ago, His Holiness told a number of Western disciples that this is the only book you need to read to understand emptiness and become enlightened. This text is for acquiring prajna or transcendental wisdom, although it also teaches the importance of cultivating character and provides much of the homework shown in Appencix E we need to do that.

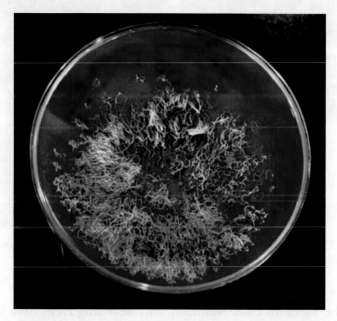

FIGURE 93: Three-color Nectar Bestowed by the Buddhas at the Holy Miracles Temple

FIGURE 94: Witnessing the bestowal of holy nectar at the dharma assembly to congratulate the publishing of the treasure scripture *Imparting the Absolute Truth through the Heart Sutra*.

FIGURE 95: Dress Rehearsal of processional making offerings at Dharma Assembly for the release of *Imparting the Absolute Truth through the Heart Sutra* in Hong Kong

The Definitive Truth Sutra
(The Sutra on Understanding and Realizing Definitive Truth)

There are two other texts by H.H. Dorje Chang Buddha III besides *Imparting the Absolute Truth through the Heart Sutra* that are useful in developing your wisdom or having an understanding of emptiness: *The Sutra on Understanding and Realizing Definitive Truth* and *A Monk Expounds the Absolute Truth to a Layperson*. The first one is included in the treasure book H.H. Dorje Chang Buddha III, but neither are yet available to the public in English. They are both delightful and use allegory to explain concepts that are beyond words. Try your best to hear them or read them.

> *"Manifesting the correct principle by not abiding in anything —*
> *That is Buddha-nature."*
>
> H.H. Dorje Chang Buddha III
> The Definitive Truth Sutra

In the *Definitive Truth Sutra*, H.H. Dorje Chang Buddha III attends a banquet in 2007 hosted by two ancient Buddhas. The conversations that occurred amongst these three Buddhas and another discussion with a wise being were recorded in the Big

Blue Treasure Book in Chinese. During the trip to the East Coast taken by His Holiness and several of his more senior disciples mentioned above, He gave a series of discourses on this sutra that are also available in Chinese. Neither these discourses nor the sutra itself have been translated into English for distribution, but preliminary translations are available at our temple in Sanger. This sutra has a very helpful discussion on why we practice the Four Limitless States of Mind and why this conditional dharma is important to train us to eventually have unconditional or ultimate and holy bodhichitta.

A Monk Expounds the Absolute Truth to a Layperson (The Monk Sutra)

This sutra was written by H.H. Dorje Chang Buddha III when he was only 20 years old for His good friend and abbot of the Baoguang Temple in Chengdu China, Dharma Master Xinji. It discusses the truth of emptiness. The sutra has not been translated into English for distribution, but again, preliminary translations of *A Monk Expounds the Absolute Truth to a Layperson* are available at our temple in Sanger.

Learning from Buddha

This important teaching from the Buddha Master was given as a discourse in America and released as Chinese CDs in 2016 and later as a small book. An English translation of the book was released in 2020 and posted online. It has three parts: One on the practice of cultivation, one on the formal practice of tantric dharma, and one on how you implement both of those practices in your daily life.

Learning from Buddha is essential for anyone wanting to become enlightened and a holy person. It is available for anyone to read and study, but you would need to take refuge and be willing to have the Three Jewels of Buddha, Dharma, and Sangha as your role models to receive the full benefits from the tantric dharmas explained therein. There are three parts in *Learning from Buddha*:

Part I: "**If You Learn Dharma but Do Not Cultivate Yourself, You Cannot Attain Accomplishment**," which focuses on cultivation of your behavior or character — how you treat others and develop bodhichitta.

Part II: "**If You Cultivate Yourself, But Do Not Learn Dharma, You Cannot Generate Realization Powers**," which explains how you do tantric meditation practice with a yidam including the preliminary, formal, and concluding practices. This section also explains the importance and practice of the dedication of your merit to help other living beings.

243

Part III: "If You Do Not Put Into Practice the Lessons You Have Heard on Cultivation and Dharma, It Will Be Like Trying to Scoop Up the Reflection of the Moon on Water," which tells you how to apply the other two parts to your daily life. The Buddha Master tells us we need to stop and reflect on what we have learned from the Buddha three times during the day. We have revised our daily morning and evening chants to enable us to do just that. It also includes background on "Kuan Yin Bodhisattva's Great Compassion Empowerment" mentioned earlier.

This little book has been so important to the Chinese students that they dare not go to see the Buddha Master without having it with them. They were tested on their understanding of all three parts by the nuns before they would be allowed to see the Buddha Master. The book also contains photos of H.H. Dorje Chang Buddha III before and after He changed His appearance from a wrinkled old man to a beautiful youth that was discussed in an earlier chapter. (FIGURE 96) It also includes a discourse He gave about the event insisting He is just an ordinary man. However, He told us that He does have what Buddhists need, the highest-level great Dharma of the Tathagata to attain perfect liberation and accomplishment; this is also the invariant Dharma jointly possessed by all Buddhas in the ten directions.

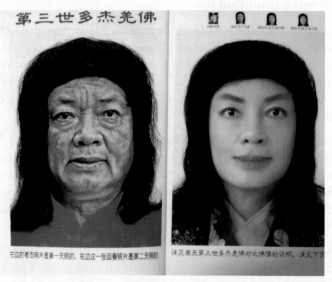

FIGURE 96: Photos taken on October 18, 2012 (left) and October 19, 2012 (right) of H.H. Dorje Chang Buddha III

The blue text below is a complete transcript of the words spoken by H.H. Dorje Chang Buddha III regarding the publication of the photos. H.H. Dorje Chang Buddha III said:

United International World Buddhism Association Headquarters has requested permission to publish and distribute these two photos of me and asked me to say a few words. First of all, I will not accept any money from the sale of the photos. However, your Headquarters should set a low price for those who purchase them. The name on the photos is Dorje Chang Buddha III. Whether I agree or not, this will be the way the name is written. This is my name, which was recognized and corroborated in official documents issued by leaders of many Buddhist sects throughout the world! It was legally affirmed by the government! It is not a name I conferred upon myself. Although the title of Buddha has been legally affirmed in my name, nevertheless, I am very humbled, and this title means nothing to me. I am not a Bodhisattva, not an Arhat, not a venerable one, not a Dharma king, and not a rinpoche. I am not a holy person. I am one with a heart of humility. When your Headquarters publishes the photos, do not add "Namo" to my name. I am not qualified to be honored with the title "Namo."

I previously vowed to bear karma on behalf of living beings. My physical strength greatly weakened. I quickly became exhausted, and an aged appearance emerged. Rather than saying I bore karma on behalf of living beings, it would be better to say that my humble body was weak and sickly. Recently, United International World Buddhism Association Headquarters insisted on using my photo to perform the Vajra Fa-Man Determination by Holy Selection Dharma. Regardless of what selection method you use to determine my status, I will not accept it. That is because I am just an ordinary person. The photo of my youthful appearance was the result of having washed my face with medicine given to me by an elder virtuous one. Actually, more cosmetic treatment methods already exist in the field of medicine nowadays. I do not know the Buddha Dharma to reverse old age and return to a youthful appearance. As time goes on, I will gradually become old again. This is because I am a person who is just like you, with no ability to stop the process of impermanence. However, I have one thing that is different from you! I have what Buddhists need, the highest-level great Dharma of the Tathagatas to attain perfect liberation and accomplishment. This is also the same Dharma possessed by all Buddhas in the ten directions:

Stay far away from feudal superstition, strange or heretically induced phenomena, evil masters, deceivers, non-Buddhists under the guise of Buddhism, cults, evil teachings, and evil books. Strictly abide by the precepts and disciplinary rules of Buddhism. Establish great compassion as your foundation. Do not do anything that is evil. Do all things that are good. Give up self-interests and benefit others. Patiently endure humilia-

tion and adversity. Practice humility. Purify the mind. When encountering living beings, regardless of whether they are handicapped, deficient, sick, or healthy, treat them all equally as family members. Know that all phenomena are governed by causality. With good causes, you receive good retributions. Good retributions yield good fruits. Good fruits enable you to receive the true Dharma. Relying on the Dharma, you can achieve perfect good fortune and wisdom. Then you can step into the state of accomplishment, break away from the sufferings that living beings experience, cease transmigrating in the cycle of birth and death, and accomplish the perfect enlightenment of a Buddha!

These are the teachings and precepts that I practice and uphold. I say without the slightest ambiguity that the Buddha Dharma I impart is absolutely the true Dharma of the Tathagatas possessed by all Buddhas in the ten directions! I cannot be modest about this. Why? I must speak true words. Otherwise, I would mislead practitioners. If you truly practice the *Supreme and Unsurpassable Mahamudra of Liberation*; thoroughly comprehend *Imparting the Absolute Truth Through the Heart Sutra*; often listen to my audio-recorded Dharma discourses that have not been altered or spoken in my stead by other people and, best of all, read published books that record the Dharma I imparted; and if you are truly devout toward all Buddhas, then I, Dorje Chang Buddha III, guarantee that you will learn great Dharma to achieve perfect good fortune and wisdom and will attain accomplishment in your current lifetime!

If you are a master with disciples, you must at least study in depth some sutras and commentaries as a foundation, such as the *Heart Sutra*, the *Diamond Sutra*, the *Avatamsaka Sutra*, the *Lotus Sutra*, the *Suramgama Sutra*, the *Agama Sutras*, the *Hetu-Vidya Treatise*, the *Madhyamaka Treatise*, the *Abhidharma-kosa Treatise*, the *Prajna Treatises*, the *Precepts and Discipline Treatise*, the *Consciousness-Only Treatise*, the *Lam Rim Chen Mo*, the *Bodhisattvacharyavatara Treatise*, and others. Doing so will reduce the possibility of leading others astray in the process of teaching.

Some people have now mentioned that they just want to learn my medicinal cosmetic regimen. Fine! As long as you thoroughly learn either The Xiaman Most Excellent Oceanic Mind Essence or The Ultimate Bodhicitta for Attaining Dharma-Nature True-Thusness Oceanic Mind Essence in *The Supreme and Unsurpassable Mahamudra of Liberation* and have put into actual practice what you learn, you can be assured that the highest, holiest great Dharma will be available to you for achieving perfect good fortune and wisdom, liberation, and accomplishment! At that time, why would you still need any medicinal cosmetic regimen?

Finally, I remind you that you must pay attention to something. Some people, including some who are masters, are now using my name to commit fraud in various ways. I hope that you will be careful and observe with caution. Be cautious!

Whoever distributes my above contrasting photos must be sure to include my words stated above. Anyone who removes my words and just distributes the photos is undoubtedly an evil person!

The Holy Vajrasana Temple Book of Chants

Finally, the main teachings that we have are included in the hymnal or chant book that we chant every day at the temple and again when we have classes there or at other locations as well as the weekly class we hold internationally via the internet. This is our communal homework that we do together with our personal Dharma practice. I've included part of it as Appendix E, so that you may chant these verses as well and take the time to reflect each day on how well you are doing to think, speak, and act like a Buddha or Bodhisattva. If you do this often enough, and are sincere enough, you will become one.

I will continue to hold classes on all the dharmas listed above and others that may be transmitted by my Guru as long as I am able. I pray that you will be able to read, hear, study and understand all of the above and practice them in your daily life to quickly become accomplished. If you do, you should be able to receive the initiations and empowerments that you need to become enlightened. May you have good fortune, live a blessed life, excel in the five vidyas, have true wisdom, bestow compassion, attain sainthood, and attain enlightenment as symbolized below in the Xuanfa Institute logo.

Epilogue

My thanks to the core group who traveled with us in the van or in their own cars on the Dharma Propagation Tour. This included the lamas, Puti Duxi and Hongxi Fazang from Macang Monastery who have returned to lay life, the nun Zhengxiang Shi who is now at the Holy Miracles Temple in Pasadena; and lay disciple Shannon Pattillo who handled so much of the logistics for the trip. Unfortunately for us, Shannon has left this world. We miss you Shannon. There were too many other lay disciples to mention who offered their homes, hands, and hearts in this effort as we toured the country. Gesang Suolang Rinpoche does deserve special mention for her thoughtful and helpful editorial advice. Gesang gave so much more. She was with me for much of this journey. Magnolia deserves several Oscars for the documentary on the Vajra Throne as do the cast. There were many others including Gongjue Tuji Rinpoche and Reba Jinbo Rinpoche who were my IT gurus and advisors. Also, Jiangba Luosang Rinpoche who discovered the Vajra Poles and more. Gesang, Gongjue, Reba, and Jiangba are also supportive Board members of the Xuanfa Institute. I am also very indebted to Benxin Chiren (Jason Wu), Jue Hui Fa Shih, and Bodi Wentu for their translation support, and to my dear former roommate Akou Lamo for her inspiration and kindness.

I also want to thank all the many donors who gave so generously to help us develop the temple. It is still not finished. The temple itself is up to code, but we still have parking, irrigation, and other infrastructure work to be done. Those who invested in the Tibetan columns, copper prayer wheels, and requests for blessings with the wheels provide the foundation for what I still hope to install. These projects await word on what can be done at Holy Heavenly Lake in Hesperia. Bhikshu Gunaratana also gets special thanks for the gift of the Bodhi Tree which he received from Lanka Rama Vihara, a Sri Lankan temple located in La Puenta, California.

Of course, I have to extend a very special thanks to the International Buddhism Sangha Association, Hua Zang Si, Macang Monastery, Sanger Mission, the Master Wan Ko Yee International Cultural Institute, and the many groups and individuals who contributed so generously to the Dharma Propagation Tour including Ven. Henghsing Gyatso Kudun Zunzhe Yongzhong Rinpoche from Taiwan. We could not have done this without the help of all these people and organizations. May the merit from this effort be shared with all so that we can all quickly become liberated and free from samsara.

The other person to whom I owe a great shout of gratitude is my friend and supporter, Helen Pan, who not only offered me shelter in Pasadena, and a venue for the English Dharma classes in Southern California but served as my Chinese advisor on so many matters.

I do not have the words to thank my Guru and Buddha Master, H.H. Dorje Chang Buddha III. In 2006 I wrote a "Hymn of Devotion to my Buddha Master". This was before I knew He was a Buddha. I did revise it to reflect this new insight once I knew the truth. I could add many verses to reflect all that has happened since then, but I am leaving it as it was then and including it as Appendix C. It is so much more today. None of what I have written would have been remotely possible without His kindness, teachings, and love. I hope in some small way this humble pigeon or chicken can share her experiences to help others find the way and I know how very much I still need to continue my cultivation and practice to rise up like the phoenix He has been training me to be.

I have wanted to do another book tour when the *Supreme and Unsurpassable Mahamudra of Liberation* is released. If I am at all physically able to do so, I will and promote this book as well to help Westerners have some indigenous context with which to understand it. All profits from the sale of this book will be donated to the Xuanfa Institute to help promote its missions and specifically to help build a second Holy Vajrasana Temple and stupa at Holy Heavenly Lakes in Hesperia, California.

May the true Dharma fill the hearts of living beings throughout the land and all obtain good fortune and wisdom. May our dear Buddha Master, H.H. Dorje Chang Buddha III, guide us and bless us with the infinite wisdom and compassion of the Buddhas.

Bibliography—Annotated

Most of the following is taken from the curriculum of the Xuanfa Five Vidyas Institute (XFVU) and reflects the major categories of classes that were offered by the XFVU. It includes the actual words of the Buddhas and also the classic commentaries, treatises, or shastras on those words. Books about the major sects that we now have in our melting pot called America are also listed along with the biographies and autobiographies of the patriarchs, matriarchs, and other saints in the various traditions to provide some background on how others have followed the paths to liberation established by the Buddhas. One of the assignments at XFVU when we studied these texts was to assess if the writers and/or those who were written about held any of the 128 Evil or Erroneous Views. You should do so as well and be careful.

Words of the Buddha—Shakyamuni

The Nikayas —Theravada:

The Pali Canon of the *Digha Nikaya*, the *Majjhima Nikaya*, the *Makkhima Nikaya*, the *Samyutta Nikaya*, the *Anguttara Nikaya*, and the *Khuddaka Nikaya*. The *Khuddaka Nikaya* also includes the *Dhammapada*, a popular collection of sayings of the Buddha in verse form. This body of teachings represent what is sometimes called the "First Turning of the Wheel." The Agama Sutras that are translated from the Sanskrit are similar to the Nikayas.

Avatamsaka Sutra (The Sutra of the Garland of Flowers)—Mahayana:

It is among the largest and greatest of the scriptures of Mahayana Buddhism. It consists of 12 volumes in Chinese, and 1656 pages in the English edition translated by Thomas Cleary. As with most Mahayana scriptures, it treats Buddha not as merely a man of ancient India, but as a cosmic principle. Differing from the austere and non-theist Theravada scriptures, it is full of gods and goddesses, heavens, jeweled trees and heavenly beings. The Avatamsaka Sutra became very influential in Chinese Buddhism and was responsible for the creation of the Hua-Yen school.

Prajnaparamita Sutras—Mahayana:

Many volumes. *The Large Sutra on Perfect Wisdom* translated by Edward Conze or *The Perfection of Wisdom in 8,000 lines and Its Verse Summary* translated by Donald Lopez. Also see *The Prajnaparamita Heart Sutra* by Avalokiteshvara Bodhisatta or *Imparting the Absolute Truth through the Heart Sutra* by H.H. Dorje Chang Buddha III and the *Diamond Sutra*.

Sukhavatiyuha (Pure Land) Sutras—Mahayana:

Several sutras exist that describe the "Land of Bliss" or Sukhavati, the Western Paradise of Amitabha Buddha, the Buddha of Infinite Light. These sutras describe how Amitabha Buddha came to preside over this marvel-filled paradise and describe the layout and wonders of the Pure Land. They also describe the preconditions that lead to rebirth in this Buddhist paradise. They form the spiritual foundation for the Pure Land schools of Buddhism.

Shurangama Sutra—Mahayana:

It is said that the *Shurangama Sutra* was translated from Sanskrit into Chinese during the Tang Dynasty by Shramana Paramiti of Central India, although no Sanskrit copies of this sutra have been found. In this sutra 25 sages explain to Manjushri Bodhisattva the various methods that they used to pierce the knots of the senses, transcend the realm of birth and death, and attain enlightenment. It was translated from Chinese into English by The Buddhist Text Translation Society, USA. The full title is known as *The Sutra of the Foremost Shurangama at the Great Buddha's Summit Concerning the Tathagata's Secret Cause of Cultivation, His Certification to the Complete Meaning and all Bodhisattvas' Myriad Practices.* There are other translations of this sutra as well.

Lankavatara Sutra—Mahayana:

The *Lankavatara Sutra* is one of the six orthodox writings of the Yogachara school. Furthermore, it is the keystone of Chinese Ch'an and Japanese Zen Buddhism. It was brought by the Indian Bodhidharma to China at the end of the fifth century and reached Japan in the eight-century and Tibet in the ninth. The Sutra deals critically with the Brahmanist schools of Indian philosophy like the Sankhya and the Pasupata. Furthermore, characteristic topics of the Yogachara doctrine are discussed such as the doctrine of the Tathagatagarbha and the eight types of consciousness. The essence of the sutra revolves around the term Cittamatra which characterizes the totality of the mental-spiritual as the basis for the manifoldness of all phenomena. Cittamatra can be translated as mind-only. All the objects of the world, and the names and forms of experience, are merely manifestations of the mind. Several English translations of this sutra are available.

Saddharmapundarika (Lotus Sutra)—Mahayana:

The *Lotus Sutra of the Wonderful Law* is filled with teachings, stories and fabulously visual scenes depicting the splendor and magnificence of the great beings. In the *Lotus Sutra*, the Buddha shows us the path to Buddhahood—the Great Vehicle taken by the Bodhisattvas. Many, many examples of how Buddhas became Buddhas can be found in this text. Several schools of Buddhism developed around this text including the T'iantai (Tendai) and Nichiren sects. Many translations exist.

Mahaparinirvana Sutra—Mahayana:

Also called the Nirvana Sutra, this is the Mahayana sutra that records the last words of Shakyamuni Buddha to His disciples and espouses the concept of the Tathagatagarbha, recognizing the hidden reality of the unconditioned, egoless Buddha-Self in all beings—the Buddha-Nature. Several translations are available.

Words of the Buddha—Dorje Chang (Vajradhara)

Vimalakirti Nirdesa Sutra—Mahayana:

In this short sutra the second manifestation of Dorje Chang Buddha in this world, the layman Ven. Vimalakirti, offers very profound teachings on the nature of reality to the Arhat students of Shakyamuni Buddha and other beings. It is noted for its humor and imagery. There are two translations from the Chinese Canon by Burton Watson and Charles Luk and a third from the Tibetan by Robert Thurman. Some translations are available online.

NOTE: The following sutras are by H.H. Dorje Chang Buddha III and are discussed in Chapter Twenty-Five. All are available in Chinese and translations of *The Dharma of Cultivation* and *The Great Dharma of Zen,* are both currently available online and in print in English, *Learning from Buddha* is also online in English, while the *SAUMOL* will hopefully be available in English soon.

> *The Monk Sutra (A Monk Expounds the Absolute Truth to a Layperson)*
>
> *The Dharma of Cultivation Transmitted by H.H. Dorje Chang Buddha III (What Is Cultivation?)*
>
> *The Great Dharma of Zen* (See Appendix A)
>
> *The Definitive Truth Sutra*
>
> *The Supreme and Unsurpassable Mahamudra of Liberation (SAUMOL)*
>
> *Imparting the Absolute Truth through the Heart Sutra*
>
> *Learning from Buddha*

Classic Commentaries, Treatises, or Shastras

These are the commentaries studied in Mahayana and Vajrayana monasteries and universities. The Buddha Master tells us we must understand, at the very least, five treatises: Master Asanga's *The Jewel of Realization (Abhisamaya-lamkara)*, a commentary on the *Prajnaparamita Sutras* that he received from Maitreya

Bodhisattva; Master Nagarjuna's *The Fundamental Wisdom of the Middle Way (Mulamadhyamakakarika Treatise)* or Master Chandrakirti's *Guide or Introduction to the Middle Way (Madhyamakavatara* or *Madhyamaka Treatise)*; Master Vasubandhu's *Abhidharmakosa Treatise*; Master Dharmakirti's *The Commentary on Valid Perception (Pramana Varttika* or *Hetu-Vidya Treatise)*; and Master Gunaprabha's *A Summary of Vowed Morality (Vinayasutra)*, also referred to as the *Precepts and Discipline Treatise*. He has also listed Master Asanga's *Mind-Only Treatise (Bodhisattvabhumi* or the entire *Yogācārabhūmi shastra)*, Lord Tsongkapa's *Broad Commentary on Levels of the Bodhi Path (Lam Rim Chen Mo)*, and Shantideva's *A Guide to the Bodhisattva's Way of Life (Bodhisattvacharyavatara Treatise)* as being important. Not all of these are available yet in English, or at least I have not found them. A translation of part of Asanga's *Bodhisattvabhumi* only recently appeared in English. All of these are recommended for anyone wanting to take disciples. Ordinary students can just focus on understanding *Imparting the Absolute Truth Through the Heart Sutra*, which explains the essence of most of these other treatises in a much clearer and precise language. However, it is not readily available in English. You may read a preliminary translation in English at the Holy Vajrasana Temple.

Nagarjuna (150-250),

Indian Mahasiddha—*Mulamadhyamakakarika Treatise (The Fundamental Wisdom of the Middle Way):* This classic text expresses the doctrine that all phenomena are empty of inherent existence, that is, that nothing exists substantially or independently. Despite lacking any essence, Nagarjuna argues, phenomena nonetheless exist conventionally, and that indeed conventional existence and ultimate emptiness are in fact the same thing. This represents the radical understanding of the Buddhist doctrine of the two truths, or two levels of reality. It represents the Profound Division of the Mahayana based on the "Second Turning of the Wheel" teachings.

Aryadeva (2nd century),

Indian Mahasiddha— *Chatuhshataka (Four Hundred Verses on the Yogic Deeds of Bodhisattvas):* Aryadeva was the main disciple of Nagarjuna. Both Nagarjuna and Aryadeva urge those who want to understand reality to induce direct experience of ultimate truth through philosophic inquiry and reasoning. Aryadeva's text is more than a commentary on Nagarjuna's *Treatise on the Middle Way* because it also explains the extensive paths associated with conventional truths.

Asanga (294-376),

Indian Mahasiddha—*Yogācārabhūmi Shastra (Treatise on the Levels of Spir-

itual Practitioners) was partially translated by Art Engle as the *Treatise on the Stages of the Practice of Yoga or The Bodhisattva Path to Unsurpassed Enlightenment (Bodhisattvabhumi)*: It represents the stages of the path, and the training and education of a Bodhisattva. It was taught and studied at the great Nalanda University. It not only outlines the practice of meditation and cultivation of the six perfections (generosity, ethics, patience, effort, meditation, and wisdom), but encourages mastery of all five of the vidyas in the pursuit of enlightenment. It is one of the main works of the Yogachara or Mind Only School. There appear to be differences of opinion on this text between Tibetan and Chinese scholars. It has been very difficult to find any translations of this work in English, but the Buddha Master often refers to it (See the section on the Five Vidyas for more). This partial translation was released in 2016. It follows the format of the *Mahayanasutralamkara (The Universal/Mahayana Vehicle Discourses)* also referred to as *The Ornament of the Great Vehicle Discourses*, one of the five treatises or shastras transmitted in the fourth century by Maitreya Bodhisattva, the fifth and future Buddha of this fortunate age, to Venerable Asanga.

The *Abhisamaya Allamkara (Gone Beyond: The Prajnaparamita Sutras, The Clear Realization and Its Commentaries)* by Karl Brunnholzl) was also transmitted from Maitreya Bodhisattva, to Venerable Asanga as one of five treatises. It comprises one of the major foundations of the Method Division of Mahayana Buddhism based on the "Third Turning of the Wheel" teachings. The focus of this text is, like the works of Nagarjuna, the *Prajnaparamita* teachings, but taken a different approach or view. This approach to emptiness reveals the hidden meaning of the *Prajnaparamita sutras* by examining the five paths and spiritual levels. Through this approach one understands how emptiness is realized. This text is from the perspective of the Nyingma and the Karma Kagyu traditions.

The *Uttaratantra Shastra* or Ratnagotravibhaga (Exposition of the Jeweled Lineage), another of the five treatises said to have been dictated to Asanga by the Bodhisattva Maitreya, presents the Buddha's definitive teachings on how we should understand this basis of enlightenment and clarifies the nature and qualities of buddhahood. All sentient beings without exception have Buddha Nature—the inherent purity and perfection of the mind, untouched by changing mental states. Thus, there is neither any reason for conceit in deeming oneself better than others nor any reason for self-contempt, thinking of oneself as inferior and unable to reach enlightenment. This seeing is obscured by veils which are removable and do not touch the inherent purity and perfection of the nature of the mind as such. Several translations of this work exist including Karl Brunnholzl's *When the Clouds Part: The Uttaratantra and Its Meditative Tradition as a Bridge between Sutra and Tantra.*

The other two Treatises of Maitreya transmitted to Asanga are the *Dharmad-harmatavibhaga ("Distinguishing Phenomena and Pure Being"),* a short Yogachara work discussing the distinction and correlation between phenomena and reality and the *Madhyantavibhagakarika ("Distinguishing the Middle and the Extremes"),* another key work in Yogachara philosophy.

Vashubandhu (312-396),

Indian Mahasiddha—*Abhidharmakosakariks (the Abhidharma Kosa Bhasyam):* It is one of the five classic treatises that is studied in all the Tibetan monastic traditions. It not only represents the compilation of the various abhidharma texts that existed in ancient India, but it includes Vashubandhu's commentary as well. Vashubandhu is the younger half-brother of Asanga.

Chandrakirti (7th century),

Indian Mahasiddha—*Madhyamakavatara (Introduction to the Middle Way):* This work is an introduction to the Madhyamaka teachings of Nagarjuna, which are themselves a systematization of the *Prajnaparamita,* or "Perfection of Wisdom" literature, the sutras on the crucial but elusive concept of emptiness.

Shantideva (650-750),

Indian Mahasiddha—*Bodhisattvacharyavatara (The Way of the Bodhisattva* or *A Guide to the Bodhisattva's Way of Life):* Composed while Shantideva was at Nalanda University, it is one of the classic works describing how to follow the path of a Bodhisattva. Shantideva was believed to be an emanation of Manjushri Bodhisattva or at the very least, received direct guidance from this holy being. There are many English translations of this short text. The account of how he gave this as a discourse while a student at Nalanda, the great ancient Indian Buddhist University is interesting. The other students thought he was a very poor student and not qualified to study with them. He never appeared to study or participate in classes or anything. They conspired to embarrass him so that he would leave in humiliation. They asked him to give a discourse, thinking he would not be able to do so. They invited everyone and erected a dais or high platform upon which he would deliver his talk. When he arrived, he saw what they had done and asked them which they would prefer to hear: a commentary on something they were studying or something original? They snickered and said the latter, thinking it would be even more impossible for him to do. As I remember the story, they didn't provide stairs to get up on the dais either. However, that did not upset Shantideva in the least. He merely flew up to his seat and proceeded to give this classic and profound teaching on the Six Paramitas. It did not take the other students long to realize they had made a major mistake. This was the work of a great holy being, not an ordinary person like themselves. When he got to the chapter on the sixth Paramita of wisdom or prajna,

Shantideva disappeared into the clouds, but they could continue to hear him. He flew away and never went back to the university no matter how much the students begged him to do so.

Shantarakshita (8th century),

Indian Mahasiddha—*Madhyamakalankara (The Adornment* or *Ornament of the Middle Way):* It effects a synthesis between the Madhyamaka of Nagarjuna, the Mind-Only or Yogachara (cittamatra) teachings traced back to Asanga, and the logico-epistemological tradition of Dignaga and Dharmakirti. This great work marks the final stage in the evolution of Madhyamaka and was the last major development of Buddhist philosophy in India. Toward the end of the 19th century, the Tibetan scholar, Jamgon Mipham, composed the commentary on this commentary.

All of these great Mahasiddhas contributed to what became the esoteric Tibetan tradition or the Blessings and Practices Division that was also known as Vajrayana Buddhism.

Atisha (980-1054) / **Chekhawa** (12th century),

Indian Master who went to Tibet and Tibetan Kadampa Master—*Seven Essentials of Self-Mastery* and *Enlightened Courage: An Explanation of the Seven-Point Mind Training* by Dilgo Khyentse: Many texts exist on the practice of Tonglen or unconditional giving and taking on the suffering of others system of developing Bodhichitta, the mind of enlightenment developed by Geshe Chekhawa Yeshe Dorjel based on the teachings of Atisha and Shakyamuni Buddha.

The Various Sects or Schools of Buddhism

This and the following section include books that may offer useful insights into the various schools and sects of Buddhism and their founders. In some cases the founders or patriarchs and matriarchs are also covered in popular biographies and autobiographies listed in the following section. They have not been vetted for accuracy or if they always portray correct Buddha Dharma. They are offered for reference only and need to be studied using the "128 Evil and Erroneous Views" from the *Supreme and Unsurpassable Mahamudra of Liberation* as a guide.

Hua Yen School—Chinese Mahayana,

Entry into the Inconceivable: An Introduction to Hua Yen Buddhism by Thomas Cleary: This major Chinese Mahayana school was based on the *Avatamsaka Sutra (Hua-Yen or Flower Garland Sutra)*. It was founded by Tu-shun (557-640) and Fa-tsang (Hsien-shou 643-712) and reached its peak during the Tang Dynasty in China. In the Mahayana tradition this sutra is considered the first sermon given by the Buddha after His enlightenment and is centered on the philosophy of interpenetration and mutual containment of all phenonena, often depicted in the image of Indra's Net. It was taught to Bodhisattvas and celestial beings. Its metaphysics were completely assimilated by the Chan School. There are still followers of this tradition in the West within certain Chinese communities.

Pure Land School—Chinese Mahayana,

Sukhavatvyuha Sutra. Founded in the sixth century in China, this school focuses on the practitioner reciting the name of Amitabha Buddha and having faith that he/she will be reborn in the Western Paradise where more favorable conditions exist for obtaining enlightenment. It is based on the assumption that conditions are not suitable, and the practitioners are not capable of achieving enlightenment in this lifetime. It was exported to Japan in the 12th century. It was one of the first forms of Buddhism to come to North America, being brought here by the early Chinese immigrants in the late 19th century. Great Strength (Mahasthamaprapta or Vajrapani) Bodhisattva is a very important Bodhisattva in Pure Land Study; he is one of the two great Bodhisattvas who are the constant companions of Amitabha Buddha in the Pure Land. In pictures of Amitabha, Great Strength Bodhisattva is often shown standing to the Buddha's right, while Guan Yin Bodhisattva—Amitabha's other constant companion — stands to His left. In the *Shurangama Sutra*, Great Strength Bodhisattva explains how He attained enlightenment through Buddha recitation samadhi (gathering in the six sense faculties through continuous pure mindfulness of the Buddha to obtain samádhi.) that He learned from The Light Surpassing the Sun and the Moon Buddha.

Chan (Zen) School—Chinese Mahayana,

Living by Vow: A Practical Introduction to Eight Essential Zen Chants and Texts by Shohaku Okumura (Also see biography and teachings of Dogen, a Japanese Buddhist who brought the Soto School of Zen to Japan from China, listed below.): A form of Buddhist thought and practice that evolved in China, Chan lists Nagarjuna in its lineage and the Indian Bodhidharma as its founder and First Patriarch (6th century CE). Bodhidharma went to China in 526 A.D. Hui-neng (638-713), the Sixth Patriarch and an illiterate who was enlightened by hearing the *Diamond Sutra*, represents this school's approach to "sudden" enlightenment and transmission of the truth outside of the scriptures. The early Zen masters did focus on the Mahayana *Lankatara Sutra* which expounds the doctrine of Mind-only and stressed meditation. Chan or channa is a transliteration of the Sanskrit term dhyana, meaning meditation, while Zen is the Japanese transliteration of Chan. Chan also integrated Buddhism with many of the Chinese indigenous systems of belief, most notably Daoism. The golden age of Chan in China ended over a thousand years ago when it became formalized and lost much of its vitality. It was exported to both Japan (as Zen) and Korea (as Son) in the 12th century where it is still one of their major schools, having several subsects. The practice today primarily consists of extensive sitting meditation, ideally in a retreat or secluded environment. It is a very popular in the West, especially the Japanese Soto and Rinzai sects.

Shingon School—Japanese Vajrayana,

The Weaving of Mantra: Kukai and the Construction of Esoteric Buddhist Discourse by Ryuichi Abe: Venerable Kukai or Kobo-Daishi (774-835) who brought the esoteric practice of Buddhism from China to Japan and founded the Shingon School.

Nyingma School—Tibetan Vajrayana,

The Words of My Perfect Teacher by Patrul Rinpoche (1808-1887): A practice manual for the Nyingma sect that studies both the external or ordinary and the internal or extraordinary practices of the Longchen Nyingthig cycle as well as briefly looks at the Transfer of Consciousness.

Shangpa Kagyu School—Tibetan Vajrayana,

Timeless Rapture: Inspired Verse of the Shangpa Masters by Jamgon Kongtrul (1813-1899). Includes a glimpse into the mysticism of a tradition based mainly on the profound teaching of two women, Lady Niguma and Lady Sukhasiddhi, who obtained it directly from Dorje Chang Buddha.

Sakya School—Tibetan Vajrayana

Taking the Result as the Path: Core Teachings of the Sakya Lamdre Tradition by Cyrus Stearns: this presents the most important tantric teachings of their system of meditation.

Karma Kagyu School—Tibetan Vajrayana,

The Jewel Ornament of Liberation by Gampopa (1079-1153). This is the essential practice manual for the Karma Kagyu School from starting the path to achieving Buddhahood by one of the patriarchs and disciples of Milarepa, another patriarch of the school.

Jonang School—Tibetan Vajrayana,

Mountain Doctrine by Dolpopa Sherab Gyeltsen (1292-1361). This sect is the primary holder of the complete Dro transmission and practice lineage of the Kalachakra Tantra, the Six Yogas of the Kalachakra completion stage, and the shentong or "emptiness of other" view. Founded in the twelfth century by Yumo Mikyo Dorje. In 1650, for political reasons (The Jonang had strong ties with the

Mongolians), the Dalai Lama V prohibited the teaching of the shentong view of emptiness, sealed Jonang libraries, burned Jonang books, and forcibly converted the Jonang monasteries in Central Tibet to the Geluk. It was generally believed that the sect had become extinct. However, many remote monasteries did survive in Eastern Tibet and have continued practicing uninterrupted to this day. It is the most mystical of the Tibetan traditions with many highly accomplished practitioners including the current Dharma King H.H. Jigme Dorje.

Kadampa/Geluk School—Tibetan Vajrayana,

Lam Rim Chen Mo by Lord Tsongkhapa: This is the practice manual for the Geluk sect. *The Three Principle Teachings of Buddhism* and *Preparing for Tantra* both by Lord Tsongkhapa with commentary by Pabongka Rinpoche are both also recommended. These are derived from the Kadampa founder Atisha.

Nichiren School—Japanese Mahayana,

Writings of the school's founder, the Japanese Buddhist priest Nichiren (1222–1282):

This branch of Mahayana Buddhism focuses on the practice of chanting Nam Myoho Renge Kyo and on the *Lotus Sutra* doctrine believing that all people have an innate Buddha Nature and are therefore inherently capable of attaining enlightenment in their current form and present lifetime. Its largest subsect is the Soka Gakkai International (SGI), which is very popular in the west with several famous followers.

The Lives of Patriarchs, Matriarchs, and Other Saints and Their Teachings

This section contains biographies and autobiographies by the founders of the major sects and other famous historic Buddhists. They are included to enable you to study how holy beings lived—their thinking, speech, and actions.

Early Disciples of Shakyamuni Buddha *(5ᵗʰ-6ᵗʰ century BCE),*

Great Disciples of the Buddha Their Lives, Their Works, Their Legacy by Nyanaponika Thera & Hellmuth Hecker: Survey of the background, practice, and accomplishments of Shakyamuni Buddha's greatest disciples including Sariputta, Maha-mogallana, Mahakassapa, Ananda, Anuruddha, Mahakaccana, Great Women Disciples, Angulimala, Anathapindika,——and others.

Master Garab Dorje (6ᵗʰ century BC to 2ⁿᵈ century CE),

Indian patriarch of Nyingma sect—*The Golden Letters,* with a foreword by Namkhai Norbu Rinpoche: Study of the life and teachings of Garab Dorje and the historical origins of dzogchen including comparing and contrasting dzogchen, Kashmiri Saivism, and other similar systems.

Guru Padmasambhava (536 BCE to 8th century CE),

Indian patriarch of Nyingma and other Tibetan sects—*Natural Liberation: Padmasambhava's Teachings on the Six Bardos*, includes commentary by Gyatrul Rinpoche: This terma text is on the life and teachings of Padmasambhava including His teachings on the Bardo and specific profound instructions given to Yeshe Tsogyal.

Master Xuanzang/Hsuan Tsang (596-664),

Chinese Patriarch and Founder of the Fa-hsian School—*The Great Tang Dynasty Record of the Western Regions* (compiled by his disciple Bian-ji from Xuanzang's journals and travel records); *A Biography of the Tripitaka Master of the Great Ci'en Monastery of the Great Tang Dynasty* by monks Huili and Yancong; *Xuanzang: A Buddhist Pilgrim on the Silk Road* by Sally Wriggins; *Ultimate Journey: Retracing the Path of an Ancient Buddhist Monk Who Crossed Asia in Search of Enlightenment* by Richard Bernstein; and the famous Chinese novel based on Xuanzang's story *Journey to the West*: This seventh century Chinese monk left China against his emperor's orders and traveled to India in search of Buddhist texts that were not then available in China. After traversing the famous Silk Road, he reached his destinations, met the rulers of the land at that time, and studied his favorite text, Asanga's *Yogācārabhūmi Shastra,* under the famous teacher Shilabhadra of Nalanda University. Nearly fourteen years of his life (from 630 to 644 CE) were spent visiting Buddhist temples and monasteries, cities and places of interest in the Indian subcontinent including what is now known as Afghanistan. His study of the Bamiyan monasteries and colossal Buddhas have inspired art historians to make a thorough study of the cultural history of Afghanistan. He recorded his pilgrimage in great detail, capturing the state of Buddhism in the world at that time and documenting many sites and events. He returned to China a hero and spent his remaining years translating the many sutras and commentaries that he brought back to China.

Master Vairochana (7th to 8th centuries),

Tibetan Patriarch of the Nyingma sect--*The Great Image: The Life Story of Vairochana the Translator* by Vairochana: He was a great Tibetan dgozchen master, who like Padmasambhava is credited with bringing the highest Dharma to Tibet. His autobiography, as told to his closest disciples near the end of his life, not only tells of the great trials he endured to learn the precious doctrine, but also gives the origin and history of the dzogchen transmission itself.

Lady Yeshe Tshogyal (8th to 9th centuries),

Tibetan Matriarch of the Nyingma sect—*Mother of Knowledge:* The terma written by one of her fellow disciples tells the life-story of the major disciple of Guru Padmasambhava and the dramatic story of her flight from home, her life as a queen of Tibet, the stages of her spiritual training, and her enlightened accomplishments. The most important woman in the Nyingma lineage, she received all of Padmasambhava's teachings and was instrumental in transmitting them to future generations. This text demonstrates the qualities and attitudes essential for the pursuit of the Vajrayana.

Master Tilopa (988-1069),

Tilopa's Wisdom: His Life and Teachings on the Ganges Mahamudra by Khenchen Thrangu.

Lady Niguma (10th to 11th centuries),

Tibetan Matriarch of the Shangpa Kagyu sect--*Niguma, Lady of Illusion* by Saha Harding: Niguma was a mysterious eleventh-century Kashmiri woman who became the source of a major Tibetan Buddhist practice lineage. There are thirteen works that have been attributed to Niguma in the Tibetan Buddhist canon. These collected works form the basis of an ancient Shangpa lineage held by the great mahasiddha Tangtong Gyalpo, Kalu Rinpoche, and others.

Master Milarepa (1052-1135),

Tibetan Patriarch of the Karma Kagyu sect— *A Hundred Thousand Songs of Milarepa* and *the Life of Milarepa* by Heruka: Jetsun Milarepa is generally considered one of Tibet's most famous yogis and poets. He was a student of Marpa Lotsawa, another patriarch of this sect.

Lady Machig (Machik) Labdron (1055-1149),

Tibetan Matriarch and Founder of the Chöd lineage – *Machik's Complete Explanation: Clarifying the Meaning of Chod* by Sarah Harding: She developed a system, the Mahamudra Chöd, that takes the Buddha's teachings as a basis and applies them to the immediate experiences of negative mind states and malignant forces. Her unique feminine approach is to invoke and nurture the very demons that we fear and hate, transforming those reactive emotions into love. It is the tantric version of developing compassion and fearlessness, a radical method of cutting through ego-fixation.

Master Honen (1133-1212),

Japanese, Pure Land/Shin sect— *Honen The Buddhist Saint: Essential Writings and Official Biography* (Spiritual Masters: East and West) by Joseph A. Fitzgerald

Master Dogen (1200-1253),

Japanese Patriarch and Founder of Soto Zen sect—*Shobogenzo*: This Zen master, Eihiei Dogen Zenji, was central in bringing Zen from China to Japan.

Master Rangung Dorje (1284-1339),

Tibetan Patriarch of Karma Kagu sect— *The Third Karmapa Rangjung Dorje: Master of Mahamudra*, by Gamble Ruth.

Master Dolpopa (1292-1361),

Tibetan Patriarch of Jonang sect—*The Buddha from Dolpo* by Cyrus Stearns and *Mountain Doctrine* by Dolpopa: Dolpopa Sherab Gyaltsen was the most famous scholar of the Jonang school, who is most well-known for his articulation of the shentong view of "other emptiness."

Master Longchenpa (1308-1364),

Tibetan Nyingma Master— *Longchen Nyingthig. A Treasury Trove of Scriptural Transmission* and *The Life of Longchenpa: The Omniscient Dharma King of the Vast Expanse* by Jampa Mackenzie Stewart: Longchenpa combined the Vima Nyingtig and Khandro Nyingtig lineages to lay the ground for the fully unified system of Dzogchen teachings.

Master Tsongkhapa (1357-1419),

Tibetan Patriarch of the Geluk sect-- *Tsongkhapa: A Buddha in the Land of Snows* by Thupten Jinpa.

Master Tangtong Gyalpo (1361-1485),

Tibetan Patriarch of the Shangpa Kalpa— *King of the Empty Plain* by Cyrus Stearns: Known as the wild engineer-saint of both Tibet and Bhutan, this heroic mahasiddha was known for his accomplishments in technology (he invented a process for building iron bridges that were amazing structures that lasted until modern times), the arts (he founded the first Tibetan Opera Drama troupe), medicine (some of his cures are still used in Tibetan medicine), and transmission of the highest Dharmas of liberation. Although most unconventional in appearance and methods, he was also the most traveled of the early Tibetan holy men, traveling all over India, Afghanistan, probably Sri Lanka, and visiting the holy Mt. Wu-Tai in China.

Master Jamgon Kongtrul (1813-1899),

Tibetan founder of the nonsectarian Rime movement— *The Life of Jamgon Kongtrul The Great*: Jamgon Kongtrul Lodro Taye was one of the most prolific writers in the Tibetan world. His *Retreat Manual* on how to conduct and participate in a three-year/three-month/three-day retreat is still followed in some Tibetan traditions.

Master Dudjom Lingpa (1835-1904),

Tibetan tantric master and treasure (terma) revealer—*The Clear Mirror*, Autobiography.

Venerable Ajahn Mun (1870-1948),

Thai Theravada Master and founder of the modern Forest Tradition—*Spiritual Biography* by Maha Boowa Nanasampanno: The life and teaching of this Theravada master, who was the teacher of Ajahn Cha and other well-known Theravada masters.

Master Pabongka Rinpoche (1878-1943),

Tibetan Dharma King of the Geluk sect—*Liberation n the Palm of Your Hand: A Concise Discourse on the Path to Enlightenment.* This does include biographical material on Pabongka Rinpoche, an important 20th century Geluk rinpoche. The text is similar in content and structure to Tsongkapa's practice manual discussed earlier.

Venerable Mogok Sayadaw U Vimala (1899-1962).

Burmese Theravada Master—*In This Very Life: The Liberation Teachings of the Buddha:* The life and teachings of a well-known Burmese vipassana meditation master who stressed learning and understanding the principles of Paticcasamuppada (Dependent Origination) and the nature of impermanence before starting actual meditation practice. This was according to the method used by Shakyamuni Buddha. He is believed to have become accomplished, leaving relics as proof.

H.H. Dudjom Jigdral Yeshe Dorje (1904-1987),

The Nyingma School of Tibetan Buddhism: Its Fundamentals and History is included here because it includes short biographies of most of the major Patriarchs and Dharma Kings in the Nyingma lineage. It also includes reference to the second Dorje Chang Buddha in this world, Venerable Vimalakirti who was one who beseeched the Buddhas to send someone to continue the work of Shakyamuni Buddha after that great Buddha left this world.

H.H. Dilgo Khyentse (1910-1991),

Tibetan Dharma King of Nyingma sect—*Brilliant Moon:* Autobiography of a modern rinpoche.

Appendix A: The Great Dharma of Zen Practice

In March 2013 H.H. Dorje Chang Buddha III transmitted the Great Dharma of Zen and gave a discourse on the nature of zen and how it should be practiced. This is an English translation of that dharma discourse. It does not include the mantras that were transmitted that increase the effectiveness of practice although you can receive benefit from practicing it without them. I can transmit two of the mantras to qualified disciples, but you need to receive the third by means of a higher transmission.

Below is the complete content of "The Great Dharma of Zen Practice" expounded by H.H. Dorje Chang Buddha III. This is a transcription of a discourse on dharma given impromptu.

H.H. DORJE CHANG BUDDHA III EXPOUNDS "THE GREAT DHARMA OF ZEN PRACTICE"

Sit down, everyone.

Has everyone sat down? Is everyone ready?

(Everyone answers: "Yes.")

First, put your palms together. Recite the Taking Refuge Vows once. Generate the four immeasurable states of mind and bodhicitta. All right listen attentively. I will now begin to expound the dharma for all of you.

I summoned you disciples to gather here today mainly in response to the requests of some Westerners who are white, black, and Hispanic, as well as in response to some Asians. Some of those people are rinpoches. You have said that you especially like zen (pronounced *chan* in Chinese) and that you want to learn the practice of zen. Therefore, today I have come here to fulfill your wishes. I will transmit to all of you a high-level great dharma of zen.

Actually, all of you sitting here have heard the name "zen practice dharma." However, truthfully speaking, none of you know what is meant by zen practice. I can say that all of you present here and even many masters who teach zen practice, which include some of you sitting here today, do not understand what true zen practice is. Is what I just said going too far? I tell you unequivocally that what I just said is not going too far in the least! I will now ask you a few simple questions. What is zen practice? What is it used for? Why should one practice zen? What is the goal of zen practice? What is zen? Do you know? Can those of you who are masters and who teach zen practice answer me?

(Some people say: "We are not very clear about such things. Would the Buddha please teach such dharma?"]

I am one with a heart of humility. It would be acceptable for you to just call me Master. You say you are not very clear about such things. Actually, that is wrong. It is not that you are not very clear about such things. Even if you claimed to know, your understanding would be wrong. If you do not even understand what the concept of zen is after all, if you know nothing about the path of zen yet still want to teach it to people, that would be harming living beings and ruining people's wisdom-roots! You would have to bear the consequences of such karma. Human life is a few dozen years or a hundred years. Why would you want to commit such an offense?

Today I will first talk about zen. Zen is divided into the four kinds of zen and eight kinds of samadhi. Of course, you know about these. The sutras contain this term. What, after all, are the four kinds of zen and eight kinds of samadhi used for? Why does one engage in zen? What are the effects of zen? All of you have scanty knowledge of the answers to such questions. Many people like to engage in sitting zen. Many people like to practice zen . What do they actually want to accomplish? What do they want to obtain? What goal do they want to achieve? Everyone should first clearly understand the answers to these questions.

Within Buddhism, there are more practitioners who engage in zen practice than there are practitioners of any other dharma. Moreover, most of them are learned people. However, they are all in blind pursuit. I will not speak any more about this now. I will now directly teach zen. Zen is a dharma method. It is one type of dharma practice that is part of the Buddha-dharma taught by the Buddha. However, this dharma practice is independent. Nonetheless, the dharma-flavor and the key or essence of this dharma practice relate to the practice of any dharma method.

To put it concisely, zen is the absolute truth. The absolute truth is truth that never perishes. It is the source of the unity and equality of the three times: past, present, and future. This is the meaning of zen. Of course, there are many other ways of expressing this. I will not at this time talk about other theories. Those who engage in zen practice should understand certain simple principles. Today I will use the simplest, easiest to understand principles to teach you, principles that relate to a state when consciousness transforms.

That is, when consciousness that differentiates or discriminates changes into a state in which consciousness does not differentiate or discriminate, what is that non-conscious state? Is it devoid of wild fancy and improper thoughts? Is it nothingness? Is it very pure? Such an understanding is completely erroneous. All of you who want to thoroughly understand this non-conscious state must study *Expounding the Absolute Truth Through the Heart Sutra*[63] that I spoke. After you study *Expounding the Absolute Truth Through the Heart Sutra*, you will apprehend what we are searching for, what our goal is, what we want to find, what we want to awaken to, and what we want to realize in the religious truths of zen.

Given that, will we be able to find the thing that we want to find? We will never find that thing through searching! As long as we search for it, we will not find it! Why will we not find it? It is because when we search

---

63 *The preliminary translation of the title of this book has been changed to* Imparting the Absolute Truth Through the Heart Sutra, *although the book has yet to be published in English.*

we must use our own consciousness to search. It is like going outside and searching everywhere for your own child who is already being carried on your own back. You say, "Oh no, where did my child go? What place did my child go to?" You will never find your child since you are the one who is actually carrying the child on your back.

Therefore, you will never find zen by using consciousness, by using the mind to intentionally search. A type of practice method is necessary to find zen. Zen itself is not a practice method. However, we can find, obtain, and realize zen only through a practice method. Listen attentively because this is not at all easy to understand. If you do not listen carefully, if your thoughts are not focused, you will not understand. Today I will teach all of you this method of practicing zen.

Let's first understand the basic concept of zen. With this basis, it will be easier to obtain zen. We want to obtain a state of zen. It is called a state. Actually, there is no state. If a state appears and we are able to use our consciousness to differentiate what type of state has appeared, then that already is not zen. However, the word *state* must be used as a figure of speech; otherwise, there are no words to express this. If *state* is not used, what word should be used? There has to be a term to express it.

What thing is that state? It is a thing that enables you to not be born and not die. That thing is you. You are that thing. The word *thing* is used as a figure of speech. It is an expedient way to explain something. Otherwise, just like with the word *state*, there would be no word to express it. Precisely because of this, there is the saying, "No speaking, no activities of consciousness." Simply put, the goal of practicing zen is enlightenment! The goal of enlightenment is to obtain the thing that is not born and does not die! It is a so-called thing. There is no such thing. I am talking about a so-called thing or state. Actually, there is no such thing. That is because if such a "thing" exists, it was produced by a differentiation or discrimination made in our consciousness. It was produced out of our thoughts.

For example, this is a round thing. This is a long thing, both ends of which are black. It is a pen. This is a string of beads. This is an image of a Buddha. This is a lotus. This is an expanse of emptiness. Who told you all of that? It came from differentiations, distinctions, or identifications made in your own consciousness. If your consciousness can distinguish and identify things such as an image of a Buddha or a lotus, then you are already not zen. Instead, your mind of differentiating thoughts is that of an ordinary person.

I return to what I said. If you read and are able to understand *Expounding the Absolute Truth Through the Heart Sutra*, you will solve all forms of zen. That is, you will obtain all forms of zen! Of course, you might say, "Since I have read treatises and writings by Nagarjuna, Aryadeva, Dignaga, Candrakirti, Fuhu, Asanga, Vasubandhu, Santideva, Xuanzang, and others of prior generations, I shouldn't have to read *Imparting the Absolute Truth Through the Heart Sutra*, right?" All I can tell you today is that those treatises and writings that you read are not bad, since they are expositions by people on the level of a patriarch. However, those books do not have the effect of *Imparting the Absolute Truth Through the Heart Sutra*. So I reiterate that you must study *Imparting the Absolute Truth Through the Heart Sutra*! If you truly understand it through studying it, you will have succeeded.

Speaking of zen, there are a great many types of zen. Other than the states of the four kinds of zen and eight kinds of samadhi, there are many methods to reach awakening or enlightenment. Each of those methods is different. The relative level of each method is also different. There is tathagata zen, patriarchal zen, altar lamp zen, wooden fish zen, thought cessation zen, one sense organ zen, unification of two states zen, introspection zen, breath counting zen, pure water zen, dharma characteristics zen, focusing on moon zen, guard the orifices zen, tummo (inner-heat) zen, cold air zen, "who is chanting the name of Amitabha Buddha?" zen, afflictions elimination zen, great enlightenment zen, and immovable zen of kalachakra. Of course, there are even more zen methods, a great many more. This would include the so-called cypress tree in front of courtyard zen and the so-called no-voice, no speech zen.

There are many forms of zen. There are so many. If I were to introduce you to them one by one, it would take three to five years. Therefore, today I will not go into such detail. What you mainly want to understand is what zen is, what you want to attain as a goal in engaging in zen practice. You want to attain introspection, enlightenment, understanding of your mind and seeing your original nature. You want to see your own original nature that was not born and does not die! Do you understand? I return to that principle: After you study and understand *Imparting the Absolute Truth Through the Heart Sutra*, zen will be kid's stuff. At that time, you naturally will clearly understand in one reading the *Diamond Sutra* and the *Sutra on Understanding and Realizing the Definitive Truth*, and you will realize the sameness of principles and essence.

We engage in zen for the purpose of realizing original nature, emptiness, or dharmakaya. This dharmakaya was not born and does not die. I will give an example to all of you. Some methods of zen practice are truly inexplicable but unfathomably profound. Take, for example, the Gaomin Monastery in Yangzhou. In ancient times, a great number of people there became accomplished through the practice of zen. At the Gaomin Monastery in Yangzhou, basically every seven days one person would awaken to zen, becoming enlightened and accomplished. That being the case, how did they do their zen practice? The dharma methods that they applied were not called by any of the names of those forms of zen that I just mentioned. Those dharma methods also did not include any of the zen practice techniques of those forms of zen that I just mentioned. That is why I say that there are a great many zen dharmas.

First of all, in ancient times when someone entered the Gaomin Monastery to practice zen, that person would first have to sign an agreement.

That agreement was very simple. To put it bluntly, they agreed that they could be beaten to death with impunity. The one who beat them to death would not have to lose his own life. Additionally, they agreed to voluntarily carry out the dharma rules of the monastery. After they entered the monastery, there were many ways for them to practice zen. Here I will talk about three of those ways. They had to give up all of the dharmas that they previously learned. As soon as one arrived at Gaomin Monastery and entered the zen hall, one could not apply any previously learned dharmas.

Five people carried cudgels. Those five were called "the five great cudgel carriers." Their specific task was to beat people. The practitioners had periods of running zen, each of which lasted the time it took for a stick of incense to burn from top to bottom. The stick of incense was not long. It was only this long. The practitioners had to jog. In the zen hall, many practitioners formed a circle and jogged. As they jogged, one of the cudgel carriers would strike his cudgel against something, which made a loud noise. As soon as he struck his cudgel against something, that loud noise sounded. When the jogging practitioners heard the striking sound from the cudgel, they had to immediately stop jogging. They were not allowed to jog even one more step. When the striking sound of the cudgel sounded again, they had to immediately resume their jogging. Have any of you seen a cudgel used by a cudgel carrier in a zen hall?

(Everyone answers: "No.")

Sometime in the future I will find a time to show you a cudgel from the Gaomin Monastery in Yangzhou that was used in the past. As soon as the striking sound from his cudgel sounded, if you were still jogging, you would be taken aside and beaten to death. If you were not beaten to death, you were at the very least maimed. Thus, the minds of those practitioners were of course extremely focused. They were always focused on the sound of the cudgel. They were always fearful that they would be taken aside and severely beaten for continuing to jog after the striking of the cudgel sounded, or, if they had stopped jogging, for not immediately resuming their jogging after the striking of the cudgel sounded. Do you understand?

There was a sitting period, which lasted as long as it took for a stick of incense to burn from top to bottom. As soon as they sat down, the cudgel carriers in back of them would keep an eye on them. While sitting, the practitioners were not allowed to move in any way. The practitioners were absolutely forbidden to move. They were not permitted to recite the name of any Buddha or chant any mantra. If one was seen moving a bit, he was taken aside and severely beaten, to the extent of possible death. Therefore, after they sat down in a settled posture, as soon as the striking sound of the cudgel carrier's cudgel could be heard, they did not dare move. They had to remain stiff for as long as the incense stick burned. They did not dare move in the slightest. The focus of their minds increased a hundredfold because they feared that they would inadvertently move, be taken aside, and be beaten, resulting in injury, deformity, or death.

Another example is the drinking of water. The practitioners had to go to the east side to draw water and then carry the water with both hands to the west side. Only then could they drink the water. Additionally, the cup of water had to be completely filled. If any water spilled to the ground as they were carrying the cup with both hands, they were taken aside and severely beaten.

Thus, the consciousness of those who practiced zen there did not wander. They did not think of other things. They did not rest. When they ate, they were not even allowed to make the sound of chopsticks hitting the bowl. As a result, their consciousness was forced to naturally not dare think of other things. Do you understand? Therefore, it is only natural that after our consciousness is united, we will not think things over and will not be distracted. Everyone fears being beaten to death. Do you understand? When you fear being beaten to death and death is used to force you, then you have no other choice. You must seriously deal with the matter. That is why in such circumstances it is very easy to cut off mistaken thinking. Through force, your thoughts are cut off. When your thoughts are cut off through force, your original nature emerges. As soon as your original nature emerges, you have broken through in your zen practice.

Therefore, by and large, at each seven-day retreat someone broke through in his zen practice at that monastery. Basically, there would be one breakthrough every seven days. How did they know someone broke through? The day someone broke through, he was ordered to write a verse for others to hear, enabling the abbot of the zen hall and the zen master to recognize him. That practitioner was later tested again to see whether he truly awakened to the truth through the practice of zen, whether he understood his mind and saw his nature. Do you understand?

(Everyone answers: "I understand.")

There is a school in Buddhism called the zen (chan) school. The Sixth Patriarch of the zen (chan) school was Patriarch Huineng. His was the sudden enlightenment method. At that time there were two patriarchs. The other patriarch was called Shenxiu. His was the gradual enlightenment method. Actually, both patriarchs were accomplished. It is just that they did not have the same level of insight.

After Shenxiu attained a certain level of realization, he composed a verse. The verse that he wrote is:

The body is the bodhi tree

The mind is like a bright mirror on a stand

At all times wipe it diligently

And let no dust sully it

He was saying that his body is like the bodhi tree that symbolizes accomplishment. The meaning here is that his body represents accomplishment. In other words, his body represents liberation. He was saying his body is a state of liberation. Why is that tree called the bodhi tree? It is because Sakyamuni Buddha attained full realization and perfect enlightenment under the bodhi tree. That is why later on the phrase "realize bodhi" was understood to mean become accomplished. That is how that came to be.

Shenxiu was saying that his body is the bodhi tree but that his mind is never confused, is clear, does not violate the laws of cause and effect, and knows everything. Thus, he wrote, "The mind is like a bright mirror on a stand." Additionally, he was saying that he was cultivating himself at all times and all places, that he would correct himself whenever he discovered something not good about himself. Thus, he wrote, "At all times wipe it diligently." Here, wiping means using a feather duster. He is saying that he constantly holds a feather duster to whisk off his defilements. "And let no dust sully it" means that he would not let dirty things sully him. Here, dirty things refer to impure karma rather than dust visible to us. His meaning here was that he very seriously corrects whatever is not good about himself so as to comport with the teachings of the Buddha.

Generally, from Shenxiu's verse, people thought that he was already the bodhi tree. Moreover, he was still correcting his mistakes. Of course, that is good, isn't it? However, Huineng did not have such a view. That is because Shenxiu had not awakened to the essence of zen. That is, he had not truly realized great, complete zen enlightenment. His enlightenment was not thorough enlightenment. Huineng was very young. He was a child, but he had attained thorough enlightenment. When Huineng heard this verse by Shenxiu, he said, "I also want to write a verse." He said he also wanted to write one. Because he was illiterate, he asked a fellow-disciple to write his verse on a wall. Huineng responded to Shenxiu's verse based on the content of Shenxiu's verse.

He wrote, "Bodhi originally has no tree." That is, there is the term "bodhi tree," but there is no such tree. That tree does not exist. "The bright mirror on a stand is also not real." Although you know everything, there is no such concrete thing and there is no knower of it. Thus, there is no such real stand. Because Shenxiu said, "The mind is like a bright mirror on a stand," Huineng said, "The bright mirror on a stand is also not real." "Not a single thing has ever existed. What, then, could dust sully?" Originally, there is not one thing. Where can dust go to sully? What can dust sully? There is not one thing to be sullied by it. That is, there is no place for thoughts to abide in Buddha-nature. Since thoughts cannot arise, the zen state that is realized is one in which nothing sticks or clings. Dust or anything else does not stick to or cling to anything. That is because there is nothing to stick or cling to. Here you must carefully grasp what I am saying. Do not think this state is the emptiness of the four elements. Do not think that there is a state of emptiness. That would be a mistake. The truth is that this state of emptiness also does not exist. Thus, there is no place to be sullied by dust.

(Many Western rinpoches and scholars who are Caucasian or of another ethnicity were in attendance. Several people were all trying to translate a certain part of what the Buddha Master was teaching. Listening to them, the Buddha Master knew that their translation into English was erroneous and disordered. At once, the Buddha Master sternly criticized them for their mistaken translation. The Buddha Master told them they were not allowed to feign understanding or continue with their chaotic translation. Finally, the Buddha Master instructed Bodi Wentu Rinpoche to continue translating.)

Shenxiu had a certain thing called the bodhi tree. The Buddha-dharma state that he realized had a certain thing that he wanted to have. However, Huineng then said that in the Buddha-dharma even consciousness does not differentiate. What thing, then, could still exist? No thing exists. What, then, could be sullied? Hence, in emptiness there cannot be consciousness that differentiates. If one's consciousness differentiates, one falls into the consciousness of any ordinary person and departs from emptiness. Having departed from emptiness, one naturally has the state of an ordinary person. Without consciousness that differentiates, one enters the state of a holy person. However, it is by and large impossible for people not to have a consciousness that differentiates. That is why they must learn from the Buddhas and cultivate themselves.

I can see today that your translation requires a great deal of effort and that many translation errors have occurred. I do not want to waste time by continuing to speak about the same subject matter. Without further delay, I will teach you zen practice methods. All right, I will now directly teach you those methods.

With respect to the zen I will be transmitting to everyone today, why is it that as soon as some people sit down to meditate, if their thoughts are not scattered, then they fall asleep; and if they do not fall asleep, then they are dull-minded; and if they are not dull-minded, they are unfocused? It is mainly because of karmic hindrances, evil karma, good karma, and ignorance-based karma that have accumulated since beginning-less time spanning many eons. That is, these karmic forces that are good, bad, and even neither good nor bad have besieged us. Therefore, when we sit down to meditate, we cannot quiet down our thoughts. Being unable to quiet down our thoughts, we will be even more unable to cut off our thoughts. Being unable to cut off our thoughts, it will be totally impossible for us to realize the zen state and enter samadhi. Thus, we will have no way to attain enlightenment.

Therefore, people who practice zen usually only know about teaching people how to practice zen. They themselves practice zen. However, people who practice zen generally do not know that there is a special mantra for zen practice. We must first purify the zen practice altar area. That is, when we sit down to engage in zen practice, we first have to recite this

Altar Area Purification Mantra to remove impurities from the altar area, to completely dispel evil energy that is harmful to us, evil spirits, and other bad things. This is the first task we should do. If we are in the mountains, we should also invite the mountain spirits to guard the mountain passes, prevent the invasion of wild animals, and prevent the invasion of mountain and tree goblins. Thus, there would be two dharmas to practice. However, if we are in our homes, we do not have that problem. Still, people in some places fear typhoons, while people in some other places fear earthquakes, floods, and fires.

A very important point is that people do not have the knowledge of the dharma that prevents external hindrances while practicing the zen dharma. This dharma should first be applied to take precautions against such hindrances. There are two parts. The first part is the power of mantras. The other part is the power of one's body. With respect to mantras, there are three mantras, each of which is indispensible. If one of those three mantras is missing, it will be very difficult to have a breakthrough in one's zen practice. One's zen practice will become one of those ordinary, secular practices. The preventing external hindrances dharma is for people who practice zen inside or outside their home, who practice zen in the city rather than in the mountains.

The first mantra is called the Altar Area Purification Mantra. This Altar Area Purification Mantra does not necessarily mean purification of a mandala. Remember, altar area does not have the meaning of mandala. Altar area is the place in your home where you do your special daily dharma practice or any other place where you can sit in meditation. This is one mantra.

The second mantra, which is exclusively for the practice of zen, is to eliminate karma and contemplate emptiness. It is used in zen, specifically for those who practice zen. It can clear away one's karmic forces, temporarily removing them.

The third mantra is very important. It is the Mind Quieting Mantra. This mantra requires very strict observance of the precepts by those who practice zen. It is just as strict for all Buddhists. The conduct of anyone who chants this mantra must truly be that of a Bodhisattva. Such a person must strictly observe the precepts and disciplines, including the five precepts, and must truly carry out the three sets of pure precepts. If you commit a serious violation, this mantra will have no beneficial effect. If you commit minor violation, the mantra will produce no good results. It will be very difficult for you to attain quietude. If you cannot attain quietude, you will not be able to enter samadhi.

This mantra is also called Mantra to Read the Minds of Others. How could it be acceptable for a person to attain the power to read the minds of others if that person does not observe the precepts well and is not a true cultivator? If that were to happen, Buddha-dharma realms would fall into chaos. That is because people who do not observe the precepts well are likely to harm people and living beings and even harm Buddhas and Bodhisattvas. Evil people, deceivers, and precept violators are not allowed to enter a Buddha-dharma domain.

Moreover, transmission of this Mantra to Read the Minds of Others, this Mind Quieting Mantra, requires an initiation in which bodhi holy water is sprinkled. You must especially bear in mind that if someone who learns this mantra casually transmits it to a third person without performing an initiation in conformity with the dharma, then such a master who transmits this mantra will never in his or her lifetime attain the power to read the minds of others no matter what the status of that master is. This is indisputable!!!

Additionally, if you attain the power to read the minds of others, you may not show others that power. If you violate this rule, it is possible that you will lose your power to read the minds of others. Instead, what you truly should show others is how to benefit living beings, how to cut off attachment to self and selfishness, and how to adopt the greatly compassionate and greatly kind conduct of a Bodhisattva. What you should show others is the undertaking of a Bodhisattva. A Bodhisattva enlightens himself first and then enlightens others. Therefore, you masters who transmit this mantra should think over who you really are. Do not harm yourself in order to show off in front of others.

You can practice zen with only the first two mantras and without the Mind Quieting Mantra. It is just that the results will be not be as good. These three mantras must first be recited. Only after you have performed this task may you start your zen practice. If you have not learned these three mantras, as long as your zen practice is correct, you will also experience beneficial effects. However, the beneficial effects you will be able to experience will at most be 30% of what you would experience with such mantras. I will now transmit to you the first mantra. I will teach it to you. I will now transmit to you that mantra. I do not want to speak too long.

To learn the first mantra, put your palms together. You must be very respectful and have a very sincere heart. Close your eyes. After I have empowered all of you, I will begin to recite that mantra....Repeat after me.... All right, I have now transmitted to you the first mantra.

The first mantra is the Altar Area Purification Mantra for the practice of zen. The main function of this mantra is to purify the altar area, to totally clear away all impure, filthy things as well as all karmic impressions and obstructive karma. This is directed at the place in which one practices zen. It is not directed at oneself. Its main effect is directed at the altar area. Therefore, one's own karmic forces are still not cleared away. That is why any top-notch zen practice dharma must also include the Mantra to Remove Obstacles, Enter Samadhi, Purify Karma, and Contemplate Emptiness, which is exclusively used for the practice of zen. Everyone should now repeat after me as we recite this Mantra to Remove Obstacles, Enter Samadhi, Purify Karma, and Contemplate Emptiness. I will read a sentence, and all of you will then repeat that sentence. I will now teach the second mantra. The words of that mantra will not be written in the dharma booklet. Today I will not transmit the third mantra, the Mind Quieting Mantra, because I did not bring with me bodhi holy water necessary for such an initiation. Next time I will perform that initiation.

All right, I have finished transmitting both mantras. Having finished transmitting them, I will now teach everyone the methods of practicing zen. There are a great many principles and theories relating to the practice of zen. I will not explain them in detail. In order to save time, I will directly transmit to you the methods! I hope that you will bear in mind that because the dharmas of zen practice that I will be transmitting to you are high-level zen practices, you therefore may not casually transmit them to other people. It is also not permissible for you to go so far as to transmit them to a disciple who has violated the precepts! You must transmit them to Buddhists who abide by the rules and precepts very well. Moreover, they should be good people of moral character who have realized a state of great compassion and awakening, who sincerely learn from the Buddhas, who have the four immeasurable minds, who carry out the myriad practices subsumed within the six perfections, and who strictly abide by the precepts and disciplines. They are the ones who should learn the dharmas of zen practice. Buddha-dharma should be transmitted to good people. Do not transmit Buddha-dharma to those bad people who have serious problems. However, after such people with serious problems repent, of course we will transmit Buddha-dharma to them as well. Additionally, do not transmit Buddha-dharma to those who take bribes and bend the law or who have their hands out for other people's money or offerings. That type of person is in fact problematic. So everyone should be especially careful about this.

As I said a moment ago, in order to save time, I will not speak superfluous words. I will directly teach you. After we have sat down and become calm, we enter the practice step by step. We first start with the meditation method that Sakyamuni Buddha used under the bodhi tree. This first step is a dharma of clear observation (vipasyansa) practice categorized as pratyutpana. That is, one observes the ocean of self-nature in which prajna will appear. It is called observation of thoughts that lead to realization of emptiness.

My way of beginning here is different from that of those zen practitioners in society. I first want all of you to start with counting your breaths. You will start with the minor samatha and vipasyana method of counting breaths. However, this is not totally the same as a minor samatha and vipasyana method. We do not care about which monster or demon corresponds to which of the 12 two-hour periods into which the day was traditionally divided. Because we have three mantras, we are not afraid if those monsters or demons try to disturb us. We simply bear in mind that those who are overweight should count the exhalations. Thin people should count the inhalations. That is, when you are breathing inward, count those inwards breaths if you are thin. That way, your physical condition will improve. If you are overweight and you cannot gain too much more weight, you should count your exhalations. That way, you will avoid becoming too fat.

Of course, whether you are overweight or thin is not important. The key is teaching all of you how to count your breaths, whether you are overweight or thin. How should you count your breaths? Start counting from one. For example, if you are counting your inhalations, you count the breaths that go in. You will softly utter "one." You must say it out loud. Do not count when you exhale. When the next breath is inhaled, you utter aloud "two." If you cannot breathe in and utter aloud the numbers at the same time, then count the numbers silently in your mind. Continue like this until you count to ten, and then immediately begin counting all over again. Begin again from "one" and count until "ten." Then, once more, start all over. Make sure you do not count to "eleven" or "twelve." This is very important.

When counting, if your mind is not scattered for about a half hour, or better yet for even an hour, then at that time you should stop uttering numbers out loud and should silently count in your mind. The method of counting is the same when you silently count. It is just that you do not say the number out loud. When you inhale, you still count "one." Or when you exhale, you still count "one." When you exhale a second time, you count "two." In this manner, you count to ten time and time again, over and over again. Do not make a mistake in counting the numbers by going past "ten."

After this step, we then begin to enter the pratyutpana water stage, which is practicing the water-light observation dharma. Pour a cup of water. After the water has been poured into the cup, place the cup about three feet away from you. Use indoor lamplight or moonlight from the outdoor sky. In that water there will be light. You should fix your vision upon that light, tightly staring at it. At that time, do not count your breaths. Your mind is totally focused upon that light, never moving away from that light one bit. Your total focus is light, light, light, light. Your eyes are fixed upon that light, never moving away from that light one bit. Do not analyze the largeness or smallness of the light. Additionally, do not analyze the changes the light undergoes. Do not be concerned about the strength or weakness of the light. The longer you maintain your focus, the better.

If you can maintain your focus on that light for more than a half hour, if during that time your mind does not leave that light and is not scattered, or if you can maintain your focus on that light for more than twenty minutes and your mind does not run away, then at that time you should change to observing your inhalations or exhalations. When you exhale, you will feel an obvious sensation at the rim of your nostrils or at a certain position on your upper lip. Focus on that sensation at that particular location that stands out. You should very clearly feel that sensation when breathing in and breathing out. However, your mind absolutely may not follow your breath as it moves inward or outward. All of your effort is completely focused solely upon that small position or location on your skin or lip that feels the sensation of breaths. If your mind follows your breath inward or outward, you have already lost your concentration. So make sure to pay attention that your mind does not follow your breath as it moves. Your mind may only focus upon that particular position or location of your skin or lip that feels the breath. You should clearly feel the obvious sensation that particular position or location has when exhaling and inhaling.

That feeling will decrease or increase according to the decrease and increase of your zen practice concentration powers. There will even be some times when you will barely have any feeling at that position or location. However, there is no need to worry. The situation will improve when you focus your mind. When your power of samadhi strengthens, illusory phenomena will appear in your zen state, such as spots of light, circles of light, and figures. Do not be attached to or distracted by any of them. You must remember that if at that time your mind becomes scattered, like a wild horse, or if you are obstructed by drowsiness or sleep, then you should stop. You must switch to the dynamic mindfulness of observing waves. You should immediately hold level with both hands your cup from which you observed light. Place that cup on your hands and sit in the cross-legged posture. If you cannot sit in that posture, you may sit on a stool or bench. Hold the cup level with both hands and place it below your navel. Your hands should be resting firmly on your legs. At that time, because it is the nature of your body to slightly move, the cup you are holding will certainly move. Along with this, the light will move. The waves of water will move. You must completely fill the cup with water. Use a copper, brass, or bronze cup that is not too large. That is because if it is too large it will be too heavy.

At that time, fix your eyes upon the light inside the cup. If at that time the cup moves, the light will become blurred, which is not good. Blurred light indicates your mind has not calmed down. Therefore, you should strive to have the water not move. It should not move one bit. Not one bit. Not one bit. Not one bit. You absolutely must keep it from moving. It should be totally still. If you can sit for a half hour or an hour or even a few hours during which time the water does not move, then your skills in the practice of zen will soon mature. You must understand that the movement of waves means the movement of light, and movement of light means the movement of waves. Know that the movement of waves and light means the movement of your mind. You certainly will have become enlightened if at that time you can attain the following: "waves and light continue to come and go, yet mindfulness, remaining unchanged, is not moved."

It may be that you are unable to continue with your sitting practice. At that time, you are most susceptible to fatigue. As soon as fatigue sets in, people want to sleep. As a result, the light of the waves easily becomes scattered or your mind is sidetracked. Sometimes it is even the case that only when water spills on you do you discover how sidetracked you are. This shows that you were not in samadhi. At the very least, you lacked basic samadhi. Of course, I am not referring to tathagata samadhi. I am simply referring to a type of samadhi that is unmoving.

Given this type of situation, you should immediately stop if at that time your eyelids are heavy with sleep, your mind begins to dull, you will soon fall asleep, and you truly cannot persist. Place the cup right in front of you. Then, pull down on your earlobes with both hands. After that, rub your palms together until they are hot. Then, begin to rub your face with your palms. Rub your face. Your face will heat up. Rub softly. Continue to rub softly. At that time, after you have rubbed your face, the obstacle of drowsiness or sleep will have disappeared. Then resume your meditation.

If obstructions reappear after you have meditated for a period of time and you realize you cannot go on, then you should immediately change the dharma you are practicing. Change to what? You immediately get off of your meditation seat, fill a bucket with cold water, and recite the Using Water Mantra seven times. After that, wash your face with that cold water.

Rub the water on your face, neck, and below your neck. At that time, your vitality will be restored such that you can immediately resume your zen practice. Your eyelids will no longer feel heavy, and you will be clear-headed. At that time, resume your zen practice. Sit down and practice.

After you have resumed your sitting zen practice for a long time, it is frequently the case that you will once more be unable to continue with your practice. There is truly no way for you to continue your sitting practice. What should you do? At that time you must stop. You should stop. What should you do after you stop? You should sleep after you stop. After you awaken from your sleep, you will regain your vitality. You then continue your sitting practice.

If you had not stopped to sleep but rather tried to persevere in your zen practice even though you could not keep it up, then a zen malady will arise. At that time, such a zen malady is very serious. Why do I say it is very serious? It is because as soon as you form the habit of incurring a zen malady, you will still want to continue your zen practice when, for example, your eyelids are heavy. You will forcefully attempt to carry on even though your eyelids are still heavy with sleep. But because you sleep, you have formed a bad habit. Thus, problems arise at this time that are not easy to correct. It is possible that when you sit down to practice zen, you will want to sleep or the other three great hindrances will appear.

Therefore, when serious hindrances appear, you should immediately begin to pull on your ears and immediately begin to rub your face. If rubbing your face and pulling on your ears do not work, you should immediately get off your meditation seat and fill a bucket with cold water. Then, recite the Using Water Mantra and wash your face. If you still cannot go on after you have washed your face with cold water and have sat down and practiced zen for a short while, then at that time you immediately discontinue your zen practice. Get off your meditation seat and go to sleep without delay. After you awaken, you get up and practice zen once again.

This is very important, very important. Everyone must be very careful. You must remember that when practicing zen, if it is truly the case that the obstacle of drowsiness or sleep arrives, mental distraction arrives, wild fancy or improper thoughts arrive, or lack of focus arrives, then they must be dealt with. The obstacle of drowsiness or sleep is an especially formidable karmic obstacle. You do not know when it arrives. It causes you to fall asleep. By the time you awaken, time has already passed by. That is why that obstacle is very difficult to deal with.

Remember that it is very easy for good states to appear in the course of practicing zen. This is called zen phenomena. Such zen phenomena that may appear include light, light spots, or even unusual phenomena, such as dharma protectors, demons, and so on, or an unusual fragrance wafts your way, or you hear sounds from outside or different places. You must remember that all such phenomena are illusions. All phenomena are false. In no case may you be attached to them. You must not be attached to them. Only with non-attachment will such phenomena deepen and progress. Only with non-attachment will you progress toward entering the pure dharmakaya. This is the truth of deeply entering the zen state. When you enter the zen state, truly attaining the state of non-abiding, your Buddha-nature will naturally appear. When you are able to be imperturbable in your Buddha-nature, then birth and death naturally end. You are able to end the cycle of birth and death. If you can be in your Buddha-nature, wisdom will naturally open up. You will be able to experience numerous kinds of holy states. You will realize all holy states. All of these are within the Buddha-nature.

Of course, this is a relatively high-level type of zen practice. This is a great dharma of the true practice of zen. However, what makes it truly high-level? The empowerment of the mantras and the way of observation and contemplation make it truly high-level. Both of them have a special effect. When you have practiced well this stage, depending upon the depth of your wholesome roots, perhaps I will perform for you a State-Practice

Initiation from "The Supreme and Unsurpassable Mahamudra of Libera-tion." Such dharma is indeed high. It is supreme, great dharma that guar-antees liberation. Nonetheless, in learning and practicing "The Supreme and Unsurpassable Mahamudra of Liberation," it is imperative that one learn well and fully put into practice the two great mind essences: the "Xiaman Magnificent Oceanic Mind Essence" and the "Ultimate Bodhicitta for Attaining Dharma-Nature True-Thusness Oceanic Mind Essence." You must have these two great mind essences as your foundation. Only then will you be able to instantly receive a state-practice initiation, instantly enter that state, attain great accomplishment, and unite with the dhar-ma-realm through learning and practicing dharma of "The Supreme and Unsurpassable Mahamudra of Liberation." In this there is limitless pro-fundity.

Today I have taken the first step to teach all of you this zen practice. I have already transmitted to you the part relating to the mantras. Those mantras will not be written in the booklet. To write them down in a book-let would not be permissible. It would not be in accord with the dharma rules. Those mantras must be transmitted from master to disciple. Other-wise, it would be treating the dharma disrespectfully. Moreover, transmis-sion through different levels of initiation is the type of transmission that most accords with the dharma rules. That is why those mantras cannot be recklessly written down. In the booklet, the mantras relating to zen will not be transcribed. It will only include teachings on this high-level dharma of zen practice.

My teachings today will end here for the time being. After you have practiced well these teachings I just gave, I may perform for you a dhar-ma selection ceremony to determine the dharma with which you have a karmic connection, the dharma you should deeply learn and practice. However, this will depend upon the beneficial effects and level of accom-plishment you derive from practicing the teachings I just gave. It will also depend upon your devoutness. Remember one thing that is important.

No matter what zen dharma you practice, you cannot deviate from cultivation. That is why you must go online and learn my teaching of "What Is Cultivation?" Furthermore, you must carry out that teaching in your daily lives. Only then will your practice of zen truly succeed. All right, that will be all. May all of you soon deeply enter samadhi, soon attain perfect good fortune and wisdom, and soon realize enlightenment.

Transmitted by H.H. Dorje Chang Buddha III
Office of H.H. Dorje Chang Buddha III
December 4, 2013

Appendix B:

The Ways to Become a Holy Being or Saint

These charts represent my understanding of how one progresses on the path to Buddhahood and the belief that all sentient beings are on such a path, even if that is not yet their conscious goal. They are very simplified and do not reflect many of the details or nuances within the various categories. The first chart shows the difference in goals among the world religions and the two main branches of Buddhism. The second chart provides basic information about what the other religions and the four categories of Buddhist practice include—the level of attainment involved in each and the time required to become accomplished. The third chart lists some of the vows and actual practices done in each of these categories. Please remember that the charts represent generalizations about the various systems of belief and are not absolutely true for any given practitioner within that system.

	Other World Religions	Buddhism	
	Initial Stage	Hinayana Stage*	Mahayana Stage (open & secret)
Goal	To stop non-meritorious (evil) behavior and practice good behavior to accumulate necessary merit so as to gain high status and a favorable rebirth in the future. In Buddhism this is seen only as a provisional goal and not as an end in itself. However, mastery of this stage is necessary to progress to higher levels.	To escape suffering of samsara (cycle of birth and death). This includes Sravakas or Arhats (Lo-hans) as well as the Pratyekabuddhas who obtain liberation on their own without a teacher in their current lifetime. This is also seen as a provisional goal or respite on the way to Buddhahood whereby the conflicting emotions are eliminated but the goal of ultimate nirvana has not been reached.	The superior goal of the Bodhisattva to bring all beings to complete enlightenment or ultimate nirvana before gaining the goal of Buddhahood for one's self. Here the double veils of conflicting emotions and primitive beliefs about reality have both been lifted and one achieves complete enlightenment.

* *See note text on page 291*

	Other World Religions	Exoteric Buddhism		Esoteric Buddhism
		Hinayana	Mahayana	
Path	Path of Favorable Rebirth (Not a Buddhist Path)	Path to Liberation (Sravakayana) (Pratyekayana)	Paramita or Open Mahayana Path to Buddhahood (Bodhisattvayana)	Tantric or Secret Mahayana Path to Buddhahood (Vajrayana or Tantrayana)
Vehicle	Of Gods & Men Of Brahma	Of Sravak-as	Of Pratyeka-buddhas	Of Bodhisattvas	Of Bodhisattvas
Level of Attainment Possible	Rebirth in the 3 Higher Realms of Samsara including the various Heavens, but will still have to take unfavorable rebirths to pay off karmic debts unless they become enlightened while in these realms.	Arhat or Lohan (Sravakas)	Pratyeka-Buddha (Not True Buddhas)	Arhats ten levels or stages of Bodhisattvas	Buddhahood Twelve or Thirteen Levels of Bodhisattvas
Buddha Body Attained		None	None	Dharmakaya (Sambhoga-kaya and Nirmanakaya are both revealed but not emphasized)	Dhamakaya, Sambhogakaya, Nirmanakaya and Real Nature Body. Advanced adepts may obtain the Immortal body or Rainbow Body
Time Required		1-7 life-times to become an Arhat	100 kalpas to become a Pratyeka-Buddha	3 asaïkhya kalpas	Liberation possible in current lifetime with higher empowerments. Lower level practices can take up to 16 lifetimes.

	Non-Buddhist	Hinayana	Open Mahayana	Secret Vajrayana
Vows	Sometimes Take Refuge in the Three Jewels	Take Refuge in the Three Jewels Pratimoksha Vows for Individual Liberation	Take Refuge in the Three Jewels Bodhisattva Vows to Liberate All Beings Pratimoksha Vows	Take Refuge in Three or Four Jewels Tantric Vows (vary to fit practitioner's karma) Bodhisattva Vows Pratimoksha Vows
Major Practices training	Four Limitless States of Mind Morality Ten Good Characteristics Sometimes practice forms of concentration (meditation)	Impermanence Firm Belief in the Suffering of Samsara Cause & Effect (karma) Appreciation for human birth 12 links of Dependent Origination Four Noble Truths (Ten Good Characteristics) Four Limitless States of Mind 37 Branches of Enlightenment Morality, Concentration and Wisdom	Development of Bodhichitta** Six Paramitas Four All Embracing Bodhisattva Virtues Five Vidyas (healing, Art-Technology, Sound, Logic, Inner Realization) Perfection of Hinayana Practices***	Preliminary Practices (100,000 minimum) Various Tantric Practices (vary to fit practitioner's karma) Perfection of the Hinayana & Open Mahayana Practices***
Major Texts	*What Is Cultivation?* *SAUMOL* *Imparting the Absolute Truth Through the Heart Sutra*	*What Is Cultivation?* *SAUMOL* *Imparting the Absolute Truth Through the Heart Sutra*	*What Is Cultivation?* *SAUMOL* *Imparting the Absolute Truth Through the Heart Sutra*	*What Is Cultivation?* *SAUMOL* *Imparting the Absolute Truth Through the Heart Sutra* Tantra Practice Booklets

** *See note text on page 291*
*** *See note text on page 291*

* In most sources the term "hinayana" is used to describe the Lesser Vehicle. It is believed that this was a mistranslation of very early texts as "hina" is considered a very insulting and derogatory term in Pali and Sanskrit. The word used in Tibetan and Chinese is translated as "lesser" without that connotation to denote that a lesser goal (short of full Buddhahood) is sought. Some use the term Sravakayana as this is the vehicle of the Sravakas or Arahats. Others refer to Early Buddhism or Conservative or Fundamental Buddhism to describe those who follow this path as compared to the Mahayana path. And some only want to refer to Northern and Southern Buddhism, but that does not portray the essential differences in goals of the two groups. Whatever this path is called, it should not be considered inferior in its methods or teachings and they were taught by Shakyamuni Buddha as what was appropriate for those living when He taught and for many people today. As shown on this chart, the Mahayana followers, must also master or understand these teachings to become accomplished. However, the use of any derogatory term that is insulting in its meaning is not appropriate and should not be used.

** It is not correct to assume that those following the lesser vehicle do not develop compassion or bodhichitta. H.H. Dorje Chang Buddha III has taught that one cannot become an Arhat without having Bodhichitta. These categories should only be considered as guides and used for reference.

*** Although the truths of these practices are the same for the followers of the Lesser Vehicle and Mahayana, the levels of realization of these factors are different. You should read *Imparting the Absolute Truth Through the Heart Sutra* to understand this.

Appendix C: Hymn to Buddha Vajradhara (Dorje Chang Buddha), H.H. Great Dharma King Wan Ko Yeshe Norbu

To the magnificent Buddha Vajradhara whose brilliance outshines the suns of a billion galaxies and whose wisdom surpasses all holy and ordinary beings;

I humbly bow and offer my devotion.

To the bearer of the Holy Scepter whose emanation graces this mundane world and blesses us with His sacred words and holy actions,

I humbly bow and offer my devotion.

To He who has as disciples the Five Buddhas of the Five Directions and through whom we fortunate ones can gain realization of our true nature,

I humbly bow and offer my devotion.

To the One who teaches Buddhas and other Holy Beings the secret doctrines and delights the Universe,

I humbly bow and offer my devotion.

To the One who reincarnated as the great layman, the Honorable Vimalakirti, to teach Buddhas and Bodhisattvas as well as the close disciples of Shakyamuni Buddha,

I humbly bow and offer my devotion.

To He who is praised by Buddhas and Bodhisattvas as well as Dharma kings and enlightened beings and unenlightened beings from the six realms,

I humbly bow and offer my devotion.

To He who shows a tiny glimpse of what is possible through His incredible achievements in the Five Vidyas,

I humbly bow and offer my devotion.

To the Great Artist and Creator, who blesses us with works of such beauty and skill as to delight the senses and touch our hearts,

I humbly bow and offer my devotion.

To the Great Healer, who by using the Galloping Horse Vajra Instrument of Hayagriva eliminates our suffering and pain and who fixes all that is broken,

I humbly bow and offer my devotion.

To the Master of Sound, who can compassionately caress with soft words and roar like a lion and whose poetry and couplets inspire countless followers,

I humbly bow and offer my devotion.

To the Great Logician, who understands the workings of karma and knows our pasts and future,

I humbly bow and offer my devotion.

To the Fully Realized One, who possesses the supernormal powers that can raise the dead and confer longevity and blessings,

I humbly bow and offer my devotion.

To He who Communicates with the Buddhas and Bodhisattvas and brings us Their blessings and empowerments

I humbly bow and offer my devotion.

To the Great Compassionate and All-Generous One, who endlessly gives of himself and His wealth so that we unworthy vessels may learn and practice the True Dharma,

I humbly bow and offer my devotion.

To He who can answer any question and selflessly shares His own boundless merit to help us inferior ordinary beings find the Way,

I humbly bow and offer my devotion.

To the Fearless Leader, who gives us the shortest of lineages and the true Buddha Dharma for this dark era,

I humbly bow and offer my devotion.

To He who expounds the Truth in such simplicity and demonstrates its practice in ordinary things,

I humbly bow and offer my devotion.

To the One who enables me to expiate my negative karma through His many empowerments and blessings,

I humbly bow and offer my devotion.

To He who uses his own merit to raise the consciousness of my dear relatives so that they may go to the Buddha Lands,

I humbly bow and offer my devotion.

Even though these pitiful words are woefully inadequate in their praise and ability to express my admiration and gratitude to my priceless Master,

I humbly bow and offer them in loving devotion.

Composed by a grateful disciple with a heart of utmost devotion,

—*Zhaxi Zhuoma Rinpoche*
at Hua Zang Si in San Francisco, California on November 17, 2006
and revised when I learned He was H.H. Dorje Chang Buddha III.

Appendix D: Major Buddhas, Mahasattvas, Patriarchs, and Matriarchs in the Buddhist Lineage Refuge Tree

Exoteric	Geluk	Jonang	Sakya	Nyingma	Kagyu
Original Dharmakaya Buddha Samantabhadra Tathagata Primordial Sambhogakaya Buddha, Dorje Chang Buddha Dipankara Buddha Shakyamuni Buddha 1. Venerable Mahakasyapa 2. Venerable Ananda **Shingon** Original Dharmakaya Buddha Samantabhadra Tathagata Primordial Sambhogakaya Buddha, Dorje Chang Buddha Mahavairochana Buddha Vajrasattva Mahasattva 9. Nagarjuna Bodhisattva 3. Venerable Subhakarasimha 4.. Venerable Vajrabodhi 5. Venerable Amoghavajra 6. Venerable Huiguo 7. Venerable Kukai	Original Dharmakaya Buddha Samantabhadra Tathagata Primordial Sambhogakaya Buddha, Dorje Chang Buddha Dipankara Buddha Shakyamuni Buddha 8. Manjushri Bodhisattva 9. Nagarjuna Bodhisattva 10. Maitreya Bodhisattva 11. Asanga Bodhisattva 12. Venerable Atisha 13. Master Dromtonpa 14. Master Tsongkapa 15. *Sect Head* Dharma King Ganden Tripa Gyaltsab Je 16. Dalai Lama 17. Master Panchen Lama 18. Zhangjia Khutukhtu 19. Jebtsundamba Khutukhtu	Original Dharmakaya Buddha Samantabhadra Tathagata Primordial Sambhogakaya Buddha, Dorje Chang Buddha Dipankara Buddha Shakyamuni Buddha 20. Shambhala King Suchandra 21. Shambhala XI Kalkin King Durjana 22. Venerable Kalachakranada Jamyang Dorje 23. Master Kunpang Thukie Tsondru 24. Master Kunkhyen Dolpopa Sherab Gyaltsen 25. *Sect Head* Dharma King Jigme Dorje	Original Dharmakaya Buddha Samantabhadra Tathagata Primordial Sambhogakaya Buddha, Dorje Chang Buddha 26. Vajra Nairatmy 27. Ven. Viruipa 28. Drokmi Lotsawa 29. Khon Konchok Gyalpo 30. Sachen Kunga Nyingpo Rinpoche 31. Lopson Sonam Tsemo Rinpoche 3. Jetsen Dakpa Gyaltsen Rinpoche 33. Sakya Pandita Kunga Gyaltsen Rinpoche 34. Drogon Chogyal Phakpa Rinpoche 35. *Sect Head* Dharma King Sakya Trizin Ngawang Kunga 36. Dharma King Jigdal Dagchen Sakya	Original Dharmakaya Buddha Samantabhadra Tathagata Primordial Sambhogakaya Buddha, Dorje Chang Buddha Vajrasattva Mahasattva 37. Vajrapani Mahasattva 38. Garab Dorje 39. Master Manjushrimitra 40. Master Shri Singha 41. Master Padmasambhava 42. Master Shantarakshita 43. Master Bairotsana 44. King Trisong Deutsen 45. Yeshe Tsogyal 46. Kunkhyen Longchen Rabjampa 47. Ven. Rigzin Terdak Lingpa 48. Ven. Rigdzin Jigme Lingpa 49. Dharma King Dodrupchen 50. Dharma King Shantarakshita II 51. Dharma King Penor Rinpoche 52. *Sect Head* Dharma King Mindrolling Trichen Kunzang Wangyal Rinpoche 53. Dharma King Omniscience Jangyang Lungdok Gyaltsen	Original Dharmakaya Buddha Samantabhadra Tathagata Primordial Sambhogakaya Buddha, Dorje Chang Buddha **Karma Kagyu** 54. Master Tilopa 55. Master Naropa 56. Master Marpa 57. Master Milarepa 58. Master Gampopa 59. Dusum Chenpa Black Jewel Crown Karmapa I 60. Black Jewel Crown Karmapa XVII 61. Shamar Rinpoche Red Jewel Crown Karmapa 62. Goshir Gyaltsab Rinpoche, Orange Jewel Crown Regent 63. Tai Situ Rinpoche 64. Jamgon Kontrul Rinpoche **Shangpa Kagyu** 65. Lady Sukasiddhi 66. Lady Niguma 67. Great Dharma King Tangton Gyalpo 68. Kalu Rinpoche 69. Tangtong Gyalpo Rinpoche XVI

Appendix E: Learning from Buddha Homework

In *Learning from Buddha,* the Buddha Master told us that we should reflect on what we had learned from the Buddha when we first woke up every morning, mid-day, and before we went to bed to see just how well our three karmas of thinking, speaking, and acting had corresponded with those of the Buddhas and Bodhisattvas. We should look at what we had done well and vow to repeat that and explore what we had done wrong and vow never to do that again. To help us achieve that, we added the most critical teachings to our chant book and repeated them every day at our morning and evening services along with praises to certain Buddhas and Bodhisattvas and the concluding dedication of merit to all living beings in the six realms of samsara. Some are included here. Not included are those various hymns of praise to certain Buddhas and Bodhisattvas as well as chants or dharmas that have not yet been published in English including the "Seven Joint Preliminary Practices" and "The Xiamen Most Excellent Oceanic Mind-Essence" from the Supreme and Unsurpassable Mahamudra of Liberation. These should also be included when they are available. The translation used for the following is shown in parentheses after the title.

Refuge Vows (*Certificate of Taking Refuge & Imparting the Absolute Truth through the Heart Sutra*)

I take refuge in the Buddha

I take refuge in the Dharma

I take refuge in the Sangha

The Four Vows (*Certificate of Taking Refuge*)

Defilements are countless; I vow to put an end to them.

Dharma methods are limitless; I vow to learn them.

Living beings are innumerable; I vow to save them.

Buddhahood is unsurpassable; I vow to realize it.

Contemplation of Impermanence. (*True Stores about a Holy Monk*)

All conditional phenomena are like a dream, an illusion, a bubble, a shadow, morning dew, or a flash of lightening.

All sentient beings will definitely die.

All inanimate things will definitely perish.

This principle also applies to my body, which is composed of the four great elements.

I will be separated from my family and friends one day.

Time is pushing my age forward, early youth is followed by the robust years of life, which is followed by old age, which is followed by death.

Sounds or flowing water never return after they are gone.

The thoughts and words of this very moment have already become impermanent.

I will come closer and closer to death.

Death has no set time to it.

I could go to the next world at any moment simply because my breathing stops.

I can take no worldly possessions whatsoever with me to the next world.

These principles apply to my very own body.

I am intent upon leaving the cycle of reincarnation.

The Three Groups of Purifying Precepts *(Certificate of Taking Refuge*
& Imparting the Absolute Truth through the Heart Sutra)

I vow to cut off all evil within me. There will be no evil that I will not cut off.

I vow to practice all types of goodness. There'll be no type of goodness I will not practice.

I vow to save all living beings. There'll be no living being that I will not save.

The Eight Fundamental Right Views *("What Is Cultivation?")*

Impermanence,

Firm Belief,

Renunciation,

True Vows,

Diligence,

Precepts,

Dhyana and Samadhi, and
Bodhicitta.

Great Compassion-All Living Beings as My Mother *("What Is Cultivation?")*
Understanding who my mother is,
Bearing in mind kindness,
Repaying kindness,
Practicing loving-kindness,
Demonstrating compassion,
Renouncing greed, and
Eliminating attachment.

Bodhisattva Correspondence Bodhicitta *("What Is Cultivation?")*
Self and others are equal
Exchange between self and others
Benefit others before self
Dedicating merit,
Fearlessly protecting the Dharma,
Effectively leading others to correct practice, and
Renouncing myself to help others build good karma.

Ten Good Characteristics *(Certificate of Taking Refuge & Imparting the Absolute Truth through the Heart Sutra)*
No killing, free captive living beings,
No stealing, perform charity,
No sexual misconduct, practice chastity,
No speaking falsely, speak truth,
No trivial chit-chat or ornate, lewd, or inappropriate speech; do straight talk,
No speaking divisively, bring about peace & accord,
No speaking harshly, use gentle words,

No lust or greed, hold correct view,

No anger, have benevolence and compassion, and

No ignorance, rather know everything is a matter of causes & conditions.

Four Limitless or Immeasurable States of Mind *(Certificate of Taking Refuge & Imparting the Absolute Truth through the Heart Sutra)*

Loving-kindness,

Compassion,

Sympathetic Joy, and

Non-differentiating Generosity.

The Six Paramitas *(Certificate of Taking Refuge & Imparting the Absolute Truth through the Heart Sutra)*

Be generous, overcome greed,

Keep precepts, overcome violations,

Endure insults, overcome hate and anger,

Be energetic, overcome laziness,

Be concentrated, overcome disorder,

Develop prajna, overcome ignorance.

Seven Joint Preliminary Practices *(Supreme and Unsurpassable Mahamudra of Liberation)*

The Xiaman Most Excellent Oceanic Mind Essence *(Supreme and Unsurpassable Mahamudra of Liberation)* You may join us at the temple in a guided meditation using a preliminary translation of this mind-essence at our Sunday Service that starts at 6:00 am on Zoom every week. The link to the session can be found in my weekly BLOG at www. zhaxizhuoma.org.

Cutting off the Twenty Dharmas Relating to Ordinary Feelings *(Dharma Discourse given on the "Trip to the East Coast")*

I will cut off ordinariness and enter holiness.

I will discard and not be attached to any of the twenty dharmas of ordinary feelings including:

Fame, Gain, Prosperity, Decline, Good fortune, Gladness, Increase, Decrease, Antipathy, Resentment, Anger, Hatred, Scheming, Defamation, Seizing, Harming, Illness, Suffering, Parting, and Death.

The Wrongs of Others Are My Wrongs *(Dharma Discourse given on the "Trip to the East Coast")*

The wrongs of others are my wrongs.

To regard others and yourself as one is great compassion.

A true cultivator regards the mistakes of others as his own mistakes.

Do not talk about the wrongs of others.

Do not make known your meritorious deeds.

Speaking of your meritorious deeds shows your dark karma.

Prajna Paramita Heart Sutra *(Imparting the Absolute Truth through the Heart Sutra)*

Avalokiteshvara Bodhisattva, when practicing deeply the prajna-paramita, illuminated the five aggregates, saw that they are all empty, and crossed beyond all suffering and adversity.

Sariputra, form does not differ from emptiness; emptiness does not differ from form.

Form is emptiness; emptiness is form.

The same is true of feeling, conceptualization, volition, and consciousness.

Sariputra, emptiness is the characteristic of all dharmas.

They do not arise or perish, are not defiled or pure, do not increase or decrease.

Therefore, in emptiness there is no form, no feeling, conceptualization, volition, or consciousness;

no eyes, ears, nose, tongue, body, or mind;

no forms, sounds, smells, tastes, touches, or mental phenomena;

no realm of eyes, up to and including no realm of mind consciousness;

no ignorance and also, no ending of ignorance, up to and including no old age and death and also no ending of old age and death;

no suffering, no accumulation, no cessation, and no path; no wisdom, also no attainment.

With nothing to be attained, therefore, the Bodhisattvas rely on prajna-paramita, and thus their minds have no hindrance.

Because there is no hindrance, they have no fear.

Having forever left inverted dream-thinking, they dwell in ultimate nirvana.

All Buddhas of the three times rely on prajna-paramita and thereby attain anuttara-samyak-sambhodi.

Therefore, know that prajna-paramita is the great supernormal mantra, the great bright mantra, the supreme mantra, the unequaled mantra, which can remove all suffering and is true, not false.

So recite the prajna-paramita mantra, recite the mantra that says:

gate gate paragate parasamgate

bodhi svaha.

The chant book also includes the following dharmas: the "Tashi Tsigpa (Verses of the Eight Auspicious Ones)" in English, Spanish, and Tibetan; the "Great Compassion Mantra (Mahakaruna Dharani)" in Chinese/Sanskrit; "Gatha on Opening the Sutra"; The "Prajna-Paramita Heart Sutra" in Chinese/Sanskrit; the "Heart Mantra of Kuan Yin Bodhisattva"; more detailed "Refuge Vows"; "Samantabhadra Bodhisattva's Verse of Exhortation"; Vajrasattva's "One-Hundred-Character Bright Mantra"; and the "Wish-Fulfilling Mantra".

Index